Wildflowers
of the
Northern
Great Plains

F.R. Vance
J.R. Jowsey
J.S. McLean

University of Minnesota Press
Minneapolis

Published by the University of Minnesota Press
2037 University Avenue Southeast, Minneapolis MN 55414
Printed in Canada

This is the second (revised) edition of *Wildflowers Across the Prairies*.

Second printing, 1991

Library of Congress Cataloging in Publication Data

Vance, F. R. (Fenton R.) 1907-
    Wildflowers of the Northern Great Plains.

Rev. ed. of: Wildflowers across the prairies. 1977.
Bibliography: p.
    Includes indexes.
    Summary: A field guide to the wild flowers of western Canada and the adjoining Great Plains states of the United States, including illustrations o nearly 400 species.
    1. Wild flowers—Prairie Provinces—Identification.
2. Wild flowers—Great Plains—Identification. [1. Wild flowers. 2. Flowers] I. Jowsey, J. R. (James R.),
1925-   . II. McLean, J. S. (James S.), 1940-
III. Vance, F. R. (Fenton R.), 1907-   . Wildflowers across the prairies. IV. Title.
QK203.P7V36 1984   582.13′09712   84-5060
ISBN 0-8166-1350-8
ISBN 0-8166-1351-6 (pbk.)

Cover design by Warren Clark/GDL
Cover photograph by F. R. Vance

The University of Minnesota is an equal-opportunity educator and employer.

To Lloyd T. Carmichael, whose earlier book, Prairie Wildflowers, *provided an introduction of wildflowers to his friends and associates in natural history, we dedicate this book.*

CONTENTS

PREFACE

Wildflowers of the Northern Great Plains is a book for field use and for reading enjoyment by both the casual and serious observer of plants. It includes one or more color illustrations and line drawings of nearly 400 species of the plants which are part of the natural scene in western Canada and the adjoining Great Plains states of the United States of America. It is a book for those who have known the wild plants of the prairies and their forest edges.

It is a book for beginning students (grade 4 and up) who can see plants in flower and use the illustrations to identify the plants they see. It is a book for use by high school and university students of biology whose studies may involve recognition of native plants.

This book on wildflowers is, in general, a book to "open the eyes" of people of all ages as they look at the flowers of this region of North America. It is for travellers who come here from far lands, and for those who have lived on these prairies. It is a book for farmers and summer cottage residents, for those who visit our parks, and for those who walk or drive in cities and along the roads of Saskatchewan and neighboring areas. It is a book for all students of the natural world.

Scientific names identify each plant with certainty and provide the serious student with a reliable field guide to plants of Saskatchewan and similar adjacent areas, including Manitoba, Alberta, North West Territories, Montana, the Dakotas, and Minnesota (see Figure 1). The illustrations and Key to Plant Families, page 9, provide a useful base for plant observation throughout the whole shaded area in Figure 1. Reference to "the area" in the HABITAT section on each plant refers specifically to the settled areas of Saskatchewan up to and including the edges of the boreal forest region.

Most readers will use only the common names of the plants and may wish to add other common names to the ones used here. In general the names accepted in Canada Agriculture Publication No. 1397, *Common and Botanical Names of Weeds in Canada* (1975), are the ones used for each plant. The Canada Agriculture Publication No. 983, *Wild Plants of the Canadian Prairies* (1964), and Publication No. 1662, *Budd's Flora of the Canadian Prairie Provinces* (1979), have been used extensively in verifying field observations and preparing descriptive material. Readers may wish to personally refine locations and flowering dates. Locations and flowering dates given are intended to provide the reader with a general idea of the range of these two details of the natural history of the plant involved.

While the botanical names of the plants described in this book have been thoroughly checked in several references, serious students in botany may wish to refer to other references for the descriptions of the plant species involved or the description of related plants. The general index is supplemented with an index of the plant families which are represented by the species described.

There are over 1,300 species of plants described in Brietung's *Annotated Catalogue of the Vascular Flora of Saskatchewan*, and the plants included in *Wildflowers of the Northern Great Plains* are the ones which commonly appear in all or part of the area described. Introduced plants are included too, if their flowers are common, and even a few plants sternly designated as "weeds," like the sow-thistle, goat's-beard, and sweet clover, are included. There is beauty in their flowers too.

Our responsibility in the natural world is "to enjoy and not destroy." The land and its plants and animal life is a trust, not a feature to be exploited. Plants should not be picked thoughtlessly, but taken only if they are abundant. Several of the plants illustrated in this book are now very rare and may have vanished from the prairie scene. They have been identified as rare with suitable precautions for preserving them. This is only a guide. The responsibility of each observer goes far beyond this, otherwise many more plants may vanish from the prairies. Take care! Encourage preservation of habitat for native plants. Know which species are abundant. Enjoy the flowers as they live, that succeeding generations may do the same.

Wildflowers of the Northern Great Plains has been produced by combining the thoughts of many people, in response to frequent expressions of the need for such a book. The authors recognize that such a work would not have been possible without the financial, scientific, and other assistance they received. Detailed acknowledgments are included in the section which follows. The primary photographic responsibilities have rested with F. R. Vance; the artistic representations of flowers by sketches were the total responsibility of J. S. McLean; and the responsibility for biological accuracy, preparation of the written descriptions of plants, assembly of the manuscript, and general management of the project was borne by J. R. Jowsey.

J. R. Jowsey
March 1984

ACKNOWLEDGMENTS

The authors acknowledge with profound gratitude the many forms of assistance provided to the Prairie Wildflowers Project and the preparation of material for this book. While such a work may have been carried on as an activity of only the authors, the assistance, material and otherwise, rendered in its preparation by many persons and organizations has made it the work of a community of persons interested in properly indentifying some of the flowers of the "northern Great Plains." It is our pleasure to acknowledge these elements of assistance as follows:

For the first edition, the financial support of the Canada Council with an Explorations Program grant to J. R. Jowsey used in financing the field work through which we obtained photographic material, plant specimens for sketches, and plants for the development of a reference herbarium;

A Saskatchewan Culture and Recreation Grant administered through the Saskatchewan Museum of Natural History provided funding to supplement costs for field work and other manuscript assembly requirements for the revised edition (1984);

The support of persons who wrote on behalf of the application of J. R. Jowsey for the grant to be received under the Canada Council Explorations Program, namely Dr. G. F. Ledingham, Dr. W. A. Quick, and Dr. M. Evelyn Jonescu of the Department of Biology and Canadian Plains Research Center of the University of Regina;

The extended period of assistance of K. F. Best, Canada Agriculture Research Station, Regina, through the designing of the project, confirmation of indentification of specimens, and the checking of the manuscript for botanical accuracy and arrangement;

In this connection too, and particularly in the case of the revised edition (1984), the care, precision, and generosity with time and skill of Gwen Jones, Department of Biology, University of Regina, in checking the text for botanical accuracy and suitability of descriptive phrases;

The special assistance by F. A. Switzer, Gwen Jones, and G. F. Ledingham in slide selection and plant identification relative to the photographic material and the contributions of three persistent and skillful photographers F. A. Switzer, G. W. Seib, and J. L. Parker who contributed major numbers of photographs of plants to this book; the assistance and patience of all those who submitted slides for consideration for this book. Inclusion of slides taken by persons other than the authors has at once speeded the completion of this project and expanded the feeling of community within the group of persons involved;

The revised edition (1984) has been improved by the addition of a dichotomous key to the families of plants in which one or more species are described. The preparation of this key was possible through the skill and patience of Lesley E. Moffatt;

The role of Shirley Jowsey in the development of this book has involved contributions of skill, wisdom, and commitment substantially equivalent to those of the authors.

INTRODUCTION

Wildflowers of the Northern Great Plains includes descriptions of nearly 400 species of flowering plants of the northern tip of the "Great Plains of North America" (Figure 1). Most species are described by two color pictures: one of the flower or group of flowers, the other of a whole plant or a group of plants in their natural habitat. A sketch and a brief description of FLOWERS, FRUIT, LEAVES, GROWTH HABIT and HABITAT is also included. In the interests of accurate comparison of plants, some pages differ through the introduction of another color illustration of a similar plant of the same genus, or through replacement of the sketch with a color illustration of the fruit of the species involved. The order in which plants are arranged in this book is the traditional taxonomic order followed by botanists and others who study plants. Within plant families, the next taxonomic division, genus, has an alphabetic arrangement, as does the arrangement of species within each genus. For the general reader, use of the index will locate any plant by either common name or genus. A dichotomous key to plant families is also included.

In a few cases, plants of different genera are included on the same page. For instance, on page 241, three plants of different genera are included: the large white ground-cherry, wild tomato and black henbane. They are shown on the same page to establish a clear comparison of these three poisonous members of the potato family (Solanacae). Another page, (186), which departs significantly from the usual arrangement includes two sketches of plants commonly confused; the water-hemlock, (*Cicuta* spp.), and the water-parsnip, (*Sium* spp.). The two sketches clearly illustrate differences in the leaves and in the inflorescence of the plants involved, and a single color picture shows the water-hemlock in its natural habitat.

The line drawings or sketches used are intended to draw attention to a particular feature of the plant involved. In some cases they are magnified several times to show such features, and this should be noted if any distortion of the plant is apparent at first examination of the sketch. All sketches are based on use of fresh specimens, usually observed under field conditions, but references to a herbarium maintained for the purpose and to other herbaria in Regina supplemented the observation of the artist (JSM) in the field.

The description of terms in the section which follows this introduction has been supplemented by several figures. Figure 1 presents the major concentration of the plants of the nearly 400 species described in this book. Figures 2 through 8 are intended to provide the reader with a visual impression of such terms as *pinnate*, in the case of leaves, *corymb*, in the case of flowers, etc. These figures are reproduced from Budd and Best's *Wild Plants of the Canadian Prairies*. Since they were originally sketched by the late Arch. C. Budd, it is with particular pleasure that the authors use them in *Wildflowers of the Northern Great Plains*.

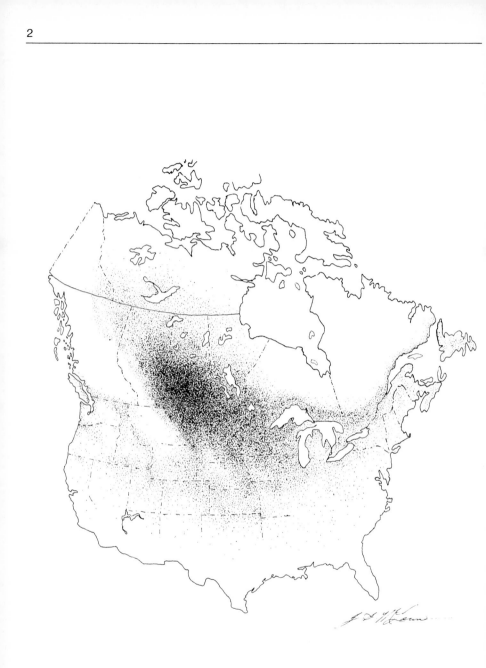

Figure 1. The shaded area indicates the extended area in western North America in which most plants described in this book are regularly observed.

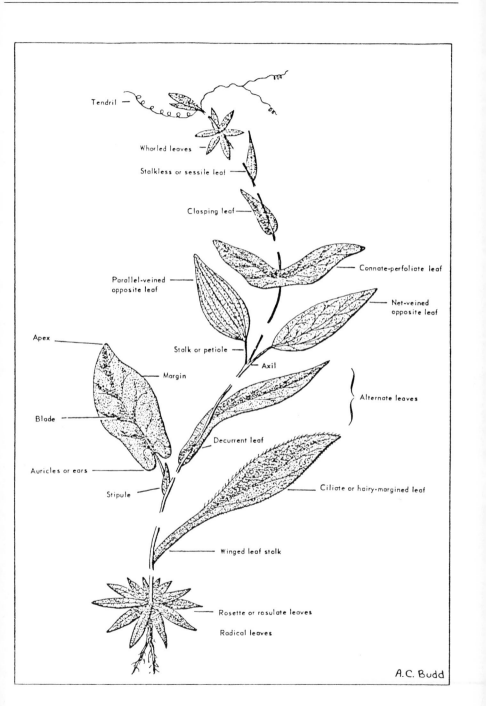

Figure 2. Leaf variations.

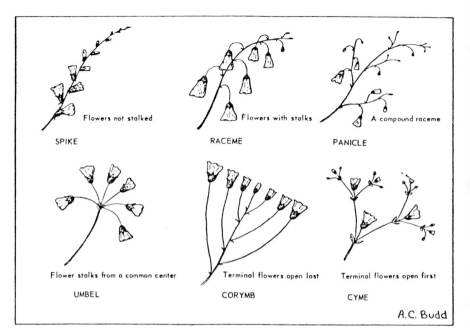

Figure 3. Types of inflorescence.

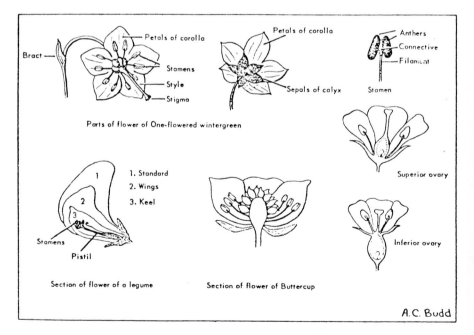

Figure 4. Flower parts.

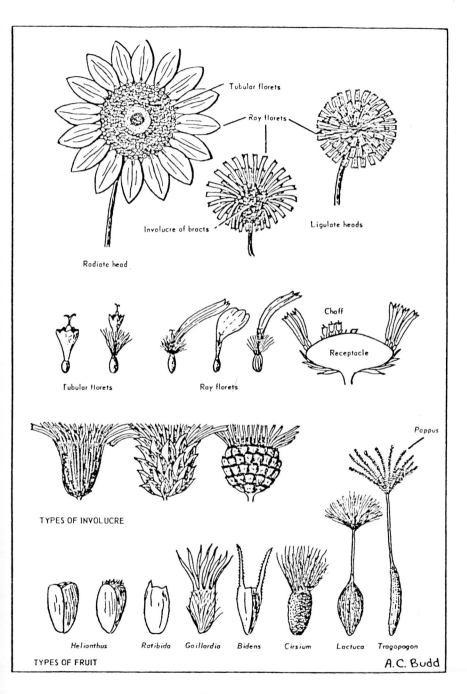

Figure 5. Characteristics of composite flowers and fruits.

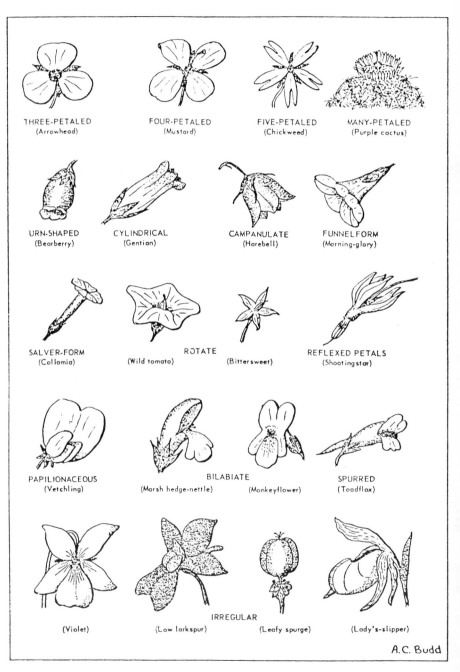

THREE-PETALED
(Arrowhead)

FOUR-PETALED
(Mustard)

FIVE-PETALED
(Chickweed)

MANY-PETALED
(Purple cactus)

URN-SHAPED
(Bearberry)

CYLINDRICAL
(Gentian)

CAMPANULATE
(Harebell)

FUNNELFORM
(Morning-glory)

SALVER-FORM
(Collomia)

ROTATE
(Wild tomato)

(Bittersweet)

REFLEXED PETALS
(Shooting star)

PAPILIONACEOUS
(Vetchling)

BILABIATE
(Marsh hedge-nettle)

(Monkeyflower)

SPURRED
(Toadflax)

(Violet)

IRREGULAR
(Low larkspur)

(Leafy spurge)

(Lady's-slipper)

A.C. Budd

Figure 6. Types of flowers.

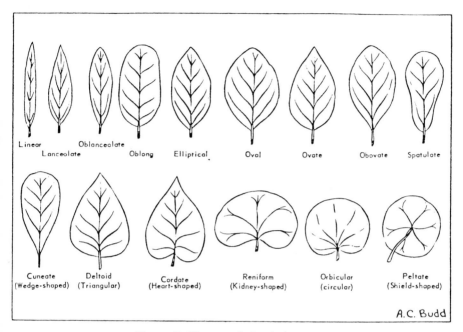

Figure 7. Shapes of simple leaves.

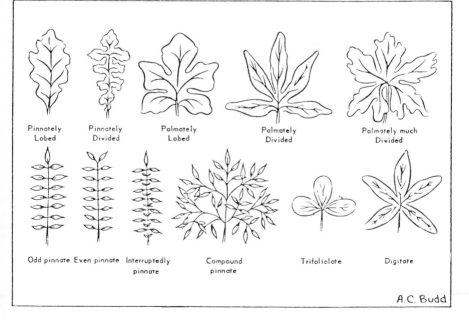

Figure 8. Types of divided leaves.

KEY TO PLANT FAMILIES

This key involves only the families of plants covered in *Wildflowers of the Northern Great Plains,* Revised Edition, 1984. Persons who wish to search for plant species other than those treated in this book should use a more comprehensive flora of the area.

Division SPERMATOPHYTA — plants producing seeds

Subdivision ANGIOSPERMAE — flowering plants

1. a) Leaves parallel veined; flower parts in 3s or 6s; embryo with 1 cotyledon; herbs . . . class **Monocotyledoneae**
   b) Leaves usually net veined; parts of flowers usually in 5s or 4s; embryo with 2 cotyledons; herbs, shrubs and trees . . . class **Dicotyledoneae**

Class **Monocotyledoneae**

1. a) Sepals and petals (perianth) lacking or inconspicuous 2
   b) Sepals and petals in two whorls, one or both brightly colored 5
2. a) Flowers in spike-like racemes 3
   b) Flowers in globose heads; fruit bur-like; marsh or aquatic plants with erect or floating stems (sepals and petals absent, or single and inconspicuous) . . . . **Sparganiaceae** (bur-reed family). p. 18
3. a) Inflorescence dense cylindrical spike 3 to 6 inches (8-15 cm) long, ⅜ to 1 inch (1-2.5 cm) thick 4
   b) Spike less than ⅜ inch (1 cm) thick; sepals and petals in two whorls, mostly inconspicuous, small and greenish; rush-like leaves all basal; plant terrestrial or semi-aquatic . . . . **Juncaginaceae** (arrow-grass family), p. 19
4. a) Inflorescence spike fleshy, subtended by, or enclosed in, a large bract; flowers usually perfect . . . . **Araceae** (arum family), p. 22
   b) Spike neither fleshy nor having a bract; flowers very small and unisexual; pistillate flowers in a thick spike, the staminate above . . . . **Typhaceae** (cattail family), p. 17
5. a) Marsh and bog plants; perianth small, with 3 green sepals and 3 greenish white petals; fruit achenes . . . . **Alismaceae** (water-plantain family), p. 20
   b) Land plants; perianth colored; carpels 3; ovaries united; fruit a capsule or berry 6

6. a) Ovary superior . . . . **Liliaceae** (lily family), p. 23
   b) Ovary inferior 7
7. a) Flowers regular, star pattern; stamens 3 . . . . **Iridaceae** (iris family), p. 34
   b) Flowers very irregular; stamens 1 or 2 . . . . **Orchidaceae** (orchid family), p. 36

Class **Dicotyledoneae**

1. a) Only 1 floral ring, lacking a corolla (inner whorl made up of petals), with a calyx (outer whorl made up of sepals) . . . . Group I
   b) Flowers with corolla and calyx both present, 2 floral rings 2
2. a) Corolla with separate petals . . . . Group II
   b) Corolla forming a tube or bell with petals more or less united . . . . Group III

Group I **Dicotyledoneae**

1. a) Either or both staminate and pistillate flowers in catkins or catkin-like heads; trees, shrubs, or herbs 2
   b) Flowers not in catkins, but often in dense heads; plants mostly with perfect flowers 6
2. a) Both staminate and pistillate flowers in catkins or catkin-like heads; trees and shrubs 4
   b) Only staminate or pistillate flowers in catkins; shrubs or herbs 3
3. a) Pistillate flowers only in catkins; staminate and pistillate flowers on separate plants (dioecious); plants climbing; leaves opposite, large and palmately lobed; herbaceous plant; fruit in catkin-like spike . . . . **Cannabinaceae** (hemp family), p. 56
   b) Staminate flowers in elongate catkin; pistillate flowers on short bud-like catkin concealed by bracts; fruit a thin-shelled nut . . . . **Betulaceae** (birch family), p. 54
4. a) Fruit a many-seeded capsule, seed with a tuft of hairs . . . . **Salicaceae** (willow family), p. 51
   b) Fruit 1 seeded, lacking a tuft of hair 5
5. a) Styles 3 or more; fruit an acorn; leaves deeply lobed . . . . **Fagaceae** (beech family), p. 55
   b) Styles 2; fruit not an acorn but nut or nutlet; leaves not as above . . . . **Betulaceae** (birch family), p. 54
6. a) Shrubs or trees 7
   b) Herbs 10
7. a) Climbing plants; flowers with colored sepals; fruit with a persistent feathery style . . . . **Ranunculaceae** (crowfoot family), p. 75
   b) Plants not climbing; fruit without a feathery style 8
8. a) Fruit a double samara, made of 2 carpels and united below . . . . **Aceraceae** (maple family), p. 165
   b) Fruit not a double samara 9
9. a) Fruit fleshy when ripe, drupe-like; leaves silvery or brownish scurfy; flowers either perfect or unisexual; plants monecious or dioecious . . . . **Elaeagnaceae** (oleaster family), p. 176

    b) Fruit dry when ripe, broad membranous wing around calyx; branches spiny; leaves pale yellowish green; staminate flowers borne on terminal spike; pistillate flowers borne singly in axils of leaves . . . . **Chenopodiaceae** (goosefoot family), p. 63

10. a) Stamens and pistils in separate flowers, borne on the same plant; plants with a milky sap . . . . **Euphorbiaceae** (spurge family), p. 162
    b) Each flower perfect 11

11. a) Leaves alternate, with stipules forming a sheath around the node . . . . **Polygonaceae** (buckwheat family), p. 59
    b) Leaves without stipules 12

12. a) Leaves opposite 13
    b) Leaves alternate, lower ones sometimes opposite 15

13. a) No true leaves; scale-like; flowers minute, sunk into the stem; plants turn bright crimson at maturity; common in saline areas . . . . **Chenopodiaceae** (goosefoot family), p. 63
    b) Leaves not scale-like 14

14. a) Erect herbs; flowers in panicles or clusters; sepals brightly colored and petal-like, often united into bell-like tube . . . . **Nyctaginaceae** (four-o'clock family), p. 66
    b) Plants with stinging hairs; flowers borne in clusters at junction of stem and leaf stalk; flowers greenish . . . . **Urticaceae** (nettle family), p. 57

15. a) Fruit a 1-seeded drupe; flowers small, greenish white, bronze or rose tinged; plant somewhat parasitic on underground parts of other plants . . . . **Santalaceae** (sandalwood family), p. 58
    b) Plants not as above; fruit varying 16

16. a) Leaves basal, compound or simple, but very deeply divided; flowering stalks bear whorl of involucral leaves; flowers at summits of long stems; fruit achenes . . . . **Ranunculaceae** (crowfoot family), p. 75
    b) Leaves not deeply divided but linear or ovate; flowers small, numerous, greenish or reddish; fruit thin walled with 1 lens-shaped seed . . . . **Chenopodiaceae** (goosefoot family), p. 63

Group II **Dicotyledoneae**

1. a) Leafless perennial plants with succulent stems covered with spines . . . . **Cactaceae** (cactus family), p. 174
    b) Plants with leaves 2

2. a) Leaves in basal rosette, leaf blades densely glandular and fringed with long reddish glandular hairs to trap insects . . . . **Droseraceae** (sundew family), p. 96
    b) Insectivorous plant; basal cluster of hollow leaves ("pitchers"), often marked with red or purple; solitary flower on erect stem . . . . **Sarraceniaceae** (pitcherplant family), p. 97
    c) Plants with "normal" leaves 3

3. a) Leaves opposite, whorled or basal 4
    b) Some or all leaves alternate 8

4. a) Low herbs with 4 large greenish white petal-like bracts surrounding minute flowers; fruit a small drupe with 2-seeded stone . . . . **Cornaceae** (dogwood family), p. 194
    b) Plants without large petal-like bracts 5

5. a) Styles single 6
    b) Styles 2 or more 7

6. a) Sepals and petals (perianth) in 4s; twice as many stamens as sepals; fruit a capsule; seeds with a tuft of silky hair; flowers in racemes or solitary in leaf axils; stigma knobbed or 4-lobed . . . . **Onagraceae** (evening-primrose family), p. 179
   b) Petals 4 to 6; stamens up to 12 . . . . **Lythraceae** (loosestrife family), p. 178
   c) Flower parts in 5s; leaves thick and leathery, usually evergreen; stamens 8 to 10; fruit a capsule . . . . **Pyrolaceae** (wintergreen family), p. 196
7. a) Sepals 4 to 5; petals 4 to 5; stems swollen at joints; fruit a capsule opening by valves at the top . . . . **Caryophyllaceae** (pink family), p. 69
   b) Sepals 2; petals 5; succulent plants; annual prostrate weed . . . . **Portulacaceae** (purslane family), p. 67
8. a) Leaves with stipules 9
   b) Leaves without stipules 14
9. a) Numerous stamens united into a column; 5 partly united sepals; 5 slightly united petals; leaves lobed or dissected, palmately veined . . . . **Malvaceae** (mallow family), p. 166
   b) Stamens usually separate, not in a column 10
10. a) Flowers irregular in shape 11
    b) Flowers regular in shape 12
11. a) Petals 5 — upper larger, 2 side wings, 2 united at bottom to form a keel; compound leaves; fruit a legume . . . . **Leguminosae** (legume family), p. 126
    b) Two kinds of flowers: 1. spring, showy flower; sepals 5 and petals 5 with 1 spurred or sac-like; 2. summer flowers; reduced corolla or none; closed and self-fertilized; fruit 3-seeded capsule . . . . **Violaceae** (violet family), p. 169
12. a) Stamens usually numerous; 5 petals, 5 sepals often with 5 bracts below; 1 to many pistils; fruits vary — dry achenes, follicles, fleshy receptacles, drupes or drupelets, or berry-like pomes . . . . **Rosaceae** (rose family), p. 104
    b) Stamens 5 or 10, ovary of 5 united carpels 13
13. a) Leaves more or less palmately divided; fruit long beaked at maturity, splits from below upward to form 5 parts, each 1-seeded and long tailed . . . . **Geraniaceae** (geranium family), p. 153
    b) Leaves of 3 leaflets, palmately divided; leaflets broadly inverted, heart-shaped; 5 petals, 5 sepals; 10 stamens; fruit a capsule, not beaked . . . . **Oxalidaceae** (wood-sorrel family), p. 156
14. a) Stamens usually more than 10 15
    b) Stamens 10 or less 18
15. a) Aquatic, perennial plants; flower solitary with fleshy sepals; leaves long petioled, blades usually floating, deeply heart-shaped; fruit large, containing many seeds . . . . **Nymphaeaceae** (water-lily family), p. 74
    b) Mostly land plants 16
16. a) Carpels separate; leaves various; fruit various — achenes, follicles, or berries . . . . **Ranunculaceae** (crowfoot family), p. 75
    b) Sepals 5, petals 10, over 1 inch long, white or pale yellow flowers, flowers solitary and terminal; biennial herb; plant armed with spine-like hairs . . . . **Loasceae** (loasa family), p. 173
17. a) Ovary inferior 18
    b) Ovary superior 19

18. a) Flowers in 3 umbels, greenish; styles 5; fruit globular, purplish black; single leaf has a tall stalk which divides into 3 parts and each part is divided into 3 to 5 leaflets . . . . **Araliaceae** (ginseng family), p. 185
    b) Flower parts in 5; sepals minute; 5 stamens, 2 styles; flowers small in umbels; fruit a mericarp consisting of 2 single-seeded carpels united into 1 capsule, generally ribbed and sometimes winged . . . . **Umbelliferae** (parsley family), p. 186
19. a) Carpels 3 to 5 20
    b) Carpels 1 or 2 22
20. a) Sepals 3, 2 small and green, the other large and spurred, 3 apparent petals and 5 stamens; fruit an explosive capsule . . . . **Balsaminaceae** (touch-me-not family), p. 159
    b) None of petals or sepals spurred; fruit not explosive 21
21. a) Regular flowers, 5 sepals, 5 petals; 5 stamens united at base; fruit a round capsule divided into 4 or 5 cells, each with 2 flat seeds; petals soon drop . . . . **Linaceae** (flax family), p. 157
    b) Perfect flowers; 4 or 5 sepals, 4 or 5 petals; stamens 8 to 10; succulent, fleshy-leaved perennials; numerous seeds in follicle-like capsule . . . . **Crassulaceae** (orpine family), p. 98
22. a) Corolla irregular in shape 23
    b) Corolla regular in shape 24
23. a) Petals 3, sepals 5, 2 large, colored, and petal-like; 3 or 5 more or less united petals; keel petal with fringed crest . . . . **Polygalaceae** (milkwort family), p. 160
    b) Petals 4, 1 of the outer pair spurred at the base, both of the outer somewhat dilated and keeled at the apex; sepals 2; stamens 6 in 2 sets; stigma 2-lobed; fruit long slender capsule . . . . **Fumariaceae** (fumitory family), p. 89
24. a) Herbs 25
    b) Shrubs 27
25. a) Sepals 5, petals 5; receptacle more or less cup-shaped; stamens 5 or 10; fruit usually a capsule . . . . **Saxifragaceae** (saxifrage family), p. 99
    b) Petals 4, sepals 4 or 2 26
26. a) Stamens 6, of equal lengths; annual herbs; often ill scented; leaves mostly with 3 leaflets; sepals 4, petals 4; fruit a pod . . . . **Capparidaceae** (caper family), p. 90
    b) Sepals 4, petals 4; stamens 6, 4 long and 2 short; fruit pods (siliques) divided into 2 compartments . . . . **Cruciferae** (mustard family), p. 91
27. a) Simple leaves opposite, turn red or purplish in the fall; shrubs or small trees; perfect flowers, sepals 4, petals 4; fruit a small white drupe . . . . **Cornaceae** (dogwood family), p. 194
    b) Leaves alternate 28
28. a) Leaves compound 29
    b) Leaves simple 30
29. a) Stamens numerous . . . . **Rosaceae** (rose family), p. 104
    b) Stamens 5; perfect and imperfect flowers; 5 sepals, 5 petals; leaves compound of 3 to many leaflets; fruit a 1-seeded drupe . . . . **Anacardiaceae** (sumach family), p. 163
30. a) Leaves small and scale-like; low shrubs, tufted and heath-like; sepals 5, outer 2 smaller than inner ones; forms mats or bushes . . . . **Cistaceae** (rock-rose family), p. 168
    b) Leaves broad, not scale-like . . . . **Rosaceae** (rose family), p. 104

14

Group III **Dicotyledoneae**

1. a) Shrubs or trees 2
   b) Herbs 6
2. a) Leaves opposite or whorled 3
   b) Leaves alternate 4
3. a) Stamens 5; fruit 1-seeded drupe; leaves large, odd-pinnate, usually 5 to 7; flowers small, numerous, in large terminal cyme . . . . **Caprifoliaceae** (honeysuckle family), p. 259
   b) Stamens usually twice as many as corolla lobes; sepals 4 to 5, corolla 4 to 5-lobed; leaves simple, leathery, persistent; fruit a capsule . . . . **Ericaceae** (heath family), p. 203
4. a) Flowers in heads; fruit 1-seeded . . . . **Compositae** (composite family), p. 268
   b) Flowers not in heads; fruit many seeded 5
5. a) Ovary inferior; shrub or shrub-like plant; calyx above the ovary; fruit crowned by the calyx; fruit a berry . . . . **Vacciniaceae** (huckleberry family), p. 207
   b) Ovary superior; shrubby plant; calyx free from the ovary; fruit a capsule, berry, or drupe . . . . **Ericaceae** (heath family), p. 203
6. a) Parasitic or saprophytic plants, lacking chlorophyll 7
   b) Plants with chlorophyll 8
7. a) Plant white, pink, yellow; mycorrhizal roots; leaves reduced to scales; flower solitary, perfect, regular, usually drooping, sepals 2 to 5, petals 4 to 5, stamens twice as many as petals . . . . **Monotropaceae** (indian-pipe family), p. 200
   b) Parasitic; pinkish or brownish herbs; leaves scale-like; flowers purplish, tubular, stamens 4; flowers irregular . . . . **Orobanchaceae** (broom-rape family), p. 255
8. a) Flowers in head or head-like form 9
   b) Flowers in long or short spikes 10
   c) Flowers in neither heads nor spikes 11
9. a) Flowers in true heads; apparent flowers in a head composed of many florets borne on a common receptacle; a large and diverse family . . . . **Compositae** (composite family), p. 268
   b) Flowers in form of head, open in irregular order; stem 4-angled; usually strong odor . . . . **Labiatae** (mint family), p. 233
10. a) Flowers inconspicuous, on long spikes; leaves all basal; flowers have a 4-lobed calyx and a 4-lobed corolla; fruit a pyxis or capsule . . . . **Plantaginaceae** (plantain family), p. 256
    b) Flowers brightly colored, perfect, irregular; petals partly united into a 2-lipped tube . . . . **Scrophulariaceae** (figwort family), p. 244
11. a) Ovary inferior 12
    b) Ovary superior 16
12. a) Tall climbing herb with branched tendrils; stem angular; leaves alternate . . . . **Cucurbitaceae** (gourd family), p. 266
    b) Not climbing plants 13
13. a) Leaves basal or alternate; milky sap 14
    b) Leaves opposite 15
14. a) Perennial herbs with milky sap; leaves simple without stipules; flowers showy, bell-shaped, or funnelform, usually blue or violet . . . . **Campanulaceae** (bluebell family), p. 265
    b) Annual or biennial herbs, small; flowers irregular . . . . **Lobeliaceae** (lobelia family), p. 267

15. a) Leaves with stipules, appear to be whorled; slender, mostly 4-sided stems; flowers small, perfect, rotate, or funnelform . . . . **Rubiaceae** (madder family), p. 257
    b) Leaves without stipules; trailing plant, flowers perfect, regular or irregular . . . . **Caprifoliaceae** (honeysuckle family), p. 259
16. a) Corolla irregular 17
    b) Corolla regular 19
17. a) Aquatic plants; leaves all basal, bearing bladders; carnivorous or insectivorous . . . . **Lentibulariaceae** (bladderwort family), p. 253
    b) Marsh or land plants 18
18. a) Stems square; leaves opposite, bearing glands; strong odor; fruit with 4 nutlets; may be growing near water . . . . **Labiatae** (mint family), p. 233
    b) Stems not square; fruit many-seeded capsule . . . . **Scrophulariaceae** (figwort family), p. 244
19. a) Plants with milky juice 20
    b) Plants without milky juice 21
20. a) Leaves opposite or whorled; flowers numerous in umbels; corolla deeply 5-parted; stamens 5, attached at the base of the corolla and united to form a tube, on stamen tube is a 5-lobed corona; pollen grains in masses; ovaries 2 with short styles . . . . **Asclepiadaceae** (milkweed family), p. 223
    b) Leaves opposite; flowers in cymes; calyx 5-lobed, corolla bell-shaped to tubular; 5 stamens joined at the base to the corolla tube; the corolla tube has 5 small appendages alternating with the 5 stamens; 2 ovaries joined by 2-lobed stigma . . . . **Apocynaceae** (dogbane family), p. 221
21. a) Twining or trailing plants; alternate leaves; corolla large, tubular, or funnelform . . . . **Convolvulaceae** (convolvulus family), p. 224
    b) Plants not twining 22
22. a) Leaves simple; flowers perfect, regular, usually 5 sepals, 5 petals; stamens as many as petals and directly opposite them . . . . **Primulaceae** (primrose family), p. 209
    b) Stamens alternating with petals or twice as many 23
23. a) Stamens 8 or 10; leaves thick and leathery . . . . **Pyrolaceae** (wintergreen family), p. 196
    b) Stamens 4 or 5 24
24. a) Fruit with 4 nutlets; style simple, from center of lobes of the ovary; 5-lobed calyx and corolla . . . . **Boraginaceae** (borage family), p. 228
    b) Fruit a berry or capsule; style terminal 25
25. a) Ovary 1-celled; flowers in cymose clusters; opposite simple leaves . . . . **Gentianaceae** (gentian family), p. 215
    b) Ovary 1-celled; leaves deeply dissected or toothed . . . . **Hydrophyllaceae** (waterleaf family), p. 227
    c) Ovary 2- or 3-celled 26
26. a) Ovary 3-celled; low growing, annual or perennial; flowers generally regular. 5 sepals, 5 petals; flowers funnel-shaped; fruit a capsule . . . . **Polemoniaceae** (phlox family), p. 225
    b) Ovary 2-celled; corolla rotate; leaves deeply lobed; flowers generally in clusters of 3; fruit smooth, green berry . . . . **Solanaceae** (potato family), p. 241

CATTAIL
Typha latifolia L.

D. HATCH

Cattail

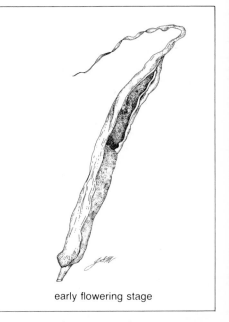

early flowering stage

FLOWERS are minute, brown and lack sepals and petals. They are arranged in a familiar dense cylindrical spike which is 3 to 6 inches (7.5-15 cm) long and about an inch (2.5 cm) in diameter. The pale green upper portion of the spike carries the male flowers and disappears, usually due to being broken off. The thicker brown section holds the female flowers. Flowers appear in July. The FRUIT is a minute, tufted achene which bears one seed. LEAVES are light olive green, parallel-veined, 10 to 20 inches (25-50 cm) in length, with a long sheath to the base of the flowering stalk. GROWTH HABIT is perennial from thick creeping roots. The flower stalk acts as the core of the plant and is surrounded by the basal leaves. The flower stem may be ¼ inch (6 mm) thick and a total height 3 to 5 feet (1-2.5 m). HABITAT includes the deeper sloughs and marshes or roadside ditches, beyond the range of sedges and bulrushes, where water persists until at least midsummer.

F. R. VANCE

Cattail

18

BROAD-FRUITED BUR-REED
Sparganium eurycarpum Engelm.

BUR-REED FAMILY

Bur-reed

Bur-reed

FLOWERS are unisexual with staminate and pistillate flowers in whitish, dense, round heads on the flower stems which arise from the leaf axils. The two to fifteen small upper heads are staminate; the lower one to three larger heads, up to ¾ inch (2 cm) in diameter, are composed of pistillate flowers, each with three to six sepals and two stigmas. FRUIT is a round, bristly head of stout-beaked achenes, ¼ to ⅜ inch (6-10 mm) long. The head is greenish brown at maturity and may be ¾ to 1 inch (2-2.5 cm) in diameter. LEAVES are light green, linear, stiff, clasping and coarsely angled, ¼ to ½ inch (6-12 mm) wide, arising along the stem to the height of the whole plant which may be up to 3 feet (1 m) but more often 8 to 10 inches (20-25 cm) tall. GROWTH HABIT is erect, rising from stout rootstocks on light floating stems. HABITAT is marshes, sloughs, and road ditches where water persists until at least late June. It is more common in the shady marshes of the parkland than elsewhere.

SEASIDE ARROW-GRASS
Triglochin maritima L.

ARROW-GRASS FAMILY

Seaside arrow-grass

Seaside arrow-grass

FLOWERS are greenish white, minute, borne in long racemes that are 8 to 18 inches (20-45 cm) long. There are three petals and three sepals in two floral rings but they appear very similar. Flowering begins in June. FRUIT is a short, stubby capsule up to ¼ inch (6 mm) long, with six carpels, held in the dried floral rings. LEAVES are basal, light to medium green, thick and linear, up to 12 inches (30 cm) long and under ¼ inch (6 mm) wide. There are four to ten leaves and they are usually encased in the leaf sheaths of the previous year. GROWTH

HABIT is perennial; total height to the top of the flowering stem may be 30 inches (75 cm). Both leaves and flowering stems arise from the same point on the bulbous rootstock. This plant is very poisonous to livestock and a substantial hazard to sheep and cattle when pastures are overgrazed. Common HABITAT is shallow marshes and roadside ditches. Soil salinity does not discourage this plant and it is widespread in the prairies and parkland to the edge of the boreal forest.

20

WESTERN WATER-PLANTAIN
Alisma triviale Pursh

Western water-plantain

Western water-plantain

FLOWERS are white, up to ⅜ inch (1 cm) diameter, with a conspicuous yellow center due to the six stamens which are longer than the light green pistil. The flowers with three white petals and three green sepals are borne separately in a much-branched arrangement and appear in June and July. FRUIT is a group of minute, flat-sided achenes with short beaks borne in a whorl. LEAVES are light green, ovate to oblong, 2 to 7 inches (5-18 cm) long, with distinct parallel veins. They have long petioles, are rounded at the base and pointed at the apex, and have smooth margins. GROWTH HABIT is perennial and erect. Both leaves and flower stem arise directly from the crown of the rootstock. Total height may be up to 3 feet (1 m). HABITAT is usually marshes, ditches, and wet slough margins where water does not persist beyond July. This water-plantain is widely distributed in the parkland and prairie.

ARROWHEAD
Sagittaria cuneata Sheld.

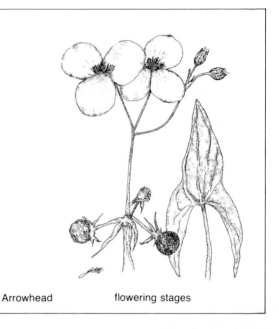

Arrowhead   flowering stages

FLOWERS (staminate and pistillate types on the same plant) are waxy white and have three petals. There is a conspicuous yellow center in the male flowers which are usually borne higher on the flowering stalk than the female flowers. Blooms are usually in whorls of three, appearing July-August. FRUITS are flattened achenes which develop from the carpels, (three to four) of the female flowers. They are arranged in a dense head. LEAVES are broad and arrow-shaped, entire margined, deep green above and lighter below. There are usually a few narrow, strap-shaped underwater leaves. Aerial leaves may be 4 inches (10 cm) long and 1½ inches (4 cm) wide. GROWTH HABIT is perennial; height may be 8 to 16 inches (20-40 cm), depending to some extent on the depth of water where the plant grows. HABITAT includes shallow sloughs, the semi-open areas of marshes, roadside ditches, etc., throughout the area.

Arrowhead

WATER CALLA
Calla palustris L.

ARUM FAMILY

Water calla

flower and spathe

FLOWERS are minute, yellowish, and lack sepals and petals. They develop in a thick spike-like spadix which is backed by a white oval spathe that is 1 to 1½ inches (2.5-4 cm) long. The modified flower stem (scape) may be up to 4 inches (10 cm) long. Flowers appear June-July. FRUIT is a red berry formed in a dense fleshy head. The white spathe rots away as the fruit develops. LEAVES are basal, broadly ovate, parallel veined, 2 to 4 inches (5-10 cm) long, on stalks of varying length, 2 to 8 inches (5-20 cm). GROWTH HABIT is perennial from thick rhizomes that root at the nodes. Total height is 4 to 8 inches (10-20 cm) but some of this is under water so plants appear shorter. HABITAT includes boggy sloughs and ditches where water remains well into August, particularly in the northern and eastern parts of the area. This plant is occasionally referred to as water-arum.

Water calla

NODDING ONION
Allium cernuum Roth

LILY FAMILY

Nodding
onion

Pink-flowered
onion

FLOWERS are pinkish lavender to white, eight to twelve in a loose nodding cluster at the end of a slender stem. Each flower is, like other onions, lily shaped, about ¼ inch (6 mm) long, with the two outer floral rings combined into six similar petals. Flowers of the pink-flowered onion, (*A. stellatum* Fraser), are similar but erect in the inflorescence, appearing June-August. FRUIT is a dry capsule, developing from the three-loculed ovary. LEAVES are fairly numerous, narrow, medium green, circular but not hollow. GROWTH HABIT is erect and the leaves and the single flower cluster arise from a rather small, coarse-necked bulb. The flower stalks are nodding when blooms are present but become erect before seeds mature. Length of the flower stalk varies from 4 to 16 inches (10-40 cm). HABITAT commonly includes open prairie and edges of scrubby patches. It is widely distributed in the same type of habitat as the prairie onion but is not as common. The pink-flowered onion is more common in the eastern and northern parts of the area.

Nodding onion

PRAIRIE ONION

LILY FAMILY

Allium textile Nels. and Macbr.

Prairie onion

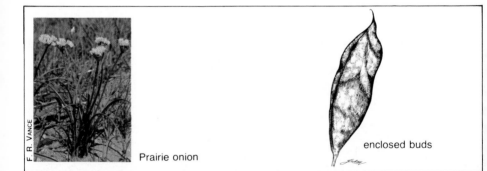

Prairie onion

enclosed buds

FLOWERS are white, occasionally tinged with pink, with the color due to similar petals and sepals (three each). They are borne in several rather tight umbels on stems which arise from the bulb, and appear May-June. FRUIT is a small, dry capsule containing four to six seeds. LEAVES are narrow, grooved and circular, characteristic of the onion family, complete with a strong odor and taste. They are not strictly hollow as are cultivated onions and wild chives, (*A. schoenoprasum* L. var. *sibiricum* [L.] Hartm.). GROWTH HABIT is erect, with several grass-like stems (leaves) arising from a bulb about ⅜ to ½ inch (10-12 mm) diameter. Height, 3 to 10 inches (7-30 cm), is usually less than that of other native onions. HABITAT commonly includes the dry prairie meadows and hillsides in the southern third of the area. It is probably the most widely distributed of the native onions.

FAIRYBELLS
LILY FAMILY
Disporum trachycarpum (S. Wats.) B. and H.

Fairybells   Fairybells

Fairybells

FLOWERS are greenish yellow to white, ½ to ¾ inch (12-20 mm) long, with the petals and sepals forming a single floral ring of six segments. From one to four blooms grow together like miniature lilies on drooping stalks among the leaves, appearing in June. FRUIT is a velvety-surfaced berry which goes through an orange stage and is red when completely ripe. The berry is ¼ to ⅝ inch (6-15 mm) diameter, soft and filled with small seeds. LEAVES are bright green, broadly ovate to lance-shaped, stalkless, parallel-veined, up to 3 inches (7.5 cm) long, and 2 inches (5 cm) wide. GROWTH HABIT is perennial, with many drooping leafy branches, 8 to 24 inches (20-60 cm) tall, usually nearer 8 inches (20 cm). Plants grow from a prominent horizontal rhizome. HABITAT includes moist wooded areas, thickets — saskatoon, chokecherry, etc., usually in association with sarsaparilla and baneberry. It is well distributed through the central part, (Qu'-Appelle Valley and its tributaries), and the east and north edges of the area.

WESTERN RED LILY

LILY FAMILY

Lilium philadelphicum L. var. *andinum* (Nutt.) Ker.

Western red lily

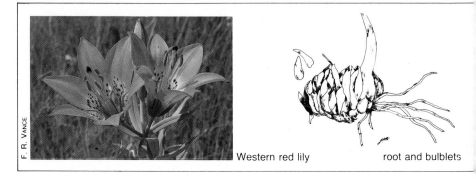

Western red lily   root and bulblets

This is Saskatchewan's floral emblem. FLOWERS are bright red, with bases of petals more orange than red and dotted with black, 2½ inches (7 cm) long and up to 3 inches (7.5 cm) across, with single or multiple blooms. Sepals and petals are both colored. Flowers appear in June. FRUIT is an elongated egg-shaped capsule in three sections. The LEAVES, linear to lance-shaped, alternate on stem with upper leaves in a whorl at the base of the flower stalk. The wood lily has all leaves in whorls. GROWTH HABIT is erect, perennial from a clump of white bulblets, usually 8-24 inches (20-60 cm) tall. Common HABITAT includes moist meadows, edges of aspen groves, thickets, and roadside ditches throughout the area.

TWO-LEAVED SOLOMON'S-SEAL (Wild lily-of-the-valley)   LILY FAMILY
Maianthemum canadense Desf. var. *interius* Fern.

Two-leaved solomon's-seal

Two-leaved solomon's-seal

FLOWERS are white, under ¼ inch (6 mm) long, clustered in a dense raceme 1 to 2 inches (2.5-5 cm) long. Each has petals, sepals, and stamens in fours and thus differs from three-leaved Solomon's-seal, *Smilacina trifolia* (L.) Desf., which has a floral ring of six parts and six stamens. Flowering occurs May to June.

FRUIT is a pale red berry, somewhat speckled, ¼ inch (6 mm) in diameter, usually containing two seeds. LEAVES are bright green, parallel veined and smooth edged, heart-shaped at the base. One basal leaf is long stalked and larger than the others, up to 2 inches (5 cm) long and ¾ inch (2 cm) wide. There are usually two short-stalked leaves on the stem, hence the common name of "two-leaved solomon's-seal." GROWTH HABIT is perennial, a low herb, 4 to 6 inches (10-15 cm), arising from branching rhizomes. Stems are very slender. HABITAT is moist woods, either deciduous or boreal, over the entire area, particularly where there is a heavy carpet of leaf mold.

FALSE SOLOMON'S-SEAL
Smilacina stellata (L.) Desf.

False solomon's-seal

False solomon's-seal

FLOWERS are small, up to ¼ inch (6 mm) in diameter, borne in a loose spike-like raceme at the end of a leafy stem. The three petals and the three sepals are white and 1/16 to ⅛ inch (3-5 mm) long. Flowers appear in early May. FRUIT is a greenish berry with brownish black stripes. LEAVES are opposite, light green, smooth above and slightly hairy underneath, from 1 to 5 inches (2.5-12 cm) long, often folded along the midrib. GROWTH HABIT is perennial, erect but on bent stems about 6 to 8 inches (15-20 cm) long and occasionally up to 18 inches (45 cm). A larger species, wild spikenard, (S. racemosa [L.] Desf.), has similar flowers but the berries are red when ripe. HABITAT includes moist woods, shores of sandy marshes and margins of scrubby patches. A similar plant often growing in the same habitat is Maianthemum canadense Desf. var. interius Fern., known as two-leaved solomon's-seal or wild lily-of-the-valley. Its height is usually under 6 inches (15 cm). It is different due to its two or three leaves and red berries.

Wild spikenard

CARRIONFLOWER

LILY FAMILY

Smilax herbacea L. var. *lasioneura* (Hook.) A. DC.

Carrionflower

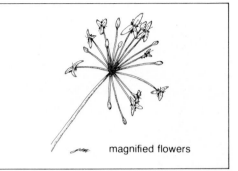

magnified flowers

FLOWERS are greenish white, small 3/32 inch or 2 mm diameter) in an umbel of twenty to forty flowers. The name of the plant comes from the carrion-like odor of the flowers. This is probably an evolutionary adaptation to attract flies which aid in fertilization. Approximate flowering date is June. FRUIT is a bluish black berry about 3/16 inch (4 mm) diameter, with a light bloom. There are usually four to six seeds per fruit. LEAVES are alternate, light green and have some netting in the arrangement of the veins. The dominant veins are parallel, as in other monocotyledons. Each leaf is 1½ to 5 inches (4-12 cm) long on petioles ½ to 2½ inches (1-7 cm) long, oval, pointed at the apex and rounded at the base. GROWTH HABIT: A climbing shrub with a weak stem and long tendrils, which attains a length of 4 to 6 feet (1.5-2m). The stems are woody but die back each year. HABITAT includes the shady moist areas of scrub, open woods and river valleys in the central and eastern part of the area.

Carrionflower

STICKY ASPHODEL
Tofieldia glutinosa (Michx.) Pers.

J. R. JOWSEY

Sticky asphodel   Sticky asphodel

FLOWERS are creamy white, tipped with a deep red which is the dominant color before they open. They are minute, with a perianth of six similar parts (sepals and petals). The inflorescence is a short, dense, spike-like raceme, up to ⅜ inch (1 cm) across and 1 inch (2.5 cm) long. Flowering occurs in late July and early August. FRUIT is a red or yellowish red ovoid capsule about ¼ inch (6 mm) diameter. The seeds have a comma-like appendage at each end. LEAVES are basal, more or less in two layers, medium green. They are long and linear, 6 to 10 inches (15-25 cm), but too broad to be considered grass-like. There are usually four to six per plant, and occasionally one or two leaf-like bracts on the flower stalk. GROWTH HABIT is perennial, up to 20 inches (50 cm) from a short rootstock and numerous fibrous roots. The flower stems are long and slightly sticky due to glands and short hairs. This species is sometimes referred to as false asphodel. HABITAT is marshy ground and recently dried slough margins and road ditches particularly on calcareous soils in the north and east at the edge of the boreal forest.

TRILLIUM (Nodding wakerobin)
Trillium cernuum L.

LILY FAMILY

FLOWERS have three dark green, pointed sepals and three white petals, occasionally tinged with pink, slightly longer than the sepals. Both sepals and petals are rolled backward. The corolla is somewhat tubular, with each petal ¾ to 1 inch (2-2.5 cm) long, ¼ to ⅜ inch (6-10 mm) across. The flowers are on a long recurved stalk, 2 to 3 inches (5-7.5 cm), and usually droop. They appear in late May or early June. FRUIT is an ovoid, reddish purple, berry-like capsule which points downward. Sepals are somewhat reflexed so they do not appear to clasp the fruit. LEAVES are ovate, pointed, smooth, and bright green with a network of fairly prominent veins. They are sessile or have short petioles, under 1 inch (2.5 cm), and are 2 to 5 inches (5-12 cm) long. There are usually three per plant. GROWTH HABIT is perennial, erect, 8 to 18 inches (20-45 cm) tall, with a single nodding flower usually somewhat hidden by the leaves. HABITAT is shady, damp, wooded areas in the northeast of Saskatchewan and throughout Manitoba. This plant is rare and worthy of rigid protection. A larger relative, *T. grandiflora* (Michx.) Salsib., is the floral emblem of Ontario.

Trillium

SMOOTH CAMAS
Zygadenus elegans Pursh

LILY FAMILY

Smooth camas

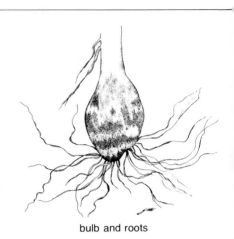

bulb and roots

Smooth camas

FLOWERS are yellowish white or greenish white and lily-shaped in an open raceme. The inner edges of the base petals and sepals (similar) are powdery yellow. They are about ⅜ inch (10 mm) long and ½ inch (12 mm) in diameter, appearing in June. FRUIT is a three-lobed, many seeded capsule, egg-shaped and ¾ inch (2 cm) long. LEAVES are pale green, mainly basal, 4 to 8 inches (10-20 cm) long, linear, keeled and almost grass-like, 1/16 inch (2 mm) wide. GROWTH HABIT is tall, 1 to 2 feet (30-60 cm) with a lily-like appearance. It is taller than death camas, *(Z. gramineus* Rydb.), and the inflorescence is much longer. HABITAT includes the moist, more saline areas of meadows and roadsides of the parkland and prairie, and scrubby areas, particularly in the east and central parts of the area. Death camas is found only in the southwest part of the area.

DEATH CAMAS
Zygadenus gramineus Rydb.

LILY FAMILY

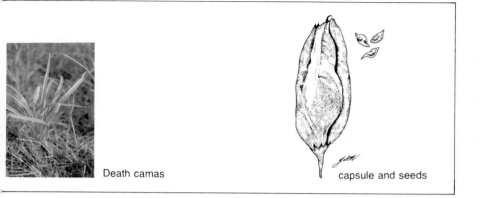

Death camas

capsule and seeds

FLOWERS are pale yellow, 3/16 inch (4 mm) long and about the same in diameter, tubular in profile. They are arranged in a dense raceme at the ends of the stems. Flowers appear May-June. The FRUIT is an oblong many-seeded capsule. LEAVES are pale green, linear, sheathed at the base, 4 to 8 inches (10-20 cm) long and about ⅛ inch (3 mm) wide. GROWTH HABIT is grass-like, 4 to 8 inches (10-20 cm), from a deep bulb. It begins growth early in the spring. This increases its hazard to ranchers because it is particularly poisonous to sheep and somewhat poisonous to cattle. HABITAT includes the higher edges of slough margins and draws and coulees of the southwest.

Death camas

BLUE FLAG
Iris versicolor L.

FLOWERS have three large violet-blue sepals which have white stripes near their centers and are occasionally tinged with yellow. A few red stripes may also be present near the base of each sepal. Sepals may be ¾ inch (2 cm) across and up to 3 inches (7.5 cm) long, but the three petals are smaller, mainly white, up to ¾ inch (2 cm) long and more linear. The pistil is more conspicuous than the petals, with three petal-like sections which arch over the stamens. Flowers, supported by a linear spathe, are borne on a round stem usually about 8 to 24 inches (20-60 cm) long. They appear in May and June. FRUIT: The ovary gives rise to an oblong capsule with three to six lobes in which several minute, flattened seeds develop. LEAVES are light to medium green, ⅜ to ⅝ inch (1-1.5 cm) wide, up to 8 inches (20 cm) long, and sharply pointed. Plants usually have only two or three leaves which are basal and distinctly parallel veined. GROWTH HABIT is perennial, erect, from woody tuber-bearing, creeping rootstocks. The stem and inflorescence is the tallest and most obvious part of the plant. HABITAT is swampy lake, slough, and stream margins in the extreme eastern parts of central and northern Saskatchewan and throughout Manitoba. This plant is rare in Saskatchewan, and it should be rigidly protected.

Blue flag

BLUE-EYED GRASS
Sisyrinchium montanum Greene

IRIS FAMILY

flower detail

Blue-eyed grass

Blue-eyed grass

FLOWERS are bright blue, ¼ inch (6 mm) diameter, with three petals and three sepals. They are distinctly star-shaped and appear June-July. FRUIT is a ¼ inch (6 mm) long, globular capsule, in three sections, containing small black seeds. LEAVES are bright green, linear and grass-like, basal with winged margins and usually ⅛ inch (3 mm) wide. GROWTH HABIT is erect, 3 to 12 inches (7-30 cm) high, often in colonies among grasses. A smaller, tufted species, *S. mucronatum* Michx., has lighter blue flowers and is more common in saline areas. HABITAT includes relatively moist areas, with the species difference in tolerance of salinity noted above. Blue-eyed grass will grow from naturally fallen seed in any reasonably moist sandy soil.

DRAGON'S MOUTH
Arethusa bulbosa L.

ORCHID FAMILY

Dragon's mouth

FLOWERS are rose pink, usually borne singly on a slender, smooth scape. The flowers have a pair of small unequal bracts at the base, and three pink linear sepals and two linear petals lateral to the lip. The pinkish white, toothed lip has purplish blotches and three to five white hairy ridges and usually droops beneath the other floral parts. It blooms in late June. FRUIT is an ellipsoidal capsule about 1 inch (2.5 cm) long, with six sharp ridges. LEAVES are light green, linear, strongly ribbed, 4 to 6 inches (10-15 cm) long, up to ¼ inch (6 mm) wide, usually single, occasionally with two other partly developed leaf sheaths clasping the scape near the base. GROWTH HABIT is perennial, a low, delicate herb growing from a small, solid, bulbous corm to a height of 6 to 12 inches (15-30 cm) which is to the top of the flowering stalk. HABITAT is cool bogs and drier humps in wet meadow openings in spruce forest.

This plant is very rare and should be rigorously protected. It has been found around Hudson Bay in Saskatchewan and at a few locations in Manitoba.

VENUS SLIPPER
Calypso bulbosa (L.) Oakes

ORCHID FAMILY

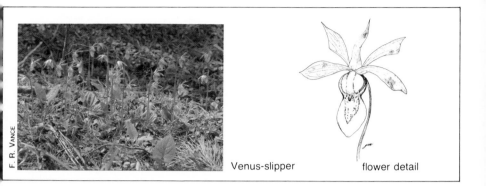

Venus-slipper   flower detail

FLOWERS are pale purple to pink with the typical orchid arrangement of sepals and petals. The whole flower is ½ to 1 inch (12-25 mm) long. The pink sac-like lip has darker purple lines on it and is more striking due to an inner tuft of yellow hairs. Flowers appear in early June. FRUIT is a brown capsule, ½ inch (12 mm) long, containing many seeds. LEAVES are dark green, one per plant, basal, wide ovate 1 to 1½ inches (2.5-4 cm) long. GROWTH HABIT is short, with the flower on a 3 to 7 inch (7-17 cm) stem. The stem is slender and the flowers may appear nearly prostrate. HABITAT is open coniferous woods, particularly under pine. This orchid, named "Calypso" for the Greek goddess of that name, favors the open shaded areas in the northern forest.

Venus-slipper

SPOTTED CORALROOT
Corallorhiza maculata Raf.

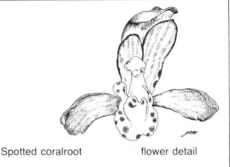

Spotted coralroot   flower detail

FLOWERS are light pink to white, liberally spotted with purple or red on sepals and petals. They are 3/16 to 5/8 inch (4-14 mm) long, with the lip, which is also spotted, about the same length. Blooms have a prominent yellowish spur. Ten to forty of them are borne in a long raceme, appearing May-June. FRUIT is a round many-seeded capsule. LEAVES are reduced to scales about ⅛ inch (3 mm) wide and an inch (2.5 cm) or more long, dark reddish brown in color. GROWTH HABIT is erect and saprophytic. They are 6 to 20 inches (15-50 cm) tall, with at least half of this height due to the raceme. HABITAT is the forest floor in deep coniferous woods. It is found on the edges of the mixed forest and in the Cypress Hills.

Spotted coralroot

STRIPED CORALROOT
Corallorhiza striata Lindl.

ORCHID FAMILY

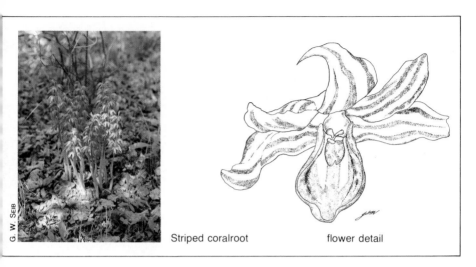

Striped coralroot   flower detail

G. W. SEIB

FLOWERS are lavender pink with dark reddish purple stripes in the lateral petals and sepals. The lip is white to light pink with five purple stripes. The flowers are about ½ inch (12 mm) long, spurless, in a raceme of fewer blooms, (10-25), than the spotted coralroot, *(C. maculata* Raf.). Approximate flowering dates range from May-June. FRUIT is a round, many-seeded capsule about 3/16 inch (4 mm) in diameter. LEAVES are reduced to long, colorless, scale-like structures which sheath the stem. GROWTH HABIT is erect and saprophytic. The coarse, stout, reddish to yellowish stems may reach a total height of 18 to 20 inches (45-50 cm) of which at least one-third is due to the flowering stalk. On average, these plants are shorter than those of spotted coralroot. HABITAT is the same for both species: deep coniferous woods. They are often found in the same area, at the boreal forest edge, and in the Cypress Hills.

F. R. VANCE

Striped coralroot

EARLY CORALROOT
Corallorhiza trifida Chat.

ORCHID FAMILY

Early coralroot

Early coralroot

FLOWERS are pale yellow with a greenish tinge, and three to twelve are borne on each stalk in an extended raceme ¾ to 2½ inches (2-6 cm) long. The white lip, sometimes dotted with red or purple, has a small tooth on each side, making it three lobed (*trifida*). The lip is slightly shorter than the two linear petals and the three linear sepals which are each about ¼ inch (6 mm) in length. Flowering occurs in early June. FRUIT is a rounded, egg-shaped capsule, ⅛ to ¼ inch (3-6 mm) long, containing many brownish seeds. LEAVES are reduced to thin, papery, yellowish scales up to ¼ inch (6 mm) long which clasp the stalk. GROWTH HABIT: A saprophytic perennial with slender yellowish stems 4 to 12 inches (10-30 cm) tall. A clump of several stems arises from a coral-red rhizome but the plant has no true roots. HABITAT is the shaded open areas in aspen groves or scrubby patches, or open spaces in coniferous woods where moisture conditions are good. It is found in the parkland and in the Cypress Hills where cultivation and drainage have not eliminated the habitat this plant requires.

STEMLESS LADY'S SLIPPER
Cypripedium acaule Ait.

ORCHID FAMILY

F. R. VANCE

Stemless lady's slipper

This is the floral emblem of Prince Edward Island. FLOWERS are dominated by a pink lip, 2 to 2½ inches (5-7 cm) long, deeply cleft near its center. Sepals and petals are lanceolate, yellow green to greenish brown. Flowers are solitary and the flowering stem is leafless and hairy. It grows from the root crown. Flowering occurs in late June. FRUIT is a brown, many-seeded capsule. LEAVES are basal, medium green, and there are only two, nearly opposite in placement. They are narrowly elliptic or oblong and sparsely hairy, about 6 inches (15 cm) long. GROWTH HABIT is erect, 6 to 15 inches (15-40 cm) tall with leaves and stems arising from coarse roots. Common HABITAT includes bogs and other moist areas among sand dunes in the open shade in northern forest areas. These flowers are rare — do not pick!

Stemless lady's slipper

RAM'S HEAD LADY'S SLIPPER
ORCHID FAMILY
Cypripedium arietinum R. Br.

Ram's head lady's slipper

Ram's head lady's slipper

G. W. SEIB

Franklin's lady's slipper

FLOWERS are greenish purple, solitary, with sepals and lateral petals ½ to 1 inch (12-24 mm) long. The lip is whitish with heavy purplish veins, ½ to ¾ inch (1-2 cm) long and ends in a spur-like horn. The other lady's slipper illustration is *C. passerinum* Richards., known by various common names: northern lady's slipper, sparrows egg lady's slipper and Franklin's lady's slipper. Generally, flowers appear in June. FRUIT is a brown capsule charac-teristic of the lady's slippers. LEAVES, three to five, are dark green and lance-shaped to elliptic. They are often folded and have marginal hairs. GROWTH HABIT is erect and slender, 4 to 15 inches (10-40 cm) high, usually nearer the former. Common HABITAT includes damp, cool sandy areas in woodlands in the north and north-east. This plant is very rare in Saskatch-ewan. Sites where it still grows should be carefully preserved.

LARGE YELLOW LADY'S SLIPPER

ORCHID FAMILY

Cypripedium calceolus L. var. *pubescens* (Willd.) Correll

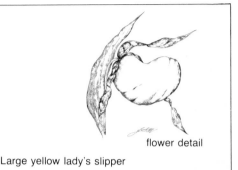

flower detail

Large yellow lady's slipper

Large yellow lady's slipper

FLOWERS are bright yellow with sepals and petals greenish to brown. The lip may be ¾ to 1½ inches (2-4 cm) long and may have a few brown or reddish purple spots near the tongue. Flowers appear in June. FRUIT is a dry, dark brown capsule with many seeds. LEAVES are light green, ovate to lanceolate with sharp points, prominently veined and with a few hairs. They are 2 to 6 inches (5-15 cm) long and up to 2 inches (5 cm) wide. GROWTH HABIT is perennial, flower stem is usually about 5 inches (12 cm) long and nearly smooth. The total plant varies in height from 6 to 16 inches (15-40 cm). HABITAT includes the edges or open spaces in aspen poplar woods or upper margins of sloughs and ditches on roads and railway grades. Both this variety and the small yellow lady's slipper, (*C. calceolus* [L.] var. *parviflorum* [Salisb.] Fern.), are rare and should only be picked or moved under special restrictions or permit.

SHOWY LADY'S SLIPPER
Cypripedium reginae Walt.

ORCHID FAMILY

Showy lady's slipper

F. R. VANCE

FLOWERS have a light pink lip with reddish purple stripes; otherwise, sepals and petals are white. The lip is often over an inch (2.5 cm) long and the total flower may be 1½ inches (4 cm) in length, blooming June-July. FRUIT is a somewhat elongated, round, many-seeded capsule to which the dried flower may be attached for many weeks. LEAVES are opposite, light green, and hairy, particularly on the underside. They are fairly numerous and each one clasps the stem over a distance of several inches. LEAVES are about 1½ inches (4 cm) across and length varies from 4 to 8 inches (10-20 cm). GROWTH HABIT is erect and perennial on rather thick hairy stems well covered with leaves. Plants are tall, usually about 15 inches (37 cm) but 2 to 2½ feet (60-75 cm) is not unusual. HABITAT includes the open shade in low spruce and pine stands, where the soil is calcareous, particularly on high calcium low magnesium soils. This plant is relatively common in Manitoba but is rare in Saskatchewan, and may have been eliminated here. Take care!

A. H. SHORTT

Showy lady's slipper

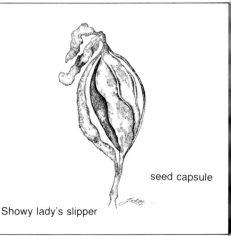

seed capsule

RATTLESNAKE-PLANTAIN
Goodyera repens (L.) Br.

ORCHID FAMILY

Lesser rattlesnake-plantain

FLOWERS are ⅛ to ¼ inch (3-6 mm) long, borne in a loose spiral or one-sided raceme where the three dark green bracts contrast with the white petals. The lateral sepals are usually widely spread and the third sepal is united with the petals above the lip. In the second species shown, *G. oblongifolia* Raf., the flowers are larger, ¼ to ⅜ inch (6-10 mm), the bracts are lighter green, and the petals greenish white. Flowers appear from mid-July to mid-August. FRUIT is a brown, oblong, reflexed capsule, about ⅛ inch (3 mm) long. LEAVES are dark green, obovate, ¼ inch (6 mm) across and up to 1⅜ inches (3.5 cm) long, very lined and mottled, like the back of a rattlesnake. Leaves of *G. oblongifolia* are more oblong and have less mottling but a more prominent whitish midrib. GROWTH HABIT is perennial and erect from creeping rootstocks and thick roots. Both species have basal leaves, but the most striking difference is height to the top of the flowering stem, which is usually less than 9 inches (23 cm) in *G. repens* and up to 12 to 18 inches (30-45 cm) in *G. oblongifolia*. HABITAT is dry to slightly moist open spaces of the boreal forest. Both species are found in coniferous woods but only *G. oblongifolia* is found in the Cypress Hills.

Lesser rattlesnake-plantain

J. R. JOWSEY

Rattlesnake-plantain

LONG-BRACTED BOG ORCHID
Habenaria bracteata (Muhl.) R.Br.

Long-bracted bog orchid   Long-bracted bog orchid

J. R. JOWSEY

FLOWERS have greenish white lateral petals and a tongue-shaped lip ⅜ inch (1 cm) long. The lip has two or three lobes at the tip and may be spotted with purple. Three ovate green sepals dominate the two petals. The spur is shorter, blunt and pouched. The flowers are ¼ to ⅜ inch (6-10 mm) long and have leaf-like bracts which are three to four times as long and curve up and over them, particularly at the base of the raceme. Flowering occurs in June and early July. FRUIT is a small, dry capsule with many seeds. LEAVES are dark green, oval to lanceolate, rather ridged, and may be as wide as 1 ¼ inches (3 cm) and 2 to 5 inches (5-12 cm) in length, with the upper leaves being shorter. They clasp the stem through about a third of their length. GROWTH HABIT is perennial and erect, 6 to 24 inches (15-60 cm) tall. A similar green orchid, *H. hyperborea* (L.) R.Br., is taller, but has less obvious bracts and smaller, greenish yellow flowers in a shorter raceme. HABITAT is open scrubby places among aspens where shade is not heavy and moisture conditions are good. Both species are found where aspens have not been cleared in the parkland and in the Cypress Hills. *H. hyperborea* is not as common and is more boreal in its distribution.

WHITE BOG ORCHID
Habenaria dilatata (Pursh) Hook.

ORCHID FAMILY

White bog orchid

FLOWERS are waxy white and fragrant, ¼ to ⅜ inch (6-10 mm) long, with the petals and sepals being similar in color. The curved spur and the tongue-shaped lip are each about ⅜ inch (1 cm) long. Flowers are in an extended spike 4 to 12 inches (10-30 cm) long and may appear from late June to early August. FRUIT is a rather linear brown capsule which contains many small seeds. LEAVES are basal, linear to lanceolate, medium green, 3 to 10 inches (7.5-25 cm) long, pointed, clasping, decreasing in size farther up the stem. GROWTH HABIT is perennial, tall, 8 to 40 inches (20-100 cm), with leaves rising to half the total height. This is probably the tallest species of bog orchid in the area and the one with the longest spike. HABITAT is wet, boggy, open areas in boreal forests of the north and east and the Cypress Hills.

G. W. SEIB

White bog orchid

NORTHERN TWAYBLADE
Listera borealis Morong.

ORCHID FAMILY

Northern twayblade

Twayblade

FLOWERS are pale green with distinct deep green veins in sepals and petals (three of each). The lip petal of the corolla is broadly oblong, green fading to yellow or white at its edges, ⅜ inch (1 cm) long, flat and lobed at its apex. Flowers are borne on short stems in a raceme about 1 inch (2.5 cm) long and appear in late June and early July. FRUIT is an egg-shaped capsule about ⅛ inch (3 mm) long which contains several minute seeds. LEAVES are opposite, dark green, broadly ovate with deep parallel veins. They may be ¾ to 2 inches (2-5 cm) long and very distinctive in their placement halfway up the stem. GROWTH HABIT is perennial with a sturdy stem for such a short plant, 3 to 6 inches (7.5-15 cm) tall, with the two large clasping leaves standing straight out from the stem. By contrast, another twayblade found farther east, *Liparis loeselii* (L.) Rich., has leaves that are basal, longer, and distinctly linear. HABITAT is the open, less shaded areas of spruce woods and swamps of the boreal forest. Both species are extremely rare but found occasionally in suitable habitat.

ROUND-LEAVED ORCHIS
Orchis rotundifolia Banks

ORCHID FAMILY

Round-leaved orchis

Round-leaved orchis

Round-leaved bog-orchid

FLOWERS are rose pink to white, ⅜ to ¾ inch (1-2 cm) long in a bracted raceme of two to eight flowers, with color mainly due to lateral petals. The lip is white with purple spots, about ⅜ inch (1 cm) long, three-lobed, with the middle lobe the largest and notched at the apex. The spur is slender, curved and much shorter than the lip. The lateral petals spread outwards and the upper sepal and petals are elevated above the lip. Flowers are greenish white in the round-leaved bog-orchid, (*Habenaria orbiculata* [Pursh] Torr.). Flowers bloom in July. FRUIT is a dry, brown, many-seeded capsule. LEAVES: This species has only one leaf. The round-leaved bog-orchid has two rounded leaves and its flower stalk is much longer. Leaves are basal in both species. GROWTH HABIT is basal, with a long, stiff flower stalk which may be 4 to 10 inches (10-25 cm) high. The leaf and flower stem arise from a scaly rootstock. HABITAT includes the boreal forest and its parkland edges, where moisture conditions are good. This plant and the *Habenaria* species described are fairly common in this habitat.

HOODED LADY'S-TRESSES
Spiranthes romanzoffiana Cham.

ORCHID FAMILY

FLOWERS are sweet scented, creamy white, about ¼ inch (6 mm) long, each on a short stalk in three spirals on a spike 1 to 3 inches (3-8 cm) long. The hood is formed of three sepals and two lateral petals, and in profile looks like the brim of a sunbonnet. The lip is fiddle-shaped, spurless, about ⅜ inch (1 cm) long and bent abruptly downward. Flower arrangement is more open on the other plant illustrated which is nodding lady's tresses, sometimes considered a separate species, *S. cernua* Rich. Blooms appear July-August. FRUIT is a small capsule which contains many seeds. LEAVES are linear to lanceolate, 2 to 6 inches (5-15 cm) long, blunt-tipped and extending along the stem rather than basal as is the case with slender lady's tresses, *(S. gracilis* [Bigel.] Beck.). GROWTH HABIT is perennial and erect, on rather stout stems, usually short but occasionally over 12 inches (30 cm) tall. HABITAT includes swampy places, meadows and open woods with light shade, lake shores, boreal and parkland areas, particularly in the north and east.

Nodding lady's-tresses

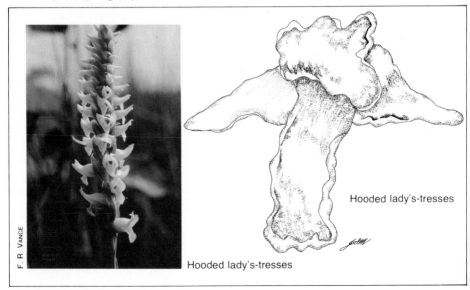

Hooded lady's-tresses

Hooded lady's-tresses

BALSAM POPLAR
Populus balsamifera L.

WILLOW FAMILY

Balsam poplar

FLOWERS are in staminate or pistillate catkins, 1 ¼ to 3 inches (3-7.5 cm) long, on separate trees. The deep red staminate catkins, which appear before the leaves, have sticky, scaly, resinous bracts. Staminate catkins are deep red before opening. They are essentially sessile and appear in May. The pistillate catkins are a chain of minute flowers and appear after leaves open. FRUIT is a smooth, oblong, brown capsule held in the scales of the flower stalks of the female flower until mid-June. Each capsule contains minute seeds attached to tufts of white hairs. LEAVES are dark green above, yellow to rusty beneath, 2 to 6 inches (5-15 cm) long, thick, often glandular and numerous, ovate to oblong, with shallow marginal teeth. Leaves are borne on a stout round petiole 1 to 2½ inches (2.5-6 cm) long. GROWTH HABIT: A tall, rough, rapidly growing tree which may attain a height of 50 to 60 feet (17-20 m). HABITAT includes marshy spots and margins of sloughs, particularly in the parkland. It extends into forest areas, but it is not as common as the aspen poplar.

Balsam poplar

ASPEN POPLAR
Populus tremuloides Michx.

Aspen poplar

FLOWERS are in staminate and pistillate catkins on separate trees. The staminate catkins appear before the leaves, and are gray and woolly, like miniature lambs' tails, 1½ to 2½ inches (4-6 cm) long, ⅛ to ¼ inch (3-6 mm) in diameter. The pistillate catkin becomes prominent just as the leaf buds open, in early June. FRUIT is a small, warty, conical capsule containing several small seeds each bearing a tuft of fine hairs. LEAVES are bright, light to medium green, broadly ovate, 1¼ to 4 inches (3-10 cm), with finely toothed indentations and a sharp tip. They are borne on flattened petioles of sufficient length, 1¼ to 2 inches (3-5 cm), that the leaves tremble in the slightest breeze, hence the common name of "trembling aspen." GROWTH HABIT: A tree of varying height, from 10 feet (3 m) in the sand dunes to forest giants 75 feet (25 m) tall, and a diameter of 12 to 22 inches (30-55 cm). The bark is light green to gray, but will be black and furrowed at the base of large trees. HABITAT includes any reasonably moist area, even in the southwest where the ground water is close to the surface. It is common in the boreal forest, sometimes to timberline.

Aspen poplar

PUSSY WILLOW
Salix discolor Muhl.

WILLOW FAMILY

Pussy willow

FLOWERS are in separate sexes on different plants. The erect male catkins appear as gray "cat's paws" and two extended pollen-laden stamens in each male flower give them a deep yellow color at maturity. Female catkins appear later and are green, more loose in arrangement, about 1¼ inches (3 cm) long, or at least twice the length of the male inflorescence. Both catkins appear well before the leaves, late April or early May. FRUIT is a somewhat conical green capsule which may be up to ⅜ inch (1 cm) long, remaining in catkins until maturity when a mass of hairs is released as the capsule opens. This stage is sometimes not obvious until after the leaves come out in June. It is more noticeable in some other species like hoary willow (*S. candida* Fluegge). LEAVES are bright green, linear lanceolate, finely serrated and smooth, on short petioles. Leaves among willow species are highly variable; those of hoary willow are gray-green above and

Hoary willow

whitish beneath due to fine hairs. GROWTH HABIT is perennial, either as small shrubs with reddish stems or occasionally maturing to small trees, 10 feet (3 m) tall, with gray-barked trunks up to 3 inches (7.5 cm) diameter. HABITAT is usually a ring around small sloughs, above the water line or as occasional trees in open spaces in aspen stands where moisture is abundant.

BEAKED HAZELNUT
Corylus cornuta Marsh.

Hazelnut

Hazelnut

G. W. SEIB

FLOWERS are of two types. The female or pistillate ones are reddish pink (cerise) about ⅛ inch (3 mm) across and ⅛ inch (3 mm) tall, lacking sepals and petals. They are a short, bud-like catkin borne in leaf axils and appear before leaves emerge. The staminate catkins are light brown, ⅜ to ¾ inch (1-2 cm) long. Both flowers are borne on the same bush (i.e. the plant is monoecious). Flowers appear in early May. FRUITS are nuts, ⅜ to ¾ inch (1-2 cm) diameter, with a very dense, brown, bony shell. They are surrounded with two hairy bractlets up to 1 ¼ inches (3 cm) long which form a leaf-like beak. The nuts grow in groups of two or three. LEAVES are alternate, medium green, oblong to ovate, 2 to 4 inches (5-10 cm) long, coarsely toothed, borne on petioles averaging ⅝ inch (1.5 cm) in length. They are numerous, particularly on the upper branches, and form a thick cover in clumps of these bushes. GROWTH HABIT is perennial, a brown-stemmed, freely branching shrub usually under 4 feet (120 cm) tall but occasionally up to 10 feet (3 m). Since the rootstocks spread, dense clumps are common. HABITAT is usually the edges of aspen groves and patches of mixed shrubs in the parkland and plains. It is widely distributed but more common in the north and east.

BUR OAK
Quercus macrocarpa Michx.

BEECH FAMILY

Bur oak

Bur oak

Bur oak

FLOWERS of male and female types are yellowish green, found on the same tree. The pistillate flowers have a bell-shaped calyx, extremely small (under 1 mm diameter). They are borne in an involucre of many bracts on twigs of the previous season. Staminate flowers are in catkins which are 1¼ to 3 inches (3-7.5 cm) in length. Flowering occurs in early May before leaves appear. FRUIT is an acorn, about ⅝ inch (1.5 cm) in diameter, held in a fringed cup formed by the thickened, rounded bracts and receptacle. They mature singly or in twos and threes in the same season as flowering. LEAVES are dark green and shiny, grayish white on the underside, obovate to oblong in outline, 4 to 8 inches (10-20 cm) long and about 2 inches (5 cm) wide, with large irregular lobes that are occasionally toothed. GROWTH HABIT: A scrubby tree rarely more than 10 to 15 feet (3-5 m) in height in Saskatchewan but occasionally to 30 feet (10 m) farther east. Bark is blackish gray and flaky and the wood is very dense. HABITAT is limited to certain soil types arising from cretaceous shales in the eastern Qu'Appelle Valley and similar areas in southern Manitoba. The stark, rough profile of these trees is an unusual feature of the valleys of rivers and creeks where it grows.

56

COMMON HOP
Humulus lupulus L.

HEMP FAMILY

Common hop

Common hop

seed stage

FLOWERS of different sexes are on different plants, (i.e., hop is dioecious.) Male flowers are green, small, in loose panicles in leaf axils, each with five sepals and five stamens. Female flowers have the calyx reduced to a single sepal. They are in drooping catkin-like spikes and are located in the leaf axils. Approximate flowering date is June. FRUIT is a resinous achene, covered with scaly, sharp, modified bracts. These clusters of bracts may be a ½ inch (12 mm) across and more than an inch (2.5 cm) long. LEAVES are numerous, opposite, light green, paimately lobed into three to seven leaflets. The upper leaves are often toothed rather than divided. The whole leaf may be 4 to 7 inches (10-18 cm) wide and has whitish or yellowish glandular spots on the underside. GROWTH HABIT is perennial. The stems are woody but usually die back each season. They twine over shrubs and may reach 20 feet (6 m) in length. HABITAT includes moist places in wooded areas, roadside ditches, etc., particularly in the Qu'Appelle Valley and tributaries, and in the eastern part of the area generally.

STINGING NETTLE
Urtrica gracilis Ait.

NETTLE FAMILY

Stinging nettle

Stinging nettle

FLOWERS are green, minute but extremely numerous in dense, branched clusters in the axils of leaves. There are no petals but there are four hairy sepals. This species is generally dioecious but both staminate and pistillate flowers may be found on the same plant. Flowers are commonly noticed in July and August but may appear earlier. FRUIT is a flattened, oblong, minute achene tightly held by the dried calyx. LEAVES are medium green, opposite, ovate to lanceolate, sharply toothed, and bearing numerous stinging hairs. They are highly variable in size, but usually 1 to 1¼ inches (2.5-3 cm) across and 2 to 5 inches (5-12 cm) long. GROWTH HABIT is perennial, erect, on slender square stems which grow to about 3 feet (1 m) but some plants may attain 6 feet (2 m). The stems arise in clumps and outer ones may fall if some support is removed. HABITAT is waste places near groves of deciduous trees, against buildings or among shrubs at garden edges or middens, or in some scrubby roadside ditches.

PALE COMANDRA
Comandra pallida A. DC.

Pale comandra   flower detail

FLOWERS are greenish white to pink, ⅛ to 3/16 inch (3-5 mm) in length, and about 3/16 inch (5 mm) across with five petals and five sepals. They are borne in clusters of three to five at the tips of stems, blooming May-June. FRUIT is a hard, olive green drupe with one seed. LEAVES are alternate, pale gray green, linear-lanceolate, ½ to 1 inch (1-2.5 cm) long, smooth, and usually lacking petioles. They are numerous and cause the plant to appear very leafy. GROWTH HABIT is erect and perennial, with many stems often arising from one point on the creeping rootstock. Plants are usually 3 to 5 inches (7-12 cm) tall but may be over 12 inches (30 cm). HABITAT includes dry sandy hillsides throughout the whole area, particularly on the open prairie.

Pale comandra

YELLOW UMBRELLAPLANT
Eriogonum flavum Nutt.

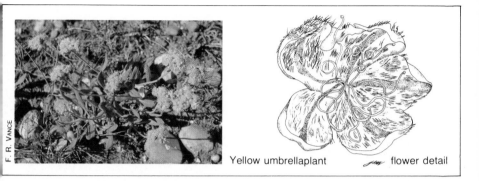

Yellow umbrellaplant   flower detail

FLOWERS are pale yellow with a tinge of orange. Petals are absent and the floral ring is formed of united sepals. Flowers are borne in fluffy clusters, about ½ inch (12 mm) diameter, which are encased with several large leaf-like bracts. Approximate flowering date is June. The FRUIT is a small, ⅛ inch (3 mm) achene, with soft matted hairs. LEAVES are basal, green above, white on the underside due to fine hairs, 1¼ to 2 inches (3-5 cm) long, linear-oblong or spatulate. GROWTH HABIT is perennial and erect, from a coarse, woody, tufted root. It is characteristically a low plant, usually 4 to 8 inches (10-20 cm) but may be as tall as 16 inches (40 cm). HABITAT includes dry eroded areas, hillsides, badland exposures and canyon walls throughout the southwest.

Yellow umbrellaplant

WATER SMARTWEED
Polygonum amphibium L.

BUCKWHEAT FAMILY

Water smartweed

Swamp smartweed

Lady's thumb

FLOWERS are reddish purple, about 1/16 inch (2 mm) in diameter, in dense spikes. The color is due to the five sepals. Petals are absent. Flowers bloom July-August. FRUIT is a small lens-shaped achene, which contains a black seed. It is a common food for ducks. LEAVES are lanceolate to ovate, 4 to 8 inches (10-20 cm) long, deep green and hairless above, often hairy beneath. A few of the lower leaves may be floating. GROWTH HABIT is perennial and more or less erect. Stems are angled and wiry but weak. Height may be up to 15 inches (38 cm) and some plants float on their stems. Swamp smartweed or persicaria, *(P. coccineum* Muhl.), also shown here, tends to have stronger stems and grow taller. The third illustration is lady's thumb, *(P. persicaria* L.), a shorter (4 to 6 inches or 10-15 cm) species. HABITAT includes shallow sloughs, slough margins and drainage ditches in the prairie and park land. Smartweed turns whole sloughs rose pink in July of some years. The swamp species and lady's-thumb take over in slightly drier terrain in marshes.

WESTERN DOCK
Rumex occidentalis S. Wats.

BUCKWHEAT FAMILY

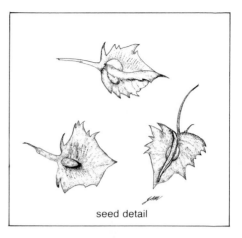

seed detail

Western dock

Western dock

FLOWERS are greenish, extremely small (under 1 mm), and densely packed in a small cluster. There are six sepals but no petals and three of the sepals are much larger than the others. Blooms appear June-July. The FRUIT is a three-sided achene enclosed in the dry papery reddish brown sepals. This gives the plants their characteristic appearance in late summer. Examination of the fruit with a microscope is about the only sure way to separate some of the species of dock. LEAVES are alternate, bright green, simple, oblong to lanceolate, thick and heart-shaped at the base. They may be up to 12 inches (30 cm) long and the lower leaves are much larger than the upper ones. GROWTH HABIT is perennial, tall, to 3 feet (1 m) or more in some cases, with a reddish stem arising from a woody taproot. Leaves are rather sparse and the plant is most noticed by its inflorescence. This may be over a foot (30 cm) long, and dark reddish brown when ripe. Other similar species are the field docks, *(R. fennicus* [Murb.]), and *(R. stenophyllus* [Ledeb.]). HABITAT includes sloughs and roadside ditches, etc., throughout the area. Field dock and narrow-leaved dock tend to be more common than western dock in similar niches in more northerly, central and eastern parts of the area.

SAND DOCK
Rumex venosus Pursh

Sand dock

Sand dock

F. R. VANCE

FLOWERS are greenish, minute, with six sepals in two circles of three and no petals. They are borne in tight clusters up to about 1½ inches (4 cm) at ends of stems. Flowers appear from May to August. FRUIT is a triangular achene which is covered with the three rose-red inner sepals which are much larger than those of other species of dock. Plants are most noticeable when the fruit is at this stage in which the calyx valves may be over ⅝ inch (1.5 cm) in diameter. LEAVES are alternate, pale green, 2 to 5 inches (5-12 cm) long, 1½ inches (4 cm) or more wide, without marginal teeth. They have short petioles and papery sheathing stipules. GROWTH HABIT is perennial and erect, but often sprawling on a stout, twisted, branching stem. Plants grow from woody, running rootstocks, and may be 4 to 8 inches (10-20 cm) in height. HABITAT is sandy soil where water is fairly near the surface. It is very common in southwest Saskatchewan but appears in many other locations on the plains where growing conditions are suitable.

STRAWBERRY BLITE
Chenopodium capitatum (L.) Aschers

GOOSEFOOT FAMILY

Strawberry blite

Strawberry blite

FLOWERS are green and minute, with five sepals and no petals. The red color is due to color change and enlargement of the ripening sepals. Several flowers are borne in a close, rounded cluster and mature to resemble a small strawberry in late July and through August. FRUIT is a thin achene with one black, lens-shaped seed enclosed by the red, fleshy calyx. LEAVES are alternate, pale green and smooth, 1 to 2¾ inches (2.5-7 cm) long, coarsely toothed and broadly spear-shaped, borne on short ⅜ inch (1 cm) petioles. GROWTH HABIT: A much-branched annual, 8 to 20 inches (20-50 cm) tall. The stem is usually longitudinally grooved and often has reddish lines or blotches. HABITAT is commonly waste places, garden edges, and moist road-sides. It is widely distributed across the continent.

RED SAMPHIRE
Salicornia rubra A. Nels.

Red samphire

FLOWERS are minute inside the fleshy, scale-like calyx which is sunk into stem tissue. There are usually three flowers in a triangular arrangement at each joint of the fruiting spike ⅜ to 2 inches (1-5 cm) long. Flowering takes place in late July and August. FRUIT is a small flattened seed covered with microscopic hairs, enclosed in the spongy, matured calyx. LEAVES are dark reddish green, triangular and scale-like, about ⅛ inch (3 mm) long, and are attached at each stem node. GROWTH HABIT: An erect, low-growing or prostrate plant with a round, succulent, reddish stem of up to 10 inches (25 cm) long which turns bright red at maturity. HABITAT is strongly saline sloughs and dry marshes of the southern prairies. Mature patches of these plants give the impression of a bright red carpet in some sloughs.

C. C. PETERS

flower detail

Red samphire

GREASEWOOD
Sarcobatus vermiculatus (Hook.) Torr.

GOOSEFOOT FAMILY

Greasewood

Greasewood

FLOWERS are yellowish green and minute. Sexes are separate with male flowers in dense, compact terminal spikes. The female flowers are very small and borne singly in leaf axils. Flowering is common by late June. FRUIT is a minute seed with a translucent seed coat in which the embryo is coiled in a green spiral. The two lips of the calyx enlarge in the fruit to form an almost circular wing up to ⅜ inch (1 cm) broad. LEAVES are alternate, pale yellow-green, ¾ to 1½ inches (2-4 cm) long, narrowly linear, and rather fleshy. They are quite numerous and give the plant a solid appearance. GROWTH HABIT is perennial, a low, rough shrub with many light green spiny branches. Stems may be quite woody and 1 inch (2.5 cm) or more in diameter. Bushes may be 2 to 3 feet (60-90 cm) tall with a whitish bark on mature stems. HABITAT is dry saline sloughs and flats in the grasslands of the southwest. It is not common and should be eradicated in pastures because it is somewhat poisonous to livestock.

UMBRELLAWORT
Mirabilis hirsuta (Pursh) MacM.

FOUR-O'CLOCK FAMILY

Hairy umbrellawort

Heart-leaved umbrellawort

Hairy umbrellawort

FLOWERS are reddish pink fading to white, about ⅜ inch (10 mm) long. They appear in groups of two to five, subtended by a bell-shaped involucral bract. There are no petals, and five sepals form a bell-like tube from which the three to five stamens and a long curved pistil project. Flowers appear in August. FRUIT is an anthocarp, i.e., a dry, one-seeded inflated cone (utricle) enclosed in the ribbed membranous base of the calyx. LEAVES are medium green, opposite without stipules, linear-lanceolate to oblong, 1 to 3 inches (2.5-7.5 cm) long, densely hairy with entire margins, sessile on the upper stems, short petioled nearer the base. Another species, heart-leaved umbrellawort, *M. nyctaginea* (Michx.) MacM., has smooth, heart-shaped, dark green leaves, a hairless stem, and flowers of a deeper pink. GROWTH HABIT is perennial, erect on light green, weak hairy stems. They are much branched and give a group of plants the appearance of a mass of vegetation, 1 to 2 feet (30-60 cm) tall, with flowering branches extending out in all directions. HABITAT is dry sandy prairie, scrubby patches and abandoned building sites in the southern third of the prairie provinces.

SPRINGBEAUTY
Claytonia lanceolata Pursh

F. R. VANCE

Springbeauty

flower detail

FLOWERS are white, occasionally with pink lines or shading on the five petals, star-shaped, about ½ inch (12 mm) across. There are only two sepals. Several blooms are borne in a loose raceme. Flowering occurs in May. FRUIT is a papery capsule about ⅛ inch (3 mm) long which contains many small black seeds. LEAVES are shiny dark green, lanceolate, ¾ to 1½ inches (2-4 cm) long, and stalkless. Occasionally plants have one or two stalked basal leaves and there are usually only two stem leaves. GROWTH HABIT is low but not exactly prostrate, growing from a ¾ inch (2 cm) corm found about 3 inches (8 cm) below ground. The reddish stems are short but may elevate plants 2 inches (5 cm) or more in a mat of dark green leaves. HABITAT commonly includes the shallow draws and south-facing slopes of the southwest. It is rare but still found in some places in the Cypress Hills.

Springbeauty

PURSLANE
PURSLANE FAMILY
Portulaca oleracea L.

Purslane

FLOWERS are yellow, saucer-shaped, up to ¼ inch (6 mm) across, and have two sepals and four to six petals. They are borne singly in the axils of leaves and are open in the sun of morning and early afternoon from July to September. FRUIT is a barrel-shaped, pointed capsule under 1 mm long which contains numerous shiny black seeds. LEAVES are alternate, dark green above and reddish gray underneath, ovate to spatulate, ¼ to ¾ inch (6-20 mm) long. They are stalkless, thick, shiny, and numerous so they may almost obscure the ground in a bad infestation. GROWTH HABIT is annual and prostrate with thick, fleshy, purplish red branching stems arising from a deep central root. Mats of a single plant may approach 16 inches (40 cm) in diameter. HABITAT is usually well cultivated fertile soil in gardens or occasionally on the edges of fields throughout the prairie provinces.

Purslane

FIELD CHICKWEED
Cerastium arvense L.

PINK FAMILY

Field chickweed   flower detail

D. GILROY

Mouse-eared chickweed

FLOWERS are white, ⅜ to ⅝ inch (10-15 mm) across, with five deeply cleft petals and five sepals. Sepals are much shorter than petals in this species, but about the same length as the petals in another common species, mouse-eared chickweed, (*C. vulgatum* L.). Flowers bloom in May. FRUIT is a capsule about ½ inch (12 mm) long which contains several reddish brown seeds. LEAVES are opposite, linear to lanceolate, ⅜ to 1½ inch (1-4 cm) long, usually hairy and consequently gray green in color. Leaves of the mouse-eared chickweed are slightly shorter and more hairy.

GROWTH HABIT is perennial and tufted, (but mouse-eared chickweed may appear as one to four distinctly separate stems). The stems are usually semi-prostrate, 6 to 10 inches (15-25 cm) long, covered with short hairs which point downward toward the base of the plant. HABITAT includes the open prairie throughout the western and central part of the area. Field chickweed and mouse-eared chickweed differ little and often grow in the same locality. The latter is more common in and near sparse stands of aspen poplar in the north and east.

BABY'S-BREATH
Gypsophila paniculata L.

PINK FAMILY

Baby's-breath

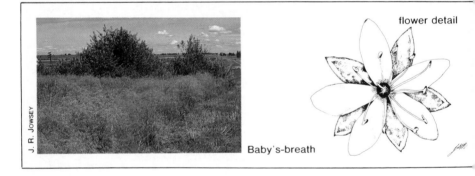

J. R. JOWSEY

Baby's-breath

flower detail

FLOWERS are white to pale pink, about ⅛ inch (3 mm) across on stalks ⅛ to ½ inch (3-12 mm) long, borne on numerous panicled cymes to give the whole plant the appearance of a puff of mist. The calyx is five lobed, smooth, bell-shaped, and encloses the five petals which may be slightly longer than the sepals. These flowers have a strikingly sweet perfume and dry well so are very useful in floral arrangements. Flowering occurs through July and August. FRUIT is a tiny ovoid to rounded capsule with four valves. Each plant produces many minute seeds which explains the sprea of this species and its occasional desig nation as a weed. LEAVES are dar green, opposite, clasping, and narrowl lanceolate. They may be up to 4 inche (10 cm) long on the lower branches bu less than 1 inch (2.5 cm) on the uppe ones. GROWTH HABIT is perennial an erect on a much-branched stem. Plant may vary in height from 8 inches to 3 fee (20-90 cm). HABITAT: An introduce plant commonly grown as a border i gardens but it has often escaped to roa allowances and field edges.

LOW WHITLOWWORT

Paronychia sessiliflora Nutt.

flower detail

Low whitlowwort

FLOWERS are minute, have no petals, but have five pointed, bristly, yellow sepals and five stamens held in a clump of silvery bracts. Flowers are not numerous but appear at the ends of some of the short branches on each plant. They appear in July and persist through August. FRUIT is a utricle, a round inflated case with one seed which is held tightly in the calyx. LEAVES are opposite, gray-green, and linear with a spiny tip. The leaves and stiff, silvery stipules overlap the short stems to cover them almost completely. GROWTH HABIT is perennial in tufts or solid patches which are formed by a net of short branches arising from the woody root crown of each plant. The mat of stems rises to about 2 inches (5 cm) above the ground and is up to 3 to 6 inches (8-15 cm) in diameter, to give the impression of a bristly cushion. HABITAT is usually dry sandy soils and south-facing slopes, throughout the prairie provinces. Pioneer naturalist John Macoun has reported it from "Fort Ellice westward to Morley [Alberta]."

Low whitlowwort

SMOOTH CATCHFLY
Silene cserei Baumgarten

PINK FAMILY

Smooth catchfly

Bladder campion

FLOWERS are numerous, white, and tubular, with flaring bi-cleft petals in a wheel-shaped corolla, ½ to ¾ inch (12-

White cockle

20 mm) across. The five sepals are united to form a bulbous structure ⅝ to 1 inch (15-25 mm) long of varying color and venation in smooth catchfly, bladder campion, *S. cucubalus* Widel, and white cockle, *Lychnis alba* Mill. The fruiting calyx in each species is marked by ten to twenty nerves running lengthwise, but there is a conspicuous network of smaller veins in bladder campion. Both *Silene* spp. have green to russet calyxes whereas *L. alba* has a larger greenish white calyx. FRUIT is an ovoid, many-seeded capsule enclosed in the calyx which opens by six teeth in *Silene* spp. and five to ten teeth in *L. alba*. LEAVES are opposite, entire margined, thick, light green, with somewhat glandular surfaces, 2 to 4 inches (5-10 cm) long, stalkless, and usually clasping. They are more glandular and sticky-hairy in the other two species. GROWTH HABIT is biennial, slightly branched (white cockle is more branching in habit), with light green, smooth stems, 8 to 30 inches (20-75 cm) in height. HABITAT: All species are widely distributed as they are imported in wildflower collections, bird seed, etc.

NIGHT-FLOWERING CATCHFLY
Silene noctiflora L.

PINK FAMILY

G. W. SEIB

Night-flowering catchfly

seed capsules

F. R. VANCE

Cow cockle

FLOWERS are white, occasionally pale pink, up to ¾ inch (2 cm) across. They are single but the plant's branching often gives the impression of a number of flowers. Sepals are united to form a sticky, oval, tubular calyx which is ½ to ¾ inch (12-20 mm) long, striped white and dark green. Each of the five petals is deeply cleft. Range of flowering dates includes June-August. FRUIT is an ovate capsule enclosed by the calyx. The small black seeds rattle about in the capsule when mature. LEAVES are opposite, dark green, oval to lance-shaped, sticky and hairy. The upper ones are stalkless, 1 to 3 inches (2.5-7 cm) long. Basal leaves have short stalks and are 2 to 5 inches (5-12 cm) long. GROWTH HABIT is erect and branched, an annual with a coarse sticky-hairy stem, usually 15 to 36 inches (38-90 cm) tall. HABITAT includes gardens, roadside ditches, and field edges. It is a persistent, introduced weed, particularly common under good moisture conditions in the south and central parts of the area. Cow cockle, (*Saponaria vaccaria* L.), is common in the same type of habitat. It has bluish pink flowers, smooth leaves and a hairless stem.

YELLOW POND-LILY
Nuphar variegatum Engelm.

Yellow pond-lily

FLOWERS are bright yellow, solitary, and 2 inches (5 cm) or more in diameter. The six sepals are petal-like, fleshy, and slightly greener than the many small, yellow petals which are almost stamen-like. Numerous stamens surround a yellow stigmatic disc formed of seven to twenty-five pistils. The small pond-lily *N. microphyllum* (Pers.) Fern. has a red central disc of pistils. FRUIT is oval, 1 inch (2.5 cm) long, many seeded, and covered with a leathery rind, purplish brown in color. LEAVES are yellowish green, heart-shaped, 4 to 10 inches (10-25 cm) long, and 3 to 6 inches (7.5-15 cm) broad on long slender petioles growing from the rootstock. There may also be some much smaller, submerged, thin, membranous leaves. GROWTH HABIT is perennial from a stout creeping rootstock. The large leaves float on the surface of slow-moving water. HABITAT is totally aquatic, in small lakes and sluggish streams and their backwaters. These plants are plentiful in the north and east and have been observed as far south as the Pipestone Creek near Moosomin, Saskatchewan.

Yellow pond-lily

F. A. SWITZER

Small pond-lily

BANEBERRY
Actaea rubra (Ait.) Willd.

CROWFOOT FAMILY

Baneberry

Baneberry   flower cluster

FLOWERS are white, ⅛ inch (3 mm) across. There are four to ten white petals and three to five petal-like sepals, which fall off soon after the flower opens. The flowers are numerous, borne in a cone-shaped cluster at the end of a slender stem, and bloom in June. FRUIT is a berry ¼ to ⅜ inch (6-10 mm) in diameter, which is red in some plants and white in others. The white form is not a separate species or sub-species. These fruits are poisonous and their bright color makes them a substantial hazard where small children are involved. LEAVES are dark green and compound, with several oval, sharply toothed leaflets. They are hairy along the veins on the underside. A whole leaf may be 3 to 5 inches (7.5-12 cm) wide. GROWTH HABIT is erect and perennial; plants are usually at least 8 inches (20 cm) tall and may be over 30 inches (80 cm). HABITAT includes the moist floor of mixed forests and aspen poplar bluffs as well as the wooded ravines of the open plains. It is reasonably common throughout the area.

CANADA ANEMONE
Anemone canadensis L.

CROWFOOT FAMILY

Canada anemone

fruit stage

FLOWERS are white, 1 to 1¼ inches (2.5-3 cm) across, due to petal-like sepals; petals are lacking. Several separate flowering stems arise from the main flowering stem at a whorl of leaf-like bracts characteristic of the genus. Flowering dates include June-July. FRUITS are achenes in a deep green globular head. Its color and mace-like shape is easily noticed in aspen poplar woods in August. LEAVES are light green, covered with fine hairs and grow up from the short stem with long petioles. They may be 1½ to 2½ inches (4-7 cm) wide, and are toothed and deeply cleft into three to five lobes. GROWTH HABIT is perennial and the slightly hairy stems grow from a bulb-like taproot. Total plant height varies from 8 to 24 inches (20-60 cm). Common HABITAT includes moist grassy areas, scrubby areas, edges of aspen poplar groves, particularly in parkland-prairie, but the plant is distributed throughout the area in suitable locations.

Canada anemone

CUT-LEAVED ANEMONE

CROWFOOT FAMILY

Anemone multifida Poir.

F. R. VANCE

Cut-leaved anemone

flower detail

FLOWERS are usually pink or reddish purple with some variation to yellow or nearly white. Each flower may be ½ to ¾ inches (12-20 mm) across and there are one to seven hairy flowering stalks which arise from the characteristic whorl of bracts below them. Flowers bloom June-July. FRUITS are achenes borne in a cylindrical head, ½ to 1 inch (12-25 mm) long, which is gray green and opens to give a "cottony" appearance due to the soft hairy achenes. LEAVES are silky hairy, 1¼ to 2½ inches (3-7 cm) across, dusty dark green, and divided into three parts. GROWTH HABIT is erect and somewhat less bushy than the Canada anemone, (*A. canadensis* L.), partly due to leaves and partly to the longer flower stalks of the cut-leaved anemone. HABITAT includes the open grasslands of the south central and southwest regions of the area in soils of reasonably good moisture supply.

F. R. VANCE

Cut-leaved anemone

PRAIRIE CROCUS
Anemone patens L. var. *wolfgangiana* (Bess.) Koch

CROWFOOT FAMILY

Prairie crocus

F. R. VANCE

Prairie crocus

seed stage

This is the floral emblem of Manitoba. FLOWERS are pale blue or mauve, occasionally white or light yellow, up to 1½ inches (4 cm) in diameter when open, borne on stems about 4 inches (10 cm) high. The sepals, five to seven, are colored and petals are absent. Flowers appear in early spring. The FRUIT is a large group of feathery achenes on a lengthened flower stalk. LEAVES are gray green, basal, stalked, and much divided. They appear after the flowers fade. GROWTH HABIT is perennial and leaves arise from a thick, woody taproot. Plants persist into September. Common HABITAT includes sandy hillsides and high meadows of the open prairie, and sandy ridges of the parkland.

SMALL-FLOWERED COLUMBINE
Aquilegia brevistyla Hook.

CROWFOOT FAMILY

seed pods

Small-flowered columbine

FLOWERS are blue and light cream nearer the centers, ⅝ to 1 inch (1.5-2.5 cm) long and ½ inch (12 mm) or more across, with a single flower on each long, drooping stalk. The five sepals give the blue color and the tube shaped petals supply the white color in the flower. The petals each end in a spur but the blade of the petal is longer than the spur. Flowers appear June-July. FRUIT is a pod, ¼ inch (6 mm) across and about ¾ inch (2 cm) long. The pods are in a tight group of five. LEAVES are dark green and slightly toothed, divided into three pointed leaflets. They are basal but grow up for 8 inches (20 cm) or more with long petioles. GROWTH HABIT is perennial; the slightly hairy, rather thin glandular stems grow from branching rootstocks to a height of 12 to 24 inches (30-60 cm). The flower stalks rise above the leaves for 8 inches (20 cm) or more. Common HABITAT includes the sunny spaces of the moist forest edges and road edges across the north and eastern sections of the area.

Small-flowered columbine

WILD COLUMBINE
Aquilegia canadensis L.

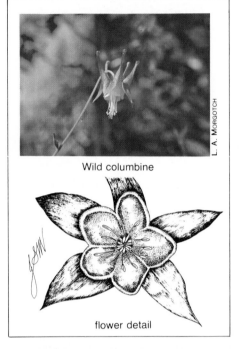

Wild columbine

flower detail

FLOWERS appear deep red due to the five sepals. The tube-like petals are yellow, tinged with red. They are 1 to 1½ inches (2.5-4 cm) across, nodding and up to 1½ inches (4 cm) long. This length includes the spurs which are straight and shorter than the petals. Flowers appear June-July. FRUIT is made up of five follicles, ¼ inch (6 mm) across and about ¾ inch (2 cm) long, with numerous black seeds. LEAVES are compound, divided into three dark green leaflets, usually with some smoothness or bloom. Leaflets may be an inch (2.5 cm) wide and over an inch (2.5 cm) long, slightly toothed and pointed at the apex. GROWTH HABIT is erect, 1 to 3 feet (30-90 cm) high, with a stout stem that may be hairy or smooth. Plants are usually somewhat branched. HABITAT commonly includes the forest edges and roadsides of the north and east, either in open spaces or partial shade, under less moist conditions than where the blue columbine, (*A. brevistyla* Hook.), is common.

Wild columbine

MARSH-MARIGOLD
Caltha palustris L.

CROWFOOT FAMILY

Marsh-marigold

F. R. VANCE

Marsh-marigold

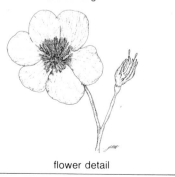

flower detail

FLOWERS are deep yellow orange ¾ to 1½ inches (2-4 cm) across, with several attached at the ends of each main stem. The two outer floral rings are not separated, but the color is uniform in the five to nine sepals. There are no true petals. The stamens are numerous and the pistil has several parts. Flowering dates include May-June. FRUITS are in a dense head of many pods which are filled with small seeds. LEAVES are dark green and thick, 1½ inches (4 cm) across. They are kidney-shaped and their bases are heart-shaped. Margins are round-toothed. GROWTH HABIT is perennial and erect, although the plants are rather squat. Height is 8 to 20 inches (20-50 cm), usually nearer 8 inches (20 cm). HABITAT includes stream edges, patches of shallow open water and roadside ditches. This plant is common throughout the north and east parts of the area, particularly where the vegetation is boreal in nature.

82

WESTERN CLEMATIS
Clematis ligusticifolia Nutt.

CROWFOOT FAMILY

Western clematis

FLOWERS are creamy white with four petal-like sepals, ¼ to ⅝ inch (6-15 mm) long. The flowers are unisexual, with the male and female flowers in leafy panicles on separate plants. The staminate flowers contain many stamens, while the pistillate ones show many feathery stigmas surrounded by sterile stamens. The flowers, ½ to ¾ inch (12-20 mm) across, appear in July and August. FRUIT is a cluster of hairy achenes, each with a persistent feathery style, 1 to 2 inches (2.5-5 cm) long, giving the whole flower a woolly appearance. LEAVES are opposite, medium green, on long stalks. They are pinnately divided into five ovate to lanceolate leaflets, deeply toothed, 2 to 2¼ inches (5-6 cm) long and ¾ inch (2 cm) across, somewhat velvety due to hairs which lie close to the surface. GROWTH HABIT is perennial, a slender climbing herb, up to 20 feet (6 m) long, with a stem that is slightly woody. The stems climb over and attach themselves to trees and shrubs by their twisted leaf stalks. HABITAT is the shrubby edges of aspen groves under moist conditions in river valleys and ravines throughout the prairies.

F. R. VANCE

Western clematis

J. R. JOWSEY

PURPLE CLEMATIS
Clematis verticellaris DC.

CROWFOOT FAMILY

FLOWERS are blue, 1 to 2 inches (3-5 cm) long, star-shaped with four blue petal-like sepals and no petals. They are borne singly, and appear in June. Flowers of western clematis, (*C. ligusticifolia* Nutt.), which flowers in late July, are white and arranged in a small cluster. FRUITS are hairy achenes with persistent feathery styles, each about 2 inches (5 cm) long. They are grouped in a head. LEAVES are alternate, medium to light green, divided into three stalked leaflets which are arranged in a pinnate fashion on the main stalk. LEAVES may be 3 to 5 inches (7.5-12 cm) long. GROWTH HABIT is trailing, up to 7 feet (2 m) in length, attached to shrubs and small trees. A leafy vine gives the impression of dense growth. HABITAT includes forest and forest margins throughout the south and southwest. Both the purple and white species are common in this area.

Purple clematis

Purple clematis

LOW LARKSPUR
Delphinium bicolor Nutt.

Low larkspur

F. R. VANCE

FLOWERS have dark blue as the prominent color due to five petal-like sepals. The four petals are blue to creamy white and somewhat hairy. The flowers are spurred, ½ to 1¼ inches (12-30 mm) long, borne in a loose spike, May-June. FRUITS are arranged in a head of a few many-seeded pods. The pods are brown, somewhat hairy, ⅝ to ¾ inch (1.5-2 cm) long. LEAVES are more or less basal, medium green and covered with fine hairs which give them a grayish appearance. They are on long stalks and are much cleft and dissected. GROWTH HABIT is perennial and erect from a thick fibrous root. The flower stalks are long and hairy and give the plant a height of 8 to 20 inches (20-50 cm). HABITAT includes sheltered open places in coulees, lower slopes of hills, particularly in the heavier soils of the southwest. The plant is very poisonous to cattle, but is not known to be poisonous to sheep. Take care! Tall larkspur, (*D. glaucum* S. Wats.), is occasionally observed in the aspen poplar stands of some areas of the southwest and northwest. It is also very poisonous to cattle.

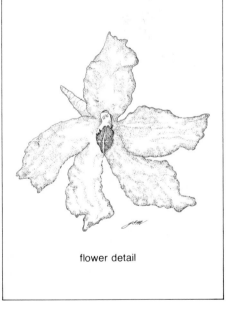

flower detail

Low larkspur

SEASIDE BUTTERCUP
Ranunculus cymbalaria **Pursh.**

CROWFOOT **FAMILY**

Macoun's buttercup

G. W. SEIB

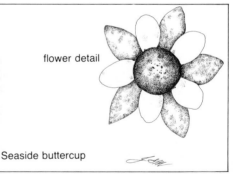

flower detail

Seaside buttercup

FLOWERS are yellow, few per plant, ¼ to 1/3 inch (6-8 mm) in diameter with petals slightly shorter than the green sepals. They have the conical arrangement of stamens and pistil characteristic of buttercups, and are borne on rather long flower stalks. The other species shown is Macoun's buttercup, (*R. macounii* Britt.), named for John Macoun, an early naturalist who travelled in Saskatchewan. Its flowers are larger, ½ inch (12 mm) and the sepals are reflexed. Approximate flowering date is June. FRUIT is small achenes which are distinctly ribbed longitudinally, formed in an oblong to cylin-drical head. LEAVES are medium green, few, small, ½ to 1 inch (12-25 mm) wide, round-toothed and mostly basal. They have rather long petioles and are ovate to heart-shaped. GROWTH HABIT is somewhat creeping with runners which root at the nodes. Plants are rarely over 3 inches (7.5 cm) in height. Stems may be smooth or hairy. HABITAT includes slough margins, creek banks and ravines, with the plant usually found in soggy ground under soil conditions which may be saline. It is widely distributed in the area.

PRAIRIE BUTTERCUP
Ranunculus rhomboideus Goldie

CROWFOOT FAMILY

Prairie buttercup

Prairie buttercup

FLOWERS are light yellow with a smooth "painted" look to the five petals which are somewhat narrow and widely spaced. The five shorter sepals are yellow also, often tinged with a lavender shade. They are ½ to ¾ inch (12-20 mm) across and relatively numerous. Flowers appear in early May. FRUITS are achenes in a globular head about 3/16 inch (5 mm) in diameter. LEAVES are dark green, rounded or oval, wavy-margined, over 1 inch (2.5 cm) wide. Basal leaves are spoon-shaped,not divided and have long petioles. The stem leaves are stalkless and deeply cleft into three to five linear lobes. In contrast, on shining-leaved buttercup, (*R. glaberrimus* Hook.), even some of the basal leaves are cleft into lobes; the petals are not as narrow and are closer together. GROWTH HABIT is erect, usually low but may grow to 18 inches (45 cm) in rare cases. Stems are densely hairy. Both species flower early in the spring but the shining-leaved buttercup is lower growing and confined to the southwest. HABITAT includes the lower areas of grasslands, not necessarily at slough margins. It is widely distributed over the grassland and parkland borders of the area.

Shining-leaved buttercup

WHITE WATERCROWFOOT
Ranunculus subrigidus W. B. Drew

CROWFOOT FAMILY

White watercrowfoot

FLOWERS are white, with five petals and five sepals, and about ½ inch (12 mm) diameter. They float on the surface of the water or rise only about an inch (2.5 cm) above it, and appear in June. Numerous stamens give the center a yellow color. FRUITS are small achenes arranged in a head. LEAVES are medium green, ½ to 1 inch (12-25 mm) long, finely dissected and all submerged. GROWTH HABIT is perennial and floating, with many long branches which spread it out in a mat at the water surface. The large number of white flowers gives the impression of total coverage in some parts of sloughs. HABITAT includes shallow sloughs, saline or fresh, where there is some slow movement of water. A yellow species, (*R. gmelinii* DC.), is not the source of yellow color in the same sloughs as white watercrowfoot. This deep yellow is due to common bladderwort, (*Utricularia vulgaris* L.).

White watercrowfoot

Yellow watercrowfoot

VEINY MEADOW-RUE
Thalictrum venulosum Trel.

CROWFOOT FAMILY

Veiny meadow-rue

pistillate flower

Tall meadow-rue

FLOWERS are unisexual, usually on separate plants, but both may be present on the same plant in large, loose clusters. There are no petals, but both types of flowers are subtended by four or five greenish white, pointed, spatulate sepals. The inflorescence of staminate flowers, each about ¼ inch (6 mm) across, is very attractive because of the numerous yellow stamens. Pistillate flowers are larger and have several light green, awn-like pistils. Flowering occurs from mid-June to July. FRUIT is a small cluster of ribbed, ovoid achenes with short beaks. LEAVES are medium to bluish green, alternate on long petioles, prominently veined, paler on the underside, palmately compounded into three to five three-lobed leaflets each ¾ to 1 ¼ inches (2-3 cm) across. GROWTH HABIT is perennial and erect on smooth, slender stems of variable height, 6 to 36 inches (15-90 cm). Another species, tall meadow rue, *T. dasycarpum* Fisch. and Lall., grows to a height of 20 to 60 inches (50-150 cm) and has darker green leaves and purplish stems. HABITAT: Fairly common in moist aspen woods and scrubby thickets throughout the parklands and into the edge of the boreal forest. It is also found in moist coulees on the prairies.

GOLDEN CORYDALIS
Corydalis aurea Willd.

FUMITORY FAMILY

flower detail

Golden corydalis

Pink corydalis

FLOWERS are deep yellow, about ½ inch (12 mm) long, and sac-like with a spur at the base about ¼ inch (6 mm) long. The spur arises from one of the four petals. There are only two sepals. Another species has pink flowers: *C. sempervirens* (L.) Pers. Flowers bloom in June. FRUIT is a narrow constricted pod-like capsule, ¾ to 1 inch (2-2.5 cm) long, which contains several dark shiny seeds. LEAVES are alternate, pale green, 2½ to 3½ inches (7-10 cm) long, compounded of many fine divi-sions. GROWTH HABIT is annual or biennial, low or nearly prostrate and much branched. Plants may spread over an area 12 to 18 inches (30-45 cm) across. HABITAT includes forest edges, road cuts, railway grades and other disturbed ground. It is found in the Qu'Appelle Valley and tributaries and up into the edge of the boreal forest as well. Here it is replaced by the pink species, which is taller, less bushy and later in flowering habit.

PINK BEE-PLANT
Cleome serrulata Pursh

CAPER FAMILY

Pink bee-plant

F. R. VANCE

F. A. SWITZER

Pink bee-plant

magnified flower

FLOWERS are lavender pink to white, ½ inch (12 mm) long, 1/16 inch (1 mm) diameter, in a nearly globose terminal raceme. The white stamens usually protrude from each flower. Approximate date of flowering is August. FRUIT is a long pod. These pods are evident on the lower parts of the raceme while the upper portion is still in flower. LEAVES are dark green, numerous, alternate, lanceolate, 1 to 3 inches (2.5-7 cm) long. Upper leaves are virtually stalkless. They are not toothed. GROWTH HABIT is annual and erect. Some plants are branched but others have a solitary stem. HABITAT includes waste places, roadsides and semi-cultivated areas of the prairies and the edge of the parkland.

REFLEXED ROCK-CRESS
Arabis retrofracta Graham

Purple rock-cress

Reflexed rock-cress

J. R. JOWSEY

FLOWERS are white to pink, the four petals about ¼ inch (6 mm) long with sepals slightly shorter. Numerous flowers are arranged in a loose terminal raceme. The flower illustration on this page is purple rock-cress, *Arabis divaricarpa* A. Nels., which is very similar. Flowers appear in May and June. FRUIT is a slender, pod-like capsule (silique) 1 to 1½ inches (2.5-4 cm) long, bent abruptly downwards on a short stalk so the pods are closely pressed to the stem. Pods on purple rock-cress are spreading or curved slightly downwards. Stem LEAVES are reflexed, linear-oblong to spatulate, and generally covered with fine hairs. They clasp the stem closely, are ¼ to 1 inch (6-25 mm) long, and entire margined. Leaves in the basal rosette are larger, more spatulate, stalked, and numerous (ten to fifteen). The lower stem leaves and basal leaves are more densely hairy than the upper leaves. GROWTH HABIT is biennial or perennial, erect, 4 to 24 inches (10-60 cm) tall, and unbranched, but several hairy stems may arise from each taproot. HABITAT: This species is widely distributed across the southern prairies.

WILD MUSTARD
Brassica kaber (D.C.) L.C. Wheeler

MUSTARD FAMILY

Wild mustard

Wild mustard

FLOWERS are bright yellow, numerous, in loose panicles on the upper stems. They have four dark green, coarse sepals and four petals extending to twice the length of the sepals. Flowers may be ⅜ to ¾ inch (1-2 cm) across. They are borne on short stalks and appear from mid-June to September. FRUIT is a long, somewhat valved, beaked, pod-like capsule (silique). The ascending pods are strongly nerved and somewhat hairy and may be up to 3 inches (7.5 cm) on large plants. Seeds are numerous and vary from yellow and orange to black. LEAVES are dark green, alternate, coarse and thick, sparsely and irregularly toothed, with a few coarse hairs, particu-larly on the underside. The lower, petioled leaves may be 4 to 6 inches (10-15 cm) long, but the upper sessile leaves are more often about 3 inches (7.5 cm) long. GROWTH HABIT: This is the introduced annual weed, 8 to 32 inches (20-80 cm) tall, that turned fields bright yellow in June before use of herbicides became general. It is probably the commonest mustard of the prairies, also characterized as *Sinapis arvensis* L. HABITAT is fields, ditches, gardens, and feedlot areas where grass has not taken over. It is a common field weed where management practices permit and moisture conditions are good.

WESTERN WALLFLOWER
Erysimum asperum (Nutt.) DC.

MUSTARD FAMILY

Western wallflower

Western wallflower

FLOWERS are pale yellow, ⅜ to ¾ inch (1-2 cm) across, wheel-shaped but enclosed in a somewhat tubular calyx. There are four sepals, petals, and sta- mens. Flowers form a tight terminal raceme and are easily noticed among prairie grasses in June. FRUIT is a four-angled, pod-like capsule (silique) 2 to 4 inches (5-10 cm) long, standing stiffly erect in the dried inflorescence. LEAVES tend to be entire margined, 1 to 3 inches (2.5-7.5 cm) long, and gray-green due to forked whitish hairs. The basal leaves are numerous, oblanceolate, the stem leaves more linear. GROWTH HABIT is usually perennial, erect, and sometimes branched. Height is highly variable from 12 inches (30 cm) to 24 inches (60 cm) or more. HABITAT is light sandy areas among sparse grass cover, road edges, and other disturbed areas of the prairie.

94

SAND BLADDERPOD
MUSTARD FAMILY

Lesquerella arenosa (Richards.) Rydb.

Sand bladderpod

Sand bladderpod

Spatulate bladderpod

FLOWERS are dull, dusty yellow, usually tinged with red or purple, with four petals and four oblong sepals. Flowers are usually quite small, no more than ¼ inch (6 mm) in diameter. They appear in a raceme-like group at the ends of upper stems in May and June. FRUIT is a small, rounded pod borne on a rather long ½ inch (12 mm) stalk. The pod is divided into two valves, each of which contains two to eight seeds. LEAVES are dark green, mostly basal, and somewhat hairy. They are oblong to lanceolate, ⅜ to 2 inches (1-5 cm) long, and narrow at both ends. GROWTH HABIT is perennial and tufted, somewhat prostrate due to weak slender stems but may reach 12 inches (30 cm) in height. A similar species, spatulate bladderpod (*L. alpina* Nutt.), occupies the same type of habitat but has more stems and is slightly shorter and more densely tufted. Common HABITAT is dry grassy slopes and uplands in the southern prairies, particularly in sandy soils.

PENNY CRESS
Thlapsi arvense L.

MUSTARD FAMILY

FLOWERS are white, ⅛ inch (3 mm) in diameter, with four sepals and four petals. They are numerous and grow on short (1 mm) stalks in raceme-like clusters at the ends of stems. Flowering time is variable but may extend from early June to September. FRUITS are coin-like, green, winged pods up to ¼ inch (6 mm) diameter, in two halves, notched at the apex, ripening to brownish orange. The six to sixteen seeds per pod are reddish brown to black with rows of curved ridges on each side. LEAVES are medium green, alternate, 3 to 4 inches (7.5-10 cm) long, ⅜ inch (1 cm) wide. Basal leaves are deeply notched and stalked and soon dry off as the plant matures. Stem leaves are sessile or clasping, shaped like an elongated arrowhead. GROWTH HABIT is annual or winter annual, erect, 3 to 24 inches (7.5-60 cm) in height, with numerous upper branches. The smaller stunted plants have only one stem. HABITAT: This is an introduced weed best known as "stinkweed" which invades standing cereal crops and gardens, particularly when moisture is in good supply. The ability of this plant to taint milk or cream is well known to dairymen but has been overcome in recent years by processing methods.

Penny cress

SUNDEW
Drosera rotundifolia L.

Round-leaved sundew

J. L. PARKER

FLOWERS are white or pink, three to ten on a naked scape in a raceme-like cluster. They are very small and commonly closed which makes them even more inconspicuous. The tubular calyx, the enclosed petals, and the stamens each have four to eight members. Flowers appear in July. FRUIT is a small capsule, inconspicuous in the calyx and containing many minute, ellipsoidal seeds. LEAVES are basal, reddish due to the fringe of colored glandular hairs which exude a sticky fluid to trap small insects. They are ¾ to 1 inch (2-2.5 cm) across and borne on sticky, hairy petioles of 1½ to 2 inches (4-5 cm) length. GROWTH HABIT is perennial with a rosette of four to twelve leaves at the base of a single flowering stem. The flowering stem may rise 4 to 10 inches (10-25 cm) above the rosette of leaves which are often covered with needles of conifers. HABITAT is the dense shade of coniferous woods in a moist or boggy situation. It is rare but found in the boreal forest and in the Cypress Hills.

G. W. SEIB

flower stalk

Round-leaved sundew

PITCHERPLANT
Sarracenia purpurea L.

Pitcherplant

This is the floral emblem of Newfound-land. FLOWERS are reddish purple due to incurved petals, nodding and borne singly on long stalks. The pistil is greenish yellow and the style is very large. Flowers appear June-July. FRUIT is a capsule, ½ to ¾ inch (12-20 mm) diameter, divided into several sections. LEAVES are bluish green with reddish veins. They are basal and pitcher-shaped, 3 to 12 inches (7.5-30 cm) long with a hood surrounded by downward pointing bristles. The bristles and the pool of water in the leaf tend to trap insects. GROWTH HABIT is basal, perennial, with leaves and the long flower stem arising from the root crown. The flower stalk may be 10 to 18 inches (25-45 cm) high. HABITAT includes black spruce bogs and other spongy areas of coniferous woods in the northeast.

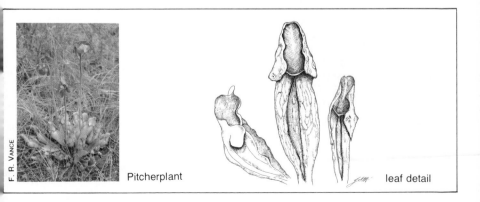

F. R. VANCE

Pitcherplant   leaf detail

NARROW-PETALED STONECROP

ORPINE FAMILY

Sedum stenopetalum Pursh

Narrow-petaled stonecrop

J. R. JOWSEY

FLOWERS are powdery orange-yellow, ⅜ inch (10 mm) across, with four or five each of petals and sepals. Petals are lanceolate, twice as long as the sepals. Several flowers develop in each cluster at the stem tips and appear in June and July. FRUIT is a small, follicle-like capsule, borne erect. LEAVES are alternate, gray-green, up to ½ to 1¼ inches (12-30 mm) long, thick and succulent. They are narrowly linear, crowded and usually overlapping, but less numerous on the flowering stalks. GROWTH HABIT is low, perennial, erect, and tufted, usually 3 to 6 inches (7.5-15 cm) high. Common HABITAT is gravelly hillsides and rocky areas. It is common in the Cypress Hills.

ALUMROOT
Heuchera richardsonii R. Br.

SAXIFRAGE FAMILY

Alumroot

FLOWERS are purple to violet, under ⅛ inch (3 mm) diameter, ⅜ inch (10 mm) long, with five petals only slightly longer than the sepals. They are in a dense spike at the end of a long leafless flower stalk and bloom in June. FRUIT is a capsule with two distinct beaks. LEAVES are basal, dark green, leathery, and have long petioles. They are round to heart-shaped and roughly toothed, 1 to 2½ inches (2.5-6 cm) across. GROWTH HABIT is erect and perennial, with basal leaves and several long flower stalks arising from a scaly rootstock. HABITAT includes all reasonably moist areas of the prairie and open parkland. It is named for the explorer, Sir John Richardson.

J. R. JOWSEY

Alumroot

flower stalk

BISHOP'S-CAP
Mitella nuda L.

SAXIFRAGE FAMILY

Bishop's-cap

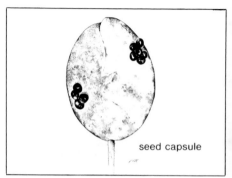

seed capsule

FLOWERS are greenish white, ¼ inch (6 mm) across, with five finely divided petals twice as long as the sepals. Each flower appears like a delicate pinwheel with rolled edges. Several flowers are borne on a short, hairy, flowering stem on upper branches in June and July. FRUIT is a minute, greenish, two-valved capsule which turns inside out to expose several black seeds. LEAVES are light green, mostly basal, rounded, heart-shaped at the base, ¾ to 2 inches (2-5 cm) across. They are smooth and round toothed and have rather long petioles. GROWTH HABIT is perennial and erect. 'The slender flower stalk grows to a height of 3 to 8 inches (7.5-20 cm). HABITAT is the cold, wet, wooded areas of heavy shade in the boreal forest and Cypress Hills.

Bishop's-cap

GRASS-OF-PARNASSUS
Parnassia palustris L.

SAXIFRAGE FAMILY

Grass-of-parnassus

F. R. VANCE

Grass-of-parnassus

flower and leaf

FLOWERS have five wide white petals with distinct green veins. They are large, up to an inch (2.5 cm) across, with sepals much smaller than petals. There are usually several flower stems per plant. Flowers appear July-September. FRUIT is an oval capsule, about ⅜ inch (1 cm) long with many seeds. LEAVES are broad, round, glossy, light green with smooth margins. They are somewhat heart-shaped and basal. A single leaf one-third to one-half way up the flower stalk characterizes this species. GROWTH HABIT is perennial and branching from a tuft of rather fibrous roots. Plant height is due to the flower stalk and varies from 4 to 14 inches (10-35 cm). HABITAT includes wet shady areas at the edge of aspen poplar groves, road ditches and railway grades. It is widely distributed, particularly in the north, central and eastern parts of the area.

WILD BLACK CURRANT
Ribes americanum Mill.

SAXIFRAGE FAMILY

Wild black currant

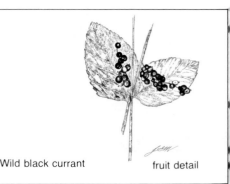

fruit detail

F. W. LAHRMAN

FLOWERS are greenish white to cream color, with five petals and five stamens. The calyx is tubular. Flowers are numerous, eight to twenty, arranged in many drooping racemes, appearing in June. Flowers of the northern gooseberry, (*R. oxyacanthoides* L.), are also illustrated. FRUIT is a round berry, 3/16 to 3/8 inch (4-10 mm) in diameter, reddish brown as it begins to ripen and black when ripe. It is not particularly palatable raw but makes excellent jelly or jam. LEAVES are alternate, bright green, toothed and divided into three to five lobes. They are heart-shaped at the base and 1 to 3 inches (2.5-8 cm) across. GROWTH HABIT: An erect shrub, branched from the base, 3 to 4 feet (90-120 cm) high. Stems are smooth and there may be fifteen to twenty-five of them in a plant. Several other black currants are also native to the area. Common HABITAT includes edges of aspen poplar groves and patches of scrub in the parkland, and the wooded ravines of the prairies.

Northern gooseberry

SWAMP RED CURRANT
Ribes triste Pall.

SAXIFRAGE FAMILY

A. C. HUME

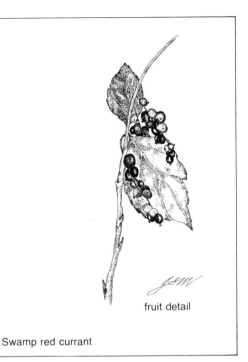

fruit detail

Swamp red currant

FLOWERS are purplish pink, several shades deeper in color than those of the wild black currant, (*R. americanum* Mill.). Sepals, (five), are longer than the petals. Flowers are borne on short stalks in a raceme, 2 to 4 inches (5-10 cm) long, and bloom in June. FRUIT is a smooth, round, bright red berry, 3/16 inch (4 mm) diameter. It has a tart pleasant taste and may be preserved as fruit or jelly. LEAVES are alternate, medium green and paler beneath due to fine hairs. They are three to five lobed and coarsely toothed, 2 to 4 inches (5-10 cm) across, on petioles about an inch (2.5 cm) long. GROWTH HABIT: A small bush up to 3 feet (90 cm) tall with many short, unarmed stems arising from the root crown. HABITAT includes low marshy ground near the edges of aspen poplar groves, in the northern edge of the parkland and in the boreal forest.

J. R. JOWSEY

Swamp red currant

AGRIMONY
Agrimonia striata Michx.

FLOWERS are bright yellow, usually ¼ to ½ inch (6-12 mm) across, with five petals which occasionally curve inwards over five to fifteen stamens. They are borne in a spike-like raceme 2 to 8 inches (5-20 cm) long, each flower surrounded by bracts and a five-lobed calyx which ends in a multitude of hooked bristles at the summit of the receptacle (hypanthium). Flowering occurs in late July and August. FRUIT is a conical, tubular receptacle ¼ inch (6 mm) long. It is deeply furrowed, has a crown of hooked bristles, and encloses two achenes. The fruiting structure is characteristic of this genus. LEAVES are dark green above, alternate, pinnately divided into seven to nine triangular leaflets, and have large stipules (one-quarter of leaf length). The leaves are on short petioles and are 1½ to 3 inches (4-7.5 cm) long and doubly toothed at the edges, slightly hairy and paler on the underside. GROWTH HABIT is perennial and erect, from a thick rhizome and fibrous roots. The stem is coarse and stiff, occasionally hairy, and bránched. Height is variable but commonly about 16 inches (40 cm) tall. HABITAT is moist, semi-wooded areas along trails through aspen stands or scrubby patches in the parklands and wooded coulees of the prairies.

J. R. JOWSEY

Agrimony

Agrimony

SASKATOON
Amelanchier alnifolia Nutt.

ROSE FAMILY

Saskatoon

F. R. VANCE

Saskatoon

fruit stages

FLOWERS are white, ⅜ to ½ inch (9-12 mm) diameter with five rounded petals and five sepals. They are borne in multiple clusters at the ends of branches and appear in June. FRUIT is a berry-like pome, variable in size, over ⅜ inch (1 cm) diameter, reddish purple, ripening to a dark purple. It is sweet and useful as food for people and for much of the native wildlife. It is also known as June-berry and service-berry. LEAVES are simple, stalked, round to oval, ½ to 2 inches (12-48 mm) long and finely toothed, particularly towards the apex. GROWTH HABIT is very variable from a small shrub under a foot (30 cm) tall to small trees of 15 feet (4.5 m). It is usually much branched, particularly at the top. HABITAT includes the margins and interiors of aspen poplar bluffs or scrubby areas of the parkland and forest edges, as well as the moist ravines of the prairies.

CHAMAERHODOS
Chamaerhodos nuttallii (T. & G.) Pickering

flower detail

Chamaerhodos

Chamaerhodos

FLOWERS are white, saucer-shaped, numerous in a branched cyme. They are ⅛ to ¼ inch (3-6 mm) in diameter, with five broad petals slightly longer than the five hairy, lanceolate sepals. There are five stamens, each opposite to a petal. Flowers appear in June and July. FRUIT is a group of small, brownish, ovoid achenes. Five to ten are produced and float free in the saucer-shaped receptacle (hypanthium) at maturity. LEAVES are medium green, the basal leaves petioled, up to 1¼ inches (3 cm) long, divided palmately into three lobes, each about ⅜ inch (1 cm) across. Basal leaves form a rosette in the first year. Stem leaves are much smaller than the basal leaves, with upper leaves sessile, resembling dissected bracts. GROWTH HABIT is biennial or perennial, an erect herb with a woody taproot. The hairy flower stem is 4 to 12 inches (10-30 cm) tall, developing in the second or later years, and may branch at the base or in its upper section. HABITAT is dry slopes, gravelly or sandy knolls on the prairies under rather severe growing conditions. The genus name is a Greek term meaning "low rose."

HAWTHORN
Crataegus spp. L.

ROSE FAMILY

Hawthorn

fruit detail

FLOWERS are white in all four species native to Saskatchewan. There are five sepals, five petals and numerous stamens. Clusters contain six to fifteen flowers, each about ½ inch (12 mm) across. Flowering occurs from May-June. FRUIT is a round, red, berry-like pome, with many seeds and little flesh. Skin color is purplish black in one species, *C. douglasii* Lindl., found in the Cypress Hills. LEAVES are dark green, alternate, doubly toothed and sometimes lobed. Leaves of the Columbian hawthorn, (*C. columbiana* Howell), are distinctly lobed and more obovate than those of the round-leaved hawthorn, (*C. chrysocarpa* Ashe). GROWTH HABIT: Columbian hawthorn is a tall shrub; the round-leaved species is more bushy. The stems are armed with stout thorns of about 1¼ to 2½ inches (3-7 cm). The main trunk may be up to 2 inches (5 cm) diameter, although most are about ¾ inch (2 cm). Height is variable up to 12 feet (4 m). HABITAT includes open woodland, coulees, margins of aspen poplar groves, or as a component of "scrubby" patches throughout the entire area. It is most common where moisture conditions are relatively good.

Hawthorn

SMOOTH WILD STRAWBERRY
Fragaria glauca (S. Wats.) Rydb.

ROSE FAMILY

Smooth wild strawberry

Smooth wild strawberry

Smooth wild strawberry

FLOWERS are white, ¾ inch (2 cm) diameter with a yellow center due to numerous stamens. There are several in a loose cluster. Stems lengthen as the fruit matures and raise it off the ground. Flowering is from May-July. FRUIT is an enlarged receptacle in which are embedded numerous dry achenes. A second species, American wild strawberry, (*F. vesca* L. var. *americana* Porter), is known in the northeast and is characterized by a lighter red, more conical fruit, with achenes nearer the surface. LEAVES are dark green, alternate, broadly ovate and coarsely toothed, three-lobed and up to 3 inches (7.5 cm) wide. They may be slightly hairy on the underside. GROWTH HABIT is basal from a rootstock. There are running stems which will send out roots. Leaf petioles and stems of fruit clusters may be 2 to 5 inches (5-12.5 cm) high depending on the habitat. HABITAT includes open shade to full sun in scrubby patches, aspen poplar groves, roadside ditches, wooded ravines, wherever moisture conditions are relatively favorable.

YELLOW AVENS
Geum aleppicum Jacq.

ROSE FAMILY

Yellow avens

Yellow avens

FLOWERS are bright yellow due to five wide petals which are slightly larger than the green, lance-shaped, reflexed sepals. The sepals alternate with five small bractlets. Flowers are ⅜ to 1 inch (1-2.5 cm) across with several in a widely branched cluster at the head of the flowering stem. Flowers appear in June and July. FRUIT is a rounded fruiting head up to ⅝ inch (15 mm) diameter, with many hooked spines. The fruiting head of snakeroot, *Sanicula marilandica* L., is similar but has shorter spines. LEAVES are bright green, mostly basal, hairy and toothed, with long petioles and large stipules. They are pinnately compound in a lyrate arrangement with a dominant center leaflet subtended by four to six smaller ones. Leaves vary widely in size, from 2 to 5 inches (5-12 cm) long. The stem leaves are alternate, smaller, sessile or with short petioles. GROWTH HABIT is perennial, erect and much branched, growing to heights of 18 to 40 inches (45-100 cm). Common HABITAT is meadows of tall grass or open woods where there is some shade and abundant moisture.

PURPLE AVENS
Geum rivale L.

flower detail

Purple avens

FLOWERS are conspicuously purple due to sepals, with the five petals more yellow with purple streaks. Stamens are numerous. Flowers appear in July. FRUITS are achenes in a bur-like head. LEAVES are basal and along the stem. The basal leaves are petioled, up to 15 inches (37 cm) long. The smaller stem leaves are divided into threes, the terminal segment of which is three-lobed. They are coarsely toothed, dark green and somewhat hairy. GROWTH HABIT is erect and perennial, a hairy stem with few branches, rising from a thick rootstock, not as large or conspicuous as that of three-flowered avens, (*G. triflorum* Pursh). Plants may be 1 to 3 feet (30-90 cm) in height. HABITAT is wet swampy ground in the north and east and in the Cypress Hills.

Purple avens

THREE-FLOWERED AVENS
Geum triflorum Pursh

Three-flowered avens

FLOWERS are reddish purple, due to sepals, ½ to ¾ inch (12-20 mm) across, nodding, and appear in threes at the end of a long flower stem. There are five smaller yellowish petals. Several flowering stems may grow from one rootstock. Flowers appear May-June. FRUITS are achenes with feathery styles about 1 inch (2.5 cm) long, grouped in a dense head. The styles persist until midsummer and are responsible for the name of "old man's whiskers." LEAVES are mostly basal, dark green, compound pinnate and finely toothed. Leaves may have ten to twenty leaflets. There is usually a small tuft of leaves halfway up the flower stem. GROWTH HABIT is basal with flower stems and leaves growing from a coarse black horizontal rootstock. Leaves may be 6 to 8 inches (15-20 cm) long and flower stems may attain a height of 6 to 18 inches (15-45 cm). Flowers appear to be barely open but they are mature at this stage. HABITAT includes open prairie, usually near trees and scrub, where plants grow in patches of ten to several hundred.

Three-flowered avens

Three-flowered avens

SILVERWEED
Potentilla anserina L.

ROSE FAMILY

Silverweed

flower detail

FLOWERS are bright yellow, up to 1 inch (2.5 cm) in diameter, with five petals and five sepals. They are borne singly on a long stalk, and appear May-September. The FRUITS are small achenes in a head. LEAVES are basal, compound (seven to twenty-five leaflets), gray green on the upper surface and whitish and woolly undernearth; hence the common name for this cinquefoil species. GROWTH HABIT is prostrate or nearly so, tufted, spreading by reddish runners. A similar species, early cinquefoil, (*P. concinna* Richards.), lacks runners and its leaves are a brighter green. HABITAT includes slough margins and other wet places, barnyards, roadside ditches, etc. It is widely distributed throughout the area.

Early cinquefoil

WHITE CINQUEFOIL
Potentilla arguta Pursh

ROSE FAMILY

White cinquefoil

FLOWERS are creamy white with a yellow center due to the numerous stamens. The five sepals are green and ovate and they elongate as the fruit matures. Several flowers, ½ to ¾ inch (12-20 mm) across, are borne in a rather crowded cyme, appearing June-July. FRUIT is a light brown achene with visible ridges in its surface. LEAVES are bright green, pinnately compound, with lower leaflets smaller than the upper ones. There are seven to eleven toothed, hairy leaflets on the basal leaves and three to five on the upper ones. Leaflets average about ½ inch (12 mm) in length, but some are over an inch (2.5 cm). GROWTH HABIT is perennial, erect and slightly branching, 12 to 30 inches (30-75 cm) high, but the whole plant gives the appearance of a single stem. HABITAT includes moist low-lying places in the prairie grasslands, slough margins and aspen poplar groves of the area, particularly in the south and central portions.

F. R. VANCE

White cinquefoil

flower detail

SHRUBBY CINQUEFOIL
Potentilla fruticosa L.

ROSE FAMILY

Shrubby cinquefoil

Shrubby cinquefoil

Prairie cinquefoil

FLOWERS are deep yellow, ¾ to 1 inch (2-2.5 cm) across with five petals and five sepals. They are borne in small dense clusters, mainly at the ends of branches, from June-August. FRUITS are achenes in a head which is densely hairy. LEAVES are alternate, gray green, with pinnate leaflets compounded in a spreading arrangement of about five leaflets closely attached to the axis. GROWTH HABIT: A bushy shrub with most branches arising from branching rootstocks and growing to 12 to 48 inches (30-120 cm) high. HABITAT includes the low moist areas of sandy soil and lower slopes of sandy areas of the south and southwest. Another yellow species, prairie cinquefoil, (*P. pensylvanica* L.), is illustrated on this page because it is often found associated with shrubby cinquefoil.

ROUGH CINQUEFOIL
Potentilla norvegica L.

ROSE FAMILY

Rough cinquefoil

Rough cinquefoil

FLOWERS are bright yellow, saucer-shaped, ¼ to ½ inch (6-12 mm) across, fairly numerous, borne in small, dense cymose clusters of leaves on the upper stems. There are five petals and five coarsely hairy sepals which are somewhat pointed and slightly longer than the petals. Flowering occurs from June to late August. FRUIT is a small group of green, ridged achenes, about ¼ inch (6 mm) across, enclosed in the enlarged hairy calyx. The achenes turn brown at maturity. LEAVES are bright green, numerous, palmately divided into three leaflets, ¾ to 4 inches (2-10 cm) long, obovate to lanceolate, hairy and coarsely toothed. Lower leaves are on long petioles but the upper leaves are sessile with large stipules. GROWTH HABIT is usually annual, a coarse, erect but rather floppy, much-branched herb with stems and leaves sparsely covered with stiff hairs. HABITAT is wet areas in land where cultivation has been abandoned, garden and road edges, and even some sandy beaches throughout the plains and parklands.

MARSH CINQUEFOIL
Potentilla palustris (L.) Scop.

ROSE FAMILY

FLOWERS have five somewhat pointed, reddish petals and five ovate, purplish, spreading, and pointed sepals, and
are ⅜ to 1¼ inches (1-3 cm) across.
Several linear bracts alternate with the
sepals and both are longer than the
petals. There are two to twenty-five reddish stamens and pistils. Flowers appear
in a cymose cluster in July and August.
FRUIT is a group of small, smooth, brown
achenes borne in a soft hairy receptacle.
LEAVES are medium green, smooth
above, paler and with fine hairs on the
underside. They are pinnately compound
with five to seven oblong, finely toothed
leaflets each 1¼ to 2½ inches (3-6 cm) in
length. The stem leaves may be reduced
to three major leaflets flanked by two
minor leaflets. Basal leaves are on long
petioles but stem leaves are essentially
sessile. GROWTH HABIT is somewhat
decumbent, supported by adjacent vegetation. They are 8 to 28 inches (20-70
cm) tall, with weak, coarse, hairy, reddish
brown stems. HABITAT is wet marshy
areas, in or near shallow water. This
species is found in the northern and
eastern parts of the parkland but also
extends to the north and west.

Marsh cinquefoil

Marsh cinquefoil

THREE-TOOTHED CINQUEFOIL
Potentilla tridentata Ait.

ROSE FAMILY

Three-toothed cinquefoil

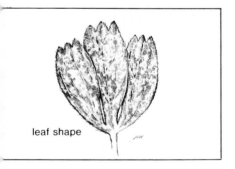

leaf shape

FLOWERS are white, ¼ to ⅜ inch (6-10 mm) across, wheel-shaped with five spreading petals, supported by five hairy, pointed sepals and a rough ring of bractlets. Stamens are numerous and give a yellowish cast to the center of each flower. Blooms (one to six) are borne in an open cyme at the ends of branches in July. FRUIT is a head of small hairy achenes held in the receptacle and surrounded by the calyx. LEAVES are dark green, borne on short petioles. They are composed of three thick leaflets, ⅜ to 1 inch (1-2.5 cm) long, entire margined except for three sharp teeth at the truncated apex of each leaflet. Leaflets are somewhat paler on the underside due to fine hairs. GROWTH HABIT is perennial, a shrubby, near prostrate plant with creeping rootstocks and a woody base from which stems arise. Flowering stems may be 12 inches (30 cm) long but are usually much shorter, and do not rise more than 3 to 4 inches (7.5-10 cm) above the ground surface. HABITAT is usually dry sandy areas in clearings or thin places in the boreal forest.

WILD PLUM
Prunus americana Marsh

ROSE FAMILY

Wild plum

Wild plum

Sand cherry

FLOWERS are white with a tinge of pink in the bud stage and may fade again to pink. They are borne in lateral sessile umbels of four to seven flowers on long smooth stalks. The five petals are ⅛ to ¼ inch (3-6 mm) across with smaller bright green sepals. Flowers open quickly in late May and soon mature and drop their petals. FRUIT is a dark red or yellow fleshy drupe up to 1 inch (2.5 cm) in diameter with a rather tough, leathery skin. The fruit of the Canada plum, *P. nigra,* is larger and more yellow-orange in color. LEAVES are bright green, narrowly obovate, with double serrations or teeth

and a pointed tip. They are 1¼ to 2½ inches (3-6 cm) long and ¾ to 1¼ inches (2-3 cm) across. In contrast, the leaves of Canada plum are broader and less sharply pointed at the apex. GROWTH HABIT: A small tree with many thorny blue-gray branches which grows to 9 to 12 feet (3-4 m) height but may reach 25 feet (8 m). The Canada plum is more tree-like than shrubby in shape and has fewer spines on its branches. HABITAT is moist woodlands and ravines in south-western and western Manitoba. It is rare in Saskatchewan, even in the Qu'Appelle and Pipestone valleys.

PIN CHERRY
Prunus pensylvanica L.f.

ROSE FAMILY

Pin cherry

Pin cherry

S. M. vanBrienen

Pin cherry

FLOWERS are white, ¼ inch (6 mm) diameter, with five petals and five sepals; stamens extend beyond petals. Flowers are short-lived and sepals drop before petals. Flowers are arranged in a round cluster and appear at the time the leaves come out, May-June. The FRUIT is a small, ¼ inch (6 mm) round drupe with a large stone. It is sour but the flavor of jelly made from it is a rare treat. LEAVES are bright green, shiny, alternate, lance-shaped and finely toothed, usually 2 to 6 inches (5-15 cm) long.

GROWTH HABIT: A small tree with a round pattern of many top branches, very variable in height but commonly about 10 feet (3 m) tall. HABITAT includes the open areas of woodlands in the parkland region, as well as wooded coulees and road edges or deeper ravines. It is also found in moist upland depressions in the southwest.

RED CHOKE CHERRY
Prunus virginiana L.

ROSE FAMILY

Black choke cherry

Red choke cherry

Red choke cherry

FLOWERS are white, ⅜ to ½ inch (1-1.5 cm) in diameter, with five petals and five sepals. The sepals soon fall. Flowers are borne on short stems in dense cylindrical clusters, May-June. FRUIT is a fleshy drupe with a fairly large stone. It is dark red but bluish black in the commoner variety, *(var. melanocarpa* [A. Nels.] Sarg.). The fruits of both show the same red color in ripening stages. They are edible, particularly as jelly. LEAVES are alternate, dark green above, lighter underneath, egg-shaped or broadly oval, smooth on both sides and sharply toothed. They are 1 to 3 inches (2.5-7.5 cm) long and relatively numerous. GROWTH HABIT is perennial in a range from a low bush to a small tree of 1½ inch (4 cm) diameter and a height of 6 to 12 feet (2-4 m). The black-fruited variety tends to grow taller than the red-fruited one. Common HABITAT includes the edges of wooded areas in the parkland, scrubby patches and deep ravines of the area up to the edge of the boreal forest.

PRICKLY ROSE

ROSE FAMILY

Rosa acicularis Lindl.

Prickly rose   ripe fruit

This is the floral emblem of Alberta. FLOWERS are a deep rose red, usually borne singly, 2-3 inches (5-7.5 cm) across, often a deeper color and with less tendency to fade than other native species. However, the color is highly variable. Flowers appear June-July. FRUIT is bright red when ripe, globular in the commonest Saskatchewan variety, (*bourgeauiana*), egg-shaped in another, with the neck constricted in both.

LEAVES are dark green, alternate, compound pinnate, with five to seven leaflets. GROWTH HABIT: A bush with several main stems and many branches, up to 4 feet (120 cm) in height. Stems are thickly covered with weak bristles. Common HABITAT includes the margins of aspen groves, scrubby patches in prairie, coulees and roadsides throughout western Canada.

Prickly rose

PRAIRIE ROSE

ROSE FAMILY

Rosa arkansana Porter

Prairie rose

FLOWERS are pink but may fade to white, or petals may be streaked with darker pink. They are usually 1¼ to 2½ inches (3-7 cm) diameter and are in a cluster of two to three blooms. The flowers are much flatter when open than those of the Wood's rose, (*R. woodsii* Lindl.), which are distinctly saucer-shaped and usually a deeper pink. Flowers appear June-August. FRUIT is a hip, almost globular and about ½ inch (12 mm) diameter. It is bright red when ripe and contains many seeds. LEAVES are medium green, pinnately compound, with nine to eleven leaflets which are smooth and shiny. GROWTH HABIT: A low branching shrub, 6 to 18 inches (15-45 cm) high, which dies off to the ground each fall. HABITAT includes open prairie, uncultivated fields and road edges. The plant is most common in the grasslands but persists into the parkland.

Prairie rose

Wood's rose

F. R. VANCE

WILD RED RASPBERRY
ROSE FAMILY

Rubus idaeus L. var. *strigosus* (Michx.) Maxim.

Wild red raspberry

Wild red raspberry

Cloudberry

FLOWERS are white, ⅝ inch (15 mm) across, with five petals, five sepals and numerous stamens. They are mainly borne at the ends of stems in several loose clusters. The cloudberry or baked-apple berry, *R. chamaemorus* L.), has similar flowers and a yellowish red fruit like a raspberry. It is shorter and its few leaves arise from the rootstock. Flowers bloom in July. FRUIT is a berry of many fleshy druplets, ½ to ¾ inch (12-20 mm) in diameter. It is bright red when ripe. LEAVES are alternate, compound pinnate with five ovate leaflets, the terminal one of which is usually three-lobed. Leaflets may be up to 4 inches (10 cm) long, toothed, and pointed at the apex. GROWTH HABIT is perennial or biennial, a shrub 3 to 4 feet (90-120 cm) high. Stems are heavily bristled and some thicker stems live beyond the second year. HABITAT includes roadside ditches, cut over and burned land, coulees, etc., throughout the area but the plant is more common in the parkland and the edges of the boreal forest. Although not considered to have an economic value, it has been a valuable addition (raw and preserved) to the diets of many people ever since man came to the plains of North America.

DEWBERRY
Rubus pubescens Raf.

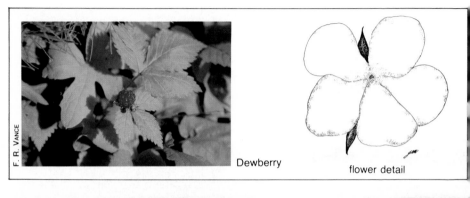

Dewberry

flower detail

Stemless raspberry

FLOWERS are white or pale pink, 3/16 to ⅝ inch (4-15 mm) across, in groups of two or three. Sepals, (five), are reflexed and are clearly visible in this state at the base of the fruit. Flowers are open, as shown in the sketch, for only a short period, and the semi-closed stage is the one most commonly observed. Flowers may appear June-July. FRUIT is a dark red edible berry, ⅜ to ⅝ inch (10-15 mm) across, not easily freed from the receptacle like that of the wild red raspberry, (*R. idaeus* L. var. *strigosus* [Michx.] Maxim.). LEAVES are alternate, light green, smooth and doubly toothed. They are compound, 3 to 4 inches (7-10 cm) across, with three to five ovate leaflets. GROWTH HABIT is trailing or climbing, with stems up to 3 feet (90 cm) but usually under 1 foot (30 cm). Flowers arise from nodes of runners or from the crown of the plant. In general appearance it is much like the stemless or Arctic raspberry, (*R. acaulis* Michx.), which has a purple pink flower and grows on the parkland-forest border and north from there. HABITAT includes deep aspen poplar woods and thickets of heavy scrub in the parkland. It also appears in the Cypress Hills.

ARROW-LEAVED MEADOWSWEET
ROSE FAMILY

Spiraea alba Du Roi

Shiny-leaved meadowsweet

magnified flower —
Narrow-leaved meadowsweet

FLOWERS are white, ⅛ inch (3 mm) diameter, with five petals and five sepals. The dense terminal raceme of many flowers gives the impression of a white brush. Flowers bloom in July. FRUIT is a short, ¼ inch (6 mm), papery pod which opens along one side and usually contains four seeds. LEAVES are dark green, alternate, narrowly lanceolate, coarsely toothed to the apex, pointed at both ends, 1 to 1½ inches (2.5-4 cm) long, paler on the underside. GROWTH HABIT is perennial, a brown stemmed shrub with a few slender branches, arising from a more or less running rootstock. Average height 8 to 30 inches (20-75 cm). Common HABITAT includes the moister areas of the prairie region, roadsides and low scrubby places, particularly in the south and central parts of the area. Another species, shiny-leaved meadowsweet, (*S. lucida* Dougl.), has a flat-topped inflorescence and may be observed in the Cypress Hills.

Narrow-leaved meadowsweet

TWO-GROOVED MILK-VETCH
Astragalus bisulcatus (Hook.) A. Gray

Two-grooved milk-vetch

F. R. VANCE

Two-grooved milk-vetch

seed pods

FLOWERS are deep purple to reddish purple, ½ inch (12 mm) long, 1/16 inch (2 mm) diameter. They are tubular and lipped, with five petals and five shorter sepals. The long dense clusters of twenty to thirty blooms have a characteristic "heavy" odor, and appear in June. The FRUIT is a narrowly oblong pod with two deep grooves. LEAVES are opposite, gray green, compound pinnate with seventeen to twenty-seven elliptic leaflets, each ⅜ to 1 inch (10-25 mm) long. GROWTH HABIT is perennial in dense clumps of many stems from one taproot. Clumps may be up to 3 feet (90 cm) across. Stems are semi-decumbent and may be up to 24 inches (60 cm) high. HABITAT includes the dry southern prairies and coulees but the plant extends into central and eastern parts of the area as well. This species and other *Astragalus* species may be poisonous to cattle and sheep, probably due to their tendency to concentrate selenium.

ANADIAN MILK-VETCH
stragalus canadensis L.

LEGUME FAMILY

Canadian milk-vetch

twenty-seven stalked leaflets which are 1 to 2 inches (2.5-5 cm) long. GROWTH HABIT is perennial with stout stems arising from the rootstock. Plants of this species may be 12 to 40 inches (30-100 cm) high with several stems, but *A. frigidus* usually has a single stem and is often shorter. HABITAT is the moist areas of margins of woods and scrubby patches. It is widely distributed throughout the parklands in low spots in open woodlands.

FLOWERS are creamy greenish white, bout ½ to ¾ inch (12-20 mm) long, in a ense spike-like raceme 1 ¼ to 4 inches 3-10 cm) in length, on a peduncle which ay be up to 8 inches (20 cm). The ower arrangement is in contrast to a imilar species, American milk-vetch, *A. rigidus* (L.) Gray, which has a loose aceme, 2 to 3 inches (5-7.5 cm) long ith the flowers widely spaced, drooping, nd reflexed at maturity. Both species ower from mid-June to July. FRUIT is a mooth, erect, stout, woody pod, ½ to ⅝ ich (12-15 mm) long, sessile, and divid-d into two cells. LEAVES are on short etioles, medium green, smooth, elliptic) oblong, odd pinnate with thirteen to

J. R. JOWSEY

American milk-vetch

128

GROUND-PLUM
Astragalus crassicarpus Nutt.

LEGUME FAMIL'

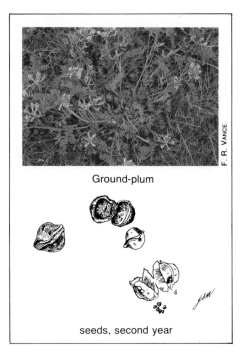

Ground-plum

seeds, second year

FLOWERS are pale violet to white, wit
the keel distinctly tinged with purple, ½ to ³
inch (12-20 mm) long. They appear in loos
racemes of eight to ten flowers at the end
of stems, May-June. The FRUIT is a po
which is nearly round, ½ inch (12 mn
diameter and reddish when mature, dryin
to a round, brown, two-valved case contair
ing many black seeds. Pods are usuall
intact the year following maturity. LEAVE
are medium green, numerous, with thirtee
to twenty-seven elliptic to oblong leaflet:
The leaflets are each ¼ to ⅝ inch (6-1.
mm) long, rounded at the apex, smooth o
the upper surface but covered with shor
stiff hairs on the lower surface. GROWTH
HABIT is perennial, decumbent in a mat
like arrangement with a mass of fifteen t
twenty prostrate stems, each 4 to 18 inche:
(10-40 cm) long. HABITAT includes the dr
plains of the south and southwest extend
ing into similar terrain in the center of th
area. It is occasionally called the buffalo
bean.

Ground-plum

DRUMMOND'S MILK-VETCH
Astragalus drummondii Dougl.

LEGUME FAMILY

Drummond's milk-vetch

Loose-flowered milk-vetch

FLOWERS are creamy white in a close, dense, spike-like raceme, 2 to 6 inches (5-15 cm) long, borne on a long stalk that ascends well above the leaves. Each flower is ½ to ¾ inch (12-20 mm) long, clasped by hairy sepals of less than half the length of the petals. Flowers hang from the inflorescence and are commonly seen in late June and July.

FRUIT is a slightly grooved, smooth, linear, medium green pod, ¾ to 1 inch (2-2.5 cm) long, which contains two rows of small seeds. Pods are spine tipped and extend well beyond the calyx on an elongated stalk (stipe). LEAVES are bright green with fine hairs on the underside, odd pinnate with twenty-one or more oblong, smooth-margined leaflets which are ½ to 1 inch (12-25 mm) long. The leaves are stalked and numerous which gives the plants a bushy appearance. GROWTH HABIT is perennial, an erect, coarse plant of 16 to 36 inches (40-90 cm) height with several thick, hairy stems arising from a woody stem base (caudex). The other species illustrated, loose-flowered milk-vetch, *A. tenellus* Pursh, has finer stems and leaves and small flowers in a short open raceme. HABITAT includes moist uplands of the southwest, especially the Cypress Hills.

MISSOURI MILK-VETCH
Astragalus missouriensis Nutt.

LEGUME FAMIL'

Missouri milk-vetch

Missouri milk-vetch

J. R. JOWSEY

FLOWERS are reddish purple to blue, ½ to ¾ inch (12-20 mm) long, enclosed by hairy, pointed sepals of about half the length of the petals. The six to ten flowers are in a loose, rounded raceme, ⅝ to 2 inches (1.5-5 cm) long, on a long stalk, and appear by late May or early June. FRUIT is an inflated, pinkish, smooth pod, ¾ to 1 inch (2-2.5 cm) long, with a sharp spine at the tip. It is slightly keelee and seeds develop in one row. Pods turn brown and leathery as they mature LEAVES are gray-green, silky-hairy, pin nate with nine to twenty-one oval to oblong leaflets, ¼ to ½ inch (6-12 mm long. They are not numerous so the plan has a rather stunted appearance GROWTH HABIT is somewhat prostrate on thin, silvery-hairy stems, but the plant may reach a height of 4 inches (10 cm) ii some cases. HABITAT: An early flower ing species of wide distribution in the southern part of the area on erode hillsides and gravelly soils where othe vegetation is sparse.

NARROW-LEAVED MILK-VETCH
Astragalus pectinatus Dougl.

LEGUME FAMILY

Narrow-leaved milk-vetch

FLOWERS are cream colored, ½ to 1 inch (12-25 mm) long in short loose clusters of eight to ten flowers, appearing in early June. FRUIT is a broad, oblong, woody pod, ½ to ¾ inch (12-20 mm) long. LEAVES are light green, compound pinnate with nine to nineteen narrow (1 mm) leaflets, each ½ to 2 inches (1-5 cm) long. GROWTH HABIT is semi-erect and much branched with "floppy" red-tinged stems up to 24 inches (60 cm) high. Plants arise from a deep taproot and have a strong tendency to concentrate selenium. They may be poisonous. The purple milk-vetch, (*A. goniatus* Nutt.), is also illustrated here. It is less erect, lower growing and more slender of stem than the narrow-leaved milk-vetch. HABITAT includes light sandy and gravelly soil with the plant often found over marine shales. It is common on the drier prairie and roadsides.

Narrow-leaved milk-vetch

F. R. VANCE

Purple milk-vetch

ASCENDING PURPLE MILK-VETCH
Astragalus striatus Nutt.

LEGUME FAMILY

Ascending purple milk-vetch

FLOWERS are purplish blue, ½ to ¾ inch (12-20 mm) long, with fifteen or more flowers in a dense spike-like raceme ⅝ to 2 inches (1.5-5 cm) long. The calyx members are usually about ¼ inch (6 mm) long, with coarse black and white hairs and a pointed spine at the end of each sepal. The inflorescence is borne on a long stalk well above the leaves, in contrast to purple milk-vetch (*A. goniatu* Nutt.), where flowering stalks are among the mat of leaves. Flowers appear in late June and early July. FRUIT is a two-valved, pointed to triangular pod, ¼ to ½ inch (6-12 mm) long. It is somewhat hairy and has a long projection at the tip. LEAVES are blue-green, alternate, with thirteen to twenty-five elliptic to oblong leaflets ⅜ to ¾ inch (1-2 cm) long, borne on erect, short petioles. They are somewhat silky-hairy on the underside with a distinct line of hairs along the midrib. GROWTH HABIT is perennial, erect, and spreading from a branched base (caudex). Stems are 4 to 18 inches (10-45 cm) long and rather weak so some plants are semi-prostrate. HABITAT: This species is widely distributed throughout the plains and parkland edges on dry slopes, open grasslands, and roadside ditches.

Ascending purple milk-vetch

J. R. JOWSEY

CUSHION MILK-VETCH
Astragalus triphyllus Pursh

LEGUME FAMILY

Cushion milk-vetch

flower detail

FLOWERS are creamy yellow, with a purple area on the keel, ½ to ¾ inch (12-20 mm) long. They are grouped in short clusters buried among the leaves of the plant, and appear May-early June. FRUIT is an oval, silvery-haired pod, partly enclosed by the sepals. LEAVES are gray green, silvery hairy and trifoliate, with leaflets ½ to ¾ inch (12-20 mm) long. Leaves grow up in a clump from the rootstock. GROWTH HABIT: A ball-like mass of leaves and flowers arising from a deep taproot. Total height rarely exceeds 4 inches (10 cm). HABITAT includes the sunny slopes and hillsides of the prairie area, particularly in the south and southwest, but extends to the Qu'Appelle River.

Cushion milk-vetch

WILD LICORICE
Glycyrrhiza lepidota (Nutt.) Pursh

LEGUME FAMILY

Wild licorice

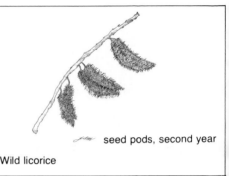

seed pods, second year

Wild licorice

FLOWERS are yellowish white, somewhat tubular with five petals and five sepals. They are borne on short stalks in dense racemes, 1 to 2 inches (2.5-5 cm) long and appear in July. FRUIT is an oblong brown bur-like pod about ⅜ inch (1 cm) long, densely covered with hooked prickles. The dry stems and pods often persist until the next season. LEAVES are opposite, pale green, compound pinnate with eleven to nineteen glandular-dotted leaflets which are about 1 inch (2.5 cm) long. GROWTH HABIT is perennial, somewhat coarse and starkly erect due to sparse leaves and short branches. The rootstock is thick and has a sweet licorice flavor. HABITAT includes the rough edges of wooded tracts and road and railway grades on wet to moderately dry sandy soils throughout the area. It is somewhat more common in the parkland and forest edge than on the plains.

HEDYSARUM
Hedysarum alpinum L.

LEGUME FAMILY

Hedysarum

FLOWERS are pinkish to violet, ½ inch (12 mm) long, usually pointing downward in a 3 to 5 inch (7.5-12.5 cm) raceme, appearing June-July. FRUIT is a flat, divided, smooth pod (loment), with slight narrowing between seeds to leave an impression of a sleeve of coins. LEAVES are opposite, medium green, smooth, pinnately compound with eleven to twenty-one oblong leaflets each ½ to 1¼ inches (12-30 mm) long. GROWTH HABIT is perennial, erect with some branching but a slim profile, height 6 to 30 inches (15-75 cm). Some lower seed pods are mature when upper blooms on the same raceme are just beginning to open. HABITAT includes the grassy areas of semi-open prairies, and borders of woodland glades from the south and southwest to the forest edge.

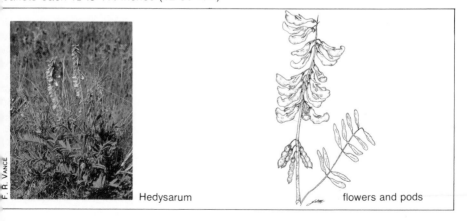

Hedysarum

flowers and pods

NORTHERN HEDYSARUM

LEGUME FAMILY

Hedysarum boreale Nutt. var. *cinerascens* (Rydb.) Rollins

Northern hedysarum

Northern hedysarum

FLOWERS are reddish purple, each ½ to ⅝ inch (12-15 mm) long, with twelve to twenty in a loose raceme 3 to 6 inches (7.5-15 cm) long. The five calyx lobes are of nearly equal length which distinguishes it from *H. alpinum,* L. var. *americanum* Michx., which has noticeably unequal calyx lobes. Each flower is borne on a short stalk. Flowering occurs in June and early July. FRUIT is the flattened, wrinkled, constricted pod (loment) about ¾ to 1 ¼ inches (2-3 cm) long, characteristic of the genus *Hedysarum,* with the dried, pointed calyx evident at its base. LEAVES are gray-green, sessile or nearly so, with nine to thirteen pinnately arranged elliptical to obovate leaflets. Both surfaces of the leaves are covered with silky hairs which are sufficient in number to give the plant a gray appearance. GROWTH HABIT is perennial, more or less erect, on thin, weak, ridged stems of 8 to 20 inches (20-50 cm) length, depending on other plants for some support. HABITAT: This variety is not common but is widely distributed on the prairies, particularly on the edges of steep coulees.

WILD PEAVINE
Lathyrus venosus Muhl.

LEGUME FAMILY

Wild peavine

Wild peavine

FLOWERS are purple with lighter violet areas on some of the petals, ½ to ⅝ inch (12-15 mm) long, typically legume in arrangement. There are twelve to twenty in each dense cluster, appearing June-August. The FRUIT is a dry, thin-walled pod, about 2 inches (5 cm) long, containing four to six seeds. They should be considered poisonous, although the action of poisons of seeds of *Lathyrus* species is not clear. LEAVES are alternate, bright green in a pinnately compound arrangement of eight to twelve oblong ovate, blunt tipped leaflets. Leaves have stipules and terminal tendrils. GROWTH HABIT is perennial and climbing to a length of 1 to 3 feet (30-90 cm). Stems are slightly branched and sometimes rather hairy. HABITAT includes margins of aspen poplar groves and relatively open areas inside such groves, particularly in the north and east. The cream-colored vetchling, (*L. ochroleucus* Hook.), overlaps its range but is more common in the central and western portions.

Cream-colored vetchling

SILVERY LUPINE
Lupinus argenteus Pursh

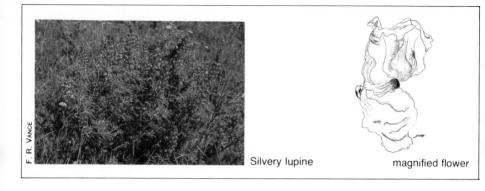

Silvery lupine   magnified flower

FLOWERS are light blue to violet, ⅜ inch (10 mm) long, ¼ inch (7 mm) across, with five petals and five sepals in the characteristic legume blossom arrangement. The keel is sickle-shaped. They are borne in loose terminal racemes of 2 to 3 inches (5-7.5 cm) in length, from June-July. The FRUIT is an upright silky-hairy pod about an inch (2.5 cm) long. It usually contains four to six seeds. LEAVES are alternate, dark green above, silvery-hairy beneath. The six to nine palmately arranged leaflets may be 1 to 2 inches (2.5-5 cm) long; leaf petioles are long. GROWTH HABIT is perennial and erect, 12 to 24 inches (30-60 cm) high with several hairy branches growing from a scaly branching rootstock. HABITAT includes the Cypress Hills and similar high plains locations in the south and southwest.

Silvery lupine

SMALL LUPINE
Lupinus pusillus Pursh

LEGUME FAMILY

Small lupine

FLOWERS are typically legume, dark blue with tinges of purple or white, about ⅜ inch (1 cm) long, on short pedicels, partly enclosed by the hairy calyx. They are borne in a short, dense raceme of five to ten blooms on a hairy stalk which is usually no more than 1 inch (2.5 cm) long. Flowers appear in June and may continue to September if moisture conditions are good, so new flowers and seed pods are often present at the same time. FRUIT is a rough, hairy, oblong pod about ¾ to 1 inch (2-2.5 cm) which contains only one or two seeds. LEAVES are dark green, alternate, palmately compound, with five leaflets usually rounded at the apex. Leaflets are ¾ to 1¼ inches (2-3 cm) long, nearly smooth on the upper surface, with long, coarse, erect hairs on the lower surface. They are borne on hairy petioles which are 1½ to 3 inches (4-7.5 cm) long. GROWTH HABIT is annual, a low, leafy, hairy plant with stout stems that branch near the base and may be decumbent. Total height is rarely more than 8 inches (20 cm). HABITAT is sandy areas often among open dunes where its presence restricts erosion. It is not common but well distributed in the south and southwest of the area.

BLACK MEDICK
Medicago lupulina L.

LEGUME FAMIL'

Black medick

Bird's foot trefoil

J. R. JOWSEY

FLOWERS are deep yellow, small and numerous, in a dense, head-like raceme about ¼ inch (6 mm) long, but larger under good moisture conditions. Flowering takes place in July and August. FRUIT is a curled, ridged pod containing one seed. The pod, which turns blacl when ripe, is usually coiled into almost a full circle. LEAVES are numerous, darl green, palmate in three parts. Leaflets are obovate to ovoid, toothed near the apex, and ⅜ to 1¼ inches (1-3 cm) long GROWTH HABIT: A prostrate or decum bent annual generating numerous branches from the root to form a dense mat of stems and leaves which ma include stems up to 2 feet (60 cm) long HABITAT: This is an introduced species from Eurasia which has spread from yards and fields to various locations throughout the parklands and forest edges. Another similar introduced le gume illustrated is bird's foot trefoil *Lotus corniculatus* L., which is semi-erec but coarser and has much larger flowers and flower heads.

ALFALFA
Medicago sativa L.

LEGUME FAMILY

Alfalfa

Alfalfa

FLOWERS are deep purple to bluish, with some white sections in the corolla. They are typical legume flowers, ¼ to ½ inch (6-12 mm) long, with a prominent keel, borne in a tight raceme ⅜ to 1¼ inches (1-3 cm) long. The pistil is held in the petals of the keel and must be released or "tripped" by foraging bees or other pollinating agents if seed is to develop. Flowers of a similar species, yellow lucerne, *M. falcata* L., are varying shades of yellow. Flowering is most common in June but harvested fields bloom again later. FRUIT is a hairy pod under ¼ inch (6 mm) curled in the two or three sepals, filled with eight to ten brown or yellow seeds. The pods of *M. falcata* are less coiled. LEAVES are numerous, dark green, divided into three oblong leaflets, with the terminal one on a short stalk. The leaflets are ⅜ to 1¼ inches (1-3 cm) long, on petioles usually longer than the leaves. GROWTH HABIT is perennial, semi-erect or prostrate, on long slender stems which may be 1 to 3 feet (30-90 cm). Some commercial varieties have been developed which are strongly creeping rooted, but a deep taproot is the characteristic that aids its growth under poor moisture conditions. HABITAT: An introduced plant from southeastern Europe now so common it is considered wild. Plants most commonly appear in ditches; field margins, and abandoned farmsteads.

WHITE SWEET-CLOVER
Melilotus alba Desr.

F. R. VANCE

White sweet-clover

seeds on spike

FLOWERS are white, about 3/16 inch (4 mm) long, densely crowded on an elongated spike-like raceme, 2 to 4 inches (5-10 cm) long. In the yellow species, (*M. officinalis* [L.] Lam.), the standard petal is shorter. Flowers bloom June-August. FRUIT is a rough thick papery pod with one and occasionally two yellow brown seeds. LEAVES are bright green, finely toothed, palmately compound of three leaflets, each ½ to 1 inch (12-25 mm) long. GROWTH HABIT is erect, biennial, and up to 7 feet (2 m) tall on woody, slightly hollow stems. The yellow species is much shorter. Their deep taproots have many branches. HABITAT This is an introduced plant of some economic importance as cattle feed and as a source of nectar for honey. Its escape to roadside ditches and some fields makes it a pioneer plant of a sort and its appearance and perfume make it a pleasant addition in many places.

Yellow sweet-clover

SAINFOIN
Onobrychis viciaefolia Scop.

LEGUME FAMILY

Sainfoin

Sainfoin

FLOWERS are light pink to lavender, prominently lined with reddish purple, ⅜ to ½ inch (10-12 mm) long, and numerous, in a tight spike in which the bottom flowers of the inflorescence mature first. The flower is somewhat tubular and enclosed in a rather hairy calyx. Flower spikes are borne on a long stalk and appear in late June and July. FRUIT is a tough, hairy, fibrous, dark brown, tightly coiled pod under ¼ inch (6 mm), which contains a single, kidney-shaped brown seed. LEAVES are odd-pinnate, numerous, gray-green, with eleven to seventeen oblong leaflets each about 1 inch (2.5 cm) long. They are entire margined and slightly hairy on the underside. GROWTH HABIT is perennial and erect to a height of 30 to 40 inches (75-100 cm). There have been various introductions of this species from Europe for use as forage. HABITAT is usually uncultivated fields or field margins. It may spread from there to road ditches, and the pink flowers will bring it to the notice of many people.

EARLY YELLOW LOCOWEED
Oxytropis macounii (Greene) Rydb.

LEGUME FAMILY

Early yellow locoweed

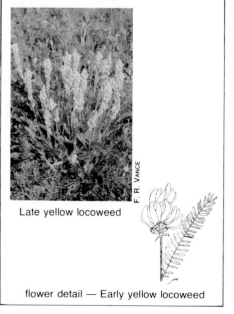

Late yellow locoweed

flower detail — Early yellow locoweed

FLOWERS are pale lemon yellow, ⅝ to ¾ inch (1.5-2 cm) long, in a dense spike of six to ten flowers. The spike is more open and flowers larger than in other *Oxytropis* species. Flowers of late yellow locoweed, (*O. gracilis* [A. Nels.] K. Schum), are shorter and creamy yellow in color. Flowers appear in May-June. FRUIT is a hairy short-beaked pod, leathery at maturity, but membranous in late yellow locoweed. LEAVES are all basal, dark gray-green, compound pinnate, silky-hairy but not woolly. The seven to twenty leaflets are oval, ½ to 1 inch (12-25 mm) long. GROWTH HABIT is low, but not densely clumped, and leaves arise from the root crown. Reported to be poisonous to livestock, it is attractive to them because of its early appearance. The late yellow locoweed is taller and flowering stems are longer. HABITAT includes the dry hillsides and open prairies of the south, southwest and central part of the area. The two species combine to provide color in stands of grasses from late May to early September. Early yellow locoweed is often confused with golden-bean, (*Thermopsis rhombifolia* [Nutt.] Richards).

SHOWY LOCOWEED
Oxytropis splendens Dougl.

Showy locoweed

Showy locoweed

detail of spike

FLOWERS are deep blue or purple, ½ inch (12 mm) long in a soft hairy dense spike of eight to twelve flowers. The spike may be 1 to 1½ inches (2.5-4 cm) long. A hairy stem projects it above the leaves. Flowers bloom June-July. Fruit is an ovoid, densely hairy, short-beaked pod, about ½ inch (12 mm) long, held in the floral spike by the sepals. LEAVES are gray green, silky-hairy, basal, numerous, pinnately compound, in a whorled arrangement 3 to 4 inches (7-10 cm) high. GROWTH HABIT is erect and perennial, in a dense clump arising from a thick rootstock, often to a height of 8 to 10 inches (20-25 cm). Several species of locoweed concentrate selenium and are known to be poisonous. HABITAT includes the grasslands of moister areas of the prairies and parkland. The variety *richardsonii* (after Sir John Richardson) has softer, more numerous hairs on leaves and is more common in the extreme southwest. Another similar species, Bessey's locoweed, (*O. besseyi* [Rydb.] Blank.), occasionally appears in the south but it is very rare and worthy of careful identification and preservation.

146

PURPLE PRAIRIE-CLOVER
Petalostemon purpureum (Vent.) Rydb.

LEGUME FAMILY

Purple prairie-clover

Purple prairie-clover

White prairie-clover

FLOWERS are numerous, dark to rose purple, small (1 mm), typically legume, in a densely packed terminal head or spike which may be ½ to 1 inch (12-25 mm) long and ¼ inch (6mm) diameter. The flowers are most often observed at the base of the spike with a bare area above, and bloom July-September. FRUIT is a short pod, and there is one of these pods in each depression in the spike. LEAVES are alternate, medium green, and compound pinnate. They are made up of seven to ten narrow, linear leaflets, ¼ to 1 inch (6-25 mm) long and occasionally slightly hairy. GROWTH HABIT is perennial, much branched, usually semi-prostrate, with stems 6 to 24 inches (15-60 cm) long. Two white flowered species, (*P. candidum* [Willd.] Michx. and *P. oligophyllum* [Torr.] Rydb.), are less common but widely distributed in the area. HABITAT is varied but the purple species is commonest on hillsides and uncultivated areas or road edges in the open prairie of the whole southern and central part of the area.

SILVERLEAF PSORALEA
Psoralea agrophylla Pursh

LEGUME FAMILY

Silverleaf psoralea

magnified flower

Silverleaf psoralea

FLOWERS are deep blue to purple, under ⅛ inch (2 mm) diameter, with unequal lobes extending out of the silvery calyx about ⅛ inch (2 mm). They are arranged in an interrupted spike of one to three whorls. The lance-leaved species, (*P. lanceolata* Pursh), is characterized by pale bluish white flowers in a short dense spike. Both bloom in July. FRUIT is an ovoid silky pod with black seeds. LEAVES are alternate, silvery gray, palmately compound, smooth and hairy on both sides. They are on short petioles about 1¼ inch (3 cm) long and have three to five oblong-ovate leaflets. GROWTH HABIT is perennial and widely branched, often 10 inches (25 cm) high but may be as tall as 40 inches (1 m). Branching is much more open than in Indian bread-root, (*P. esculenta* Pursh), and growth habit is more upright than the lance-leaved species. HABITAT includes the dry uplands of the prairies in the entire southern part of the area, to the edge of the aspen parkland. The lance-leaved species is more common in the southwest.

148

INDIAN BREADROOT
Psoralea esculenta Pursh

LEGUME FAMILY

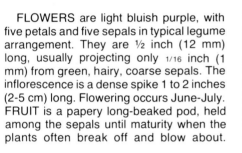

Indian breadroot

mature spike of seeds

FLOWERS are light bluish purple, with five petals and five sepals in typical legume arrangement. They are ½ inch (12 mm) long, usually projecting only 1/16 inch (1 mm) from green, hairy, coarse sepals. The inflorescence is a dense spike 1 to 2 inches (2-5 cm) long. Flowering occurs June-July. FRUIT is a papery long-beaked pod, held among the sepals until maturity when the plants often break off and blow about.

LEAVES are alternate, bright green, compound palmate with five leaflets. They are coarse and hairy, particularly on the under side, with thick hairy petioles. GROWTH HABIT is perennial, bunched in appearance due to branching and compression of leaves to stems. Plants are usually 6 to 12 inches (15-30 cm) high. HABITAT includes high, dry prairie grassland over the south central and southwest of the area.

Indian breadroot

LANCE-LEAVED PSORALEA
Psoralea lanceolata Pursh

LEGUME FAMILY

Lance-leaved psoralea

FLOWERS are bluish white to white with a blue-tipped keel, about ¼ inch (6 mm) long, borne in short dense spikes of ten to fifteen flowers in the leaf axils. The calyx is formed of five pointed sepals which are partly united and only about one-third the length of the corolla. June and July is the common time of flowering. FRUIT is a lemon-shaped pod, slightly hairy or dotted, which contains one small brown seed. LEAVES are light or yellowish green, opposite, entire margined, palmate with three linear to lanceolate, sharply pointed leaflets about ⅜ to 1¼ inches (1-3 cm) long and ¼ inch (6 mm) wide. GROWTH HABIT is perennial, usually erect but occasionally prostrate, 6 to 12 inches (15-30 cm) tall, sometimes attaining a height of 20 inches (50 cm) under good moisture conditions. Roots are long and much branched and often exposed at edges of dune sand. HABITAT is sandy unstable areas or edges of sand dunes, particularly in the southwest, rarely extending into heavier soils. Since the plant is not readily grazed by cattle, it is left in dunes where it is a substantial factor in erosion control.

Lance-leaved psoralea

GOLDEN-BEAN
Thermopsis rhombifolia (Nutt.) Richards.

LEGUME FAMILY

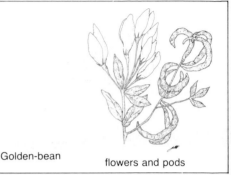

Golden-bean

flowers and pods

FLOWERS are bright golden yellow, about ½ inch (12 mm) long, with several flowers arranged in a dense terminal spike. This plant is reported to be poisonous, particularly to children, in both the flower and seed stage. Flowering dates range from May-early June. FRUIT is a grayish brown hairy curved pod, about 2 inches (5 cm) long with four to six seeds. LEAVES are alternate, composed of three dark-green ovate leaflets, ¾ to 1¼ inches (2-3 cm) long, with long stalks and large ovate stipules. GROWTH HABIT is perennial and branching, 6 to 20 inches (15-50 cm) high, usually in large patches, growing from running rootstocks. HABITAT includes the moister areas of the prairies, grassy roadside ditches, etc., where the water table is high. It is widely distributed over the southern half of the area.

Golden-bean

RED CLOVER
Trifolium pratense L.

LEGUME FAMILY

Red clover

Alsike clover

FLOWERS are red, (white and pink respectively in the two other species, *T. repens* L. or white Dutch and *T. hybridium* L. or alsike). They are in the typical legume form, each about ¼ to ½ inch (6-12 mm) long in a dense rounded head of fifteen to twenty flowers, appearing in July. FRUIT is a dry pod containing one to six seeds, usually held among the sepals in each section of the rounded head. LEAVES are smooth, dark green, up to ¾ inch (20 mm) long, ¼ inch (6 mm) wide, made up of three oval to elliptic leaflets which are pointed and slightly toothed. GROWTH HABIT is perennial and creeping, usually rather bunched, but some stems may be more than a foot (30 cm) long. HABITAT includes lawns, gardens and field edges where moisture conditions are better than average. The three species illustrated are widely distributed and red clover, (*T. pratense* L.), is more common in Alberta. Like the yellow and white sweet-clovers, they have also escaped to the point of being considered common wildflowers.

White Dutch clover

WILD VETCH
Vicia americana Muhl.

LEGUME FAMILY

Wild vetch   Tufted vetch

Wild vetch

FLOWERS are reddish purple, about 1 inch (2.5 cm) long in the legume pattern of five petals, five sepals, and ten stamens. Petals are narrower than in the vetchlings (*Lathryus* spp.). There are five to seven flowers in a loose, spike-like raceme. Flowers of vetch have a slender style with a tuft of hairs near the end. The flowers of *V. cracca* L., an introduced species, are more numerous, in a dense raceme and bluer in color. They bloom from June to August. FRUIT is a smooth, flat pod 1 to 1¼ inches (2.5-3 cm) long which contains four to seven seeds. LEAVES are alternate, pinnately compound with eight to fourteen leaflets which are prominently veined, variable in surface and margins. They are ovate to elliptic, ⅜ to 1¼ inches (1.5-3 cm) long. The terminal tendril usually branches at its origin. Stipules are sharply toothed and triangular ovate. GROWTH HABIT is perennial and twining, often as a group of decumbent stems and leaves. Stems are slender, usually below 16 inches (40 cm) in length, but occasionally up to 32 to 40 inches (80-100 cm) long. HABITAT is grassland and thickets or open wooded areas in the parkland and prairies where relatively good moisture conditions prevail.

STORK'S-BILL
Erodium cicutarium (L.) L'Her.

Stork's-bill

stork's-bill

FLOWERS are pink to light purple, ⅜ inch (1 cm) across, saucer-shaped in umbel-like clusters of two to ten. The five hairy, awn-tipped sepals overlap to some extent and are somewhat shorter than the petals. Flowers appear in late June and plants may continue to flower until September. FRUIT matures as the style extends to 1¼ to 1½ inches (3-4 cm) after flowering. The five beaked seeds with long spiral tails are formed from the style and twist in various directions to disperse the seeds. LEAVES are dark green, pinnately or bi-pinnately divided, somewhat hairy, 3 to 5 inches (7.5-12 cm) long. Lower leaves have petioles but the upper ones are stalkless. A similar species, *Geranium bicknellii* Britt., may be distinguished by the palmate arrangement of the leaflets, which are deeply dissected and thinner. GROWTH HABIT is annual and semi-prostrate, an introduced species which is a weed throughout much of northern Europe as well as North America. HABITAT is gardens and road edges near cultivation. By contrast, Bicknell's geranium is found in edges of boreal forest clearings and fields, usually in some shade.

Bicknell's geranium

Bicknell's geranium

WILD WHITE GERANIUM
Geranium richardsonii Fisch. and Trautv.

GERANIUM FAMILY

Wild white geranium

Wild white geranium

FLOWERS are white tinged with pink and show distinct purplish veins. The wheel-shaped corolla has five petals ⅜ to ¾ inch (1-2 cm) long and five bristly, lanceolate sepals about half the length of the petals. There are ten stamens. Flowers appear from late June to September. FRUIT: A pistil of five one-seeded carpels disperses the seeds; each section splits and twists outwards from the base of the pistil at maturity. The fruit has the appearance of a long beak, hence the common name of "crane's bill." LEAVES are opposite, bright green, and numerous. They are 1¼ to 6 inches (3-15 cm) across, palmately divided into three to seven coarsely toothed leaflets. GROWTH HABIT is perennial, erect, and branching, and weak, smooth stems may raise the plant to a height of 16 to 36 inches (40-90 cm) if some other support is available. HABITAT is moist edges of aspen groves and boreal forest, particularly in the west and in the Cypress Hills.

C. LETKEMAN

STICKY GERANIUM
Geranium viscosissimum Fisch. and Mey.

GERANIUM FAMILY

FLOWERS are deep lavender pink, 1¼ to 1½ inches (3-4 cm) across, with five petals and five sepals; the latter are hairy and tipped with awns. There are several blooms in a flat-topped cluster on the glandular, hairy flower stalk. This is the "windflower" of the Cypress Hills that turns meadows deep pink in June of some years. Approximate date of flowering is June-July. FRUITS arise from a stigma that is divided into five carpels, and the long-beaked capsule retains these five divisions, as shown by the sketch of the fruit of Bicknell's geranium, (*G. bicknellii* Britt.). The genus name *Geranium* is derived from the Greek word for crane because the fruit resembles the bill of this bird. LEAVES are opposite, medium green, hairy and glandular, 1½ to 4 inches (4-10 cm) wide and three to five times divided into sharply toothed segments. GROWTH HABIT is erect and perennial, with some branching. A height of 12 to 24 inches (30-60 cm) is common. HABITAT includes the open areas of wooded uplands, particularly on the south slopes of the Cypress Hills. Bicknell's and the white species, (*G. richardsonii* Fisch. and Trautv.), are more common and Bicknell's is relatively common at the north and eastern edges of the boreal forest.

F. R. VANCE

Sticky geranium

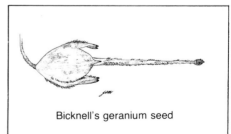

Bicknell's geranium seed

Sticky geranium

YELLOW WOOD-SORREL
Oxalis stricta L.

Yellow wood-sorrel

FLOWERS are bright, pale yellow, regular in shape with five sepals, a wheel-shaped corolla, and ten stamens arranged in two whorls. Sepals and petals are partly united in their respective floral rings. Petals are ¼ to ¾ inch (6-20 mm) long. Flowers are borne singly in umbel-like cymes on a ¼ inch (6 mm) stem and appear in August. FRUIT is a short, narrow, pointed, hairy capsule, ⅝ to 1 inch (15-25 mm) long, which when dry breaks open explosively and scatters four or five seeds. LEAVES are light green, smooth margined, palmately compound of three leaflets each about ⅜ inch (1 cm) long and ¼ inch (6 mm) wide, notched at the tip, with a prominent midvein. GROWTH HABIT: A low-growing, inconspicuous, decumbent perennial, arising from rootstocks to form a mat of leaves and flowers. Stems may be 1¼ to 2¼ inches (3-6 cm) but leaves and flowers rarely rise more than 2 inches (5 cm) above the ground surface. Flowers and leaves close at nightfall. HABITAT is watercourses in the parkland and moister areas of the plains. It is becoming common in abandoned farmsteads, yards and gardens.

WILD BLUE FLAX
Linum lewisii Pursh

FLAX FAMILY

Wild blue flax

F. A. SWITZER

Wild blue flax

seed capsule

FLOWERS are pale blue, ¾ to 1½ inches (15-35 mm) diameter. The five petals may have radiate lines of lighter blue. Several flowers are borne in a loose terminal cluster, and appear June-July. FRUIT is a round capsule, ⅛ inch (3 mm) diameter, which matures rapidly. LEAVES are linear, ⅜ to ¾ inch (7-15 mm) long, gray green and numerous. GROWTH HABIT is erect and perennial, 10 to 24 inches (25-60 cm) tall with several stems arising from each rootstock. HABITAT includes dry open places, roadsides and railway grades throughout the area; the plant is more common in the south and central part. This plant is named for the American explorer, Capt. Meriwether Lewis of the famed Lewis and Clark expedition.

YELLOW FLAX
Linum rigidum Pursh

FLAX FAMILY

Yellow flax

Yellow flax

FLOWERS are deep yellow, about ¾ inch (2 cm) in diameter, with five each of sepals, petals, and stamens. The petals open to the shape of a flat saucer but soon fall, as do the sepals. Flowering is common from late June to August. FRUIT is a small, ⅛ inch (3 mm), ovoid capsule which contains about ten small seeds, also ovoid, with a sharp tip at the apex. They scatter by wind action when the dry capsule breaks open. LEAVES are alternate, light green, narrowly linear, sharp tipped, and sessile. They soon dry up and drop off as the plant matures. GROWTH HABIT is erect, on a slender stem with a few upper branches. Plants may be as tall as 16 inches (40 cm) but are more commonly under 6 inches (15 cm). HABITAT is the drier upper ranges of the southern prairies, particularly along old trails and sandy disturbed places.

JEWELWEED
Impatiens biflora Walt.

TOUCH-ME-NOT FAMILY

Spotted touch-me-not

Western jewelweed

FLOWERS are about ⅝ inch (15 mm) long, deep orange-yellow with a pouch-like orange sepal dotted with purplish brown spots (pale yellow in western jewelweed, *I. noli-tangere* L.). Floral rings are complete but irregular; there are two small green sepals and the third forms the pouch which has a nectar-filled spur about ⅜ inch (1 cm) long. There are three lobed yellow petals which form a tube around the pistil and five stamens. Flowers appear in August. FRUIT is a pod-like capsule made up of the five carpels of the pistil. The mature capsules burst open at the slightest touch. Seeds often arise from some less conspicuous flowers that lack a pouch. LEAVES are alternate, light green, numerous, oval, and vary widely in size, ¾ to 3½ inches (2-9 cm). They are delicately thin, finely toothed, and have petioles about 1 inch (2.5 cm) in length. GROWTH HABIT is annual, a much-branched, weak-stemmed herb which may vary from 16 to 36 inches (40-90 cm) in height. HABITAT is usually open spaces near the water line of streams and lakes in forested areas of the parkland, the boreal forest, and Cypress Hills.

160

FRINGED MILKWORT
Polygala paucifolia Willd.

MILKWORT FAMILY

Fringed milkwort

White milkwort

FLOWERS are irregular, rose purple to pink due to two of the five sepals which are petal-like, and three petals each ⅜ to ¾ inch (1-2 cm) long. The keel of the corolla has a fringed crest, at least partly responsible for one of this plant's common names, "gaywings." Three or four flowers are borne in a loose raceme at the end of each stem. Another species, white milkwort, (*P. alba* Nutt.), is occasionally found in more southern parts of the area. Flowering occurs in June. FRUIT is a small two-valved capsule with only two seeds. LEAVES are alternate, entire, upper ones ovate, ⅜ to 1¼ inches (1-3 cm) long, prominently veined on the underside. Lower leaves are small and scale-like. GROWTH HABIT is essentially erect, growing from creeping rhizomes, but stems are weak. Stems are branched and the whole plant is no more than 4 to 7 inches (10-15 cm) high. HABITAT includes sunny open spaces in spruce groves of the boreal forest area. It is fairly common in moist sandy woodlands of the north and east.

Fringed milkwort

ENECA ROOT
olygala senega L.

MILKWORT FAMILY

F. R. VANCE

Seneca root

sepals, two of which resemble the petals. Flowering occurs through June and July. FRUIT is a small capsule with two seeds. LEAVES are alternate, narrow, lanceolate, ¾ to 1½ inches (2-4 cm) long, dark green and numerous, somewhat lighter on the underside. GROWTH HABIT is erect and perennial with numerous reddish stems arising from the short, branching rootstock to a height of 6 to 16 inches (15-40 cm). The plant is occasionally referred to as "seneca snakeroot" and the dried root is in demand as a flavoring in candy, medicines, and drinks. Its sale has often been a source of revenue for children and others short of cash. Common HABITAT is edges of aspen groves, scrubby patches, and moist grassy meadows of the parklands.

Seneca root

FLOWERS are minute and "closed" in appearance, greenish white, often tipped with purple, borne in a dense spike-like raceme, 1 to 2 inches (2.5-5 cm) in length. Each has three petals and five

LEAFY SPURGE
Euphorbia esula L.

SPURGE FAMILY

Leafy spurge

Leafy spurge

FLOWERS are greenish yellow, without petals and sepals, but with a peculiar "cyathium" formed of modified bracts ⅛ inch (3 mm) tall, bearing four crescent-shaped glands. Numerous male flowers, consisting of a single anther, and one female flower, a single pistil, often protruding, are found in one cyathium. Umbels of seven to ten flowers are borne at tips of main stems and upper branches and are common from late May to early August. FRUIT is a smooth, angular capsule ⅛ inch (3 mm) long, containing three seeds. Capsules burst open with some force when ripe. LEAVES are bluish green, alternate, sessile, ¾ to 3 inches (2-7.5 cm) long, linear to slightly oblong, with shorter, spade-shaped leaves forming a whorl beneath the inflorescence. GROWTH HABIT is perennial, erect and usually branching, 6 to 30 inches (15-75 cm) tall, spreading by creeping roots as well as seeds. Stems are light green, hard, smooth, and relatively bare of leaves. HABITAT is road and field edges as well as land where cultivation has been abandoned. This is a serious introduced weed that has rapidly spread into fields, particularly on sandy soils in south central Saskatchewan.

POISON-IVY
Rhus radicans L.

SUMACH FAMILY

Poison-ivy

FLOWERS are yellowish green, small, 1/16 inch (2 mm) long, with five sepals which are joined and slightly shorter than the petals. The five petals are veined with green and there are five stamens. Blooms are grouped in dense panicles in the leaf axils, and appear in early July. FRUITS are round, ¼ inch (6 mm) diameter, a cluster of greenish berries slowly ripening to dull white. LEAVES are alternate, bright green, smooth, up to 4 inches (10 cm) wide, compound, made up of three drooping, strongly-veined leaflets. Remember the saying, "leaves three — let it be." Leaflets are usually notched in an irregular fashion. They turn a brilliant red in the autumn. GROWTH HABIT: A low erect shrub which grows from a creeping rootstock to a height of 4 to 12 inches (10-30 cm). HABITAT includes deep wooded coulees and shady wooded places throughout Western Canada; the plant is very common along the Qu'Appelle River and its tributaries. It is noted for production of a powerful skin poison and irritant. All parts of the plant may exude enough of this poison to affect susceptible persons.

Poison-ivy

magnified flower group

SKUNKBUSH
Rhus trilobata Nutt.

Skunkbush

F. R. VANCE

Skunkbush   ripe fruit

FLOWERS are yellowish green, under ⅛ inch (2 mm) in diameter, in close terminal clusters. The five petals are united. Flowers appear before leaves and persist until the bushes leaf out. Approximate date of the flowering is mid-May. The FRUIT is a globular to coin-shaped dark red berry. LEAVES are dark gray green, alternate and roughly divided into three parts. Each leaflet is ½ to 1¼ inches (12-30 mm) long. GROWTH HABIT: A small bush or several plants in a bushy clump, usually under 3 feet (90 cm) in height and diameter. HABITAT includes south-facing slopes of coulees, particularly those leading into the Qu'Appelle River.

MANITOBA MAPLE
Acer negundo L. var. interius (Britt.) Sarg.

F. R. VANCE

Maple   Maple

FLOWERS are borne on separate trees (dioecious). Male flowers are most conspicuous, reddish with four to five stamens ⅝ to 1¼ inches (1.5-3 cm) long, appearing in drooping clusters before the leaves. Female flowers, greenish and minute with five sepals only, appear in a drooping raceme in early May. FRUITS consist of two samaras united at the base; the wings on each are very conspicuous, 1¼ to 2 inches (3-5 cm) long. LEAVES are light green, with long petioles, pinnately compound with three to five lanceolate, toothed, pointed leaflets, each 2 to 5 inches (5-12 cm) long. GROWTH HABIT is perennial, a roughly branched, short-lived tree up to 30 feet (10 m) tall, with reddish brown upper branches and grayish black, furrowed bark when mature. The mountain maple, A. glabrum Torr. var. douglasii (Hook.) Dippel, grows as a shrub or small tree to 10 feet (3 m) tall, has leaves that are palmately lobed but not divided, and bears either perfect flowers or both staminate and pistillate flowers on the same plant. HABITAT is commonly well watered uplands, particularly along watercourses. The Manitoba maple or "box elder" is widely used as a shade tree.

SMALL-FLOWERED MALLOW
Malva parviflora L.

Small-flowered mallow

across, with five partly united sepals and five petals united at their bases to form a wheel-shaped but semi-tubular flower They are borne in the leaf axils and are rather inconspicuous due to their size and to numerous leaves. Flowering is common in August. FRUIT is a peculiar ring of seeds, under ¼ inch (6 mm) in diameter, composed of ten to fifteen strongly ridged carpel segments which arise from a single style retained in an enlarged calyx. LEAVES are alternate medium green, ¾ to 2 inches (2-5 cm) across, roughly obovate to round, palmately veined, with six to eight wavy-margined lobes. Petioles are slender and vary in length from 2 to 4 inches (5-10 cm). GROWTH HABIT is annual, prostrate in a mat of leaves on smooth, fleshy trailing stems up to 12 inches (30 cm) long, spreading from the crown of a deep taproot. HABITAT: This species and several others in the genus have been introduced with garden seeds and have spread widely. They are found in gardens, lanes, and abandoned farmsteads usually in the black soil zone where moisture is in good supply.

FLOWERS are light pink varying to lilac and white, up to ⅜ inch (1 cm)

Small-flowered mallow

SCARLET MALLOW
Malvastrum coccineum (Pursh) A. Gray

MALLOW FAMILY

Scarlet mallow   flower detail

FLOWERS are orange red with five petals, five sepals and numerous stamens. The short, dense, leafy spikes have four to six flowers. Flowers appear May-July. FRUIT is formed of the carpels and develops in ten or more papery segments, each of which contains a single seed. LEAVES are alternate and gray green due to a covering of soft white hairs. They are divided into three to five divisions which are each lobed or forked. Each division is ½ to ¾ inches (12-20 mm) wide. GROWTH

HABIT is perennial, erect or semi-erect from a thick, scaly rootstock. Plants are 6 to 8 inches (15-20 cm) high, forming a mat of stems with several flowers on each. HABITAT includes roadsides, railway grades and other disturbed places throughout the southern half of the area. It is more common in the southwest. On the open prairie, plants are smaller and more separated. The other mallows, (*Malva* spp.), have been introduced, so this is the only native member of the family.

Scarlet mallow

168

SAND-HEATHER
Hudsonia tomentosa Nutt.

ROCK-ROSE FAMILY

Sand heather

FLOWERS are deep lemon yellow, under ¼ inch (6 mm) across, with five round tipped petals and ten to twenty stamens. There are four or five blunt sepals, two of which are green and hairy and much shorter than the others. The pistil is so slender that it is inconspicuous among the stamens. Flowers are borne in loose clumps at the ends of branches and usually appear in July. FRUIT is a tiny ovoid capsule which is tightly enclosed in the persistent calyx. It usually contains only one seed. LEAVES are alternate, pale grayish green due to a covering of gray hairs, ⅛ inch (3-5 mm) long. They are oval to oblong, pointed, and overlap the stem like shingles. GROWTH HABIT: A low to prostrate shrub with many branches, 3 to 6 inches (7.5-15 cm) tall. However, stems in some plants may grow to 8 to 10 inches (20-25 cm). HABITAT is sandy soils and dune sands, often adjacent to pine where moisture conditions are good in the boreal forest. This plant is very rare and should not be dug up.

Sand heather

NORTHERN BOG VIOLET
Viola nephrophylla Greene

VIOLET FAMILY

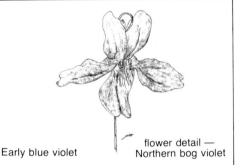

F. R. VANCE

Early blue violet

flower detail —
Northern bog violet

FLOWERS are bluish purple, up to ¾ inch (2 cm) across, borne on long stems. Petals are somewhat hairy, particularly the spur petal. It is similar to the early blue violet, (*V. adunca* J. E. Smith), which has somewhat smaller flowers. Flowers appear May-July. FRUIT is a dry, three-valved capsule which breaks open with some force to scatter the fifteen to twenty seeds it may contain. LEAVES are all basal, oval to kidney-shaped, round toothed and wavy margined, heart-shaped at the base and bluntly pointed. There are only a few per plant and they are 1½ to 2½ inches (4-7 cm) wide. GROWTH HABIT is erect, perennial, 2 to 4 inches (5-10 cm) tall to the top of the tallest flower stem. This species has no distinct stem but leaves of the early blue violet grow on a stem which is 1½ to 6 inches (4-15 cm) long. Common HABITAT includes moist edges of aspen poplar groves, sloughs and bogs. It is one of the commonest violets of the plains and forest edges in northern and eastern parts of the area, but only the early blue violet is common in moist locations on the prairie.

Northern bog violet

170

NUTTALL'S YELLOW VIOLET
Viola nuttallii Pursh

VIOLET FAMILY

Nuttall's yellow violet   Nuttall's yellow violet

Yellow meadow violet

FLOWERS are deep yellow with five sepals, five petals and five stamens. There is a short spur on the lowest petal. There are four to ten blooms per plant and they arise from the axils of the upper leaves. Another species, yellow meadow violet, (*V. vallicola* A. Nels.), is very similar except for differences in leaves. It is sometimes classed as a variety of *V. nuttallii* Pursh. Flowering occurs May-June. FRUIT is a dry, three-valved, many-seeded capsule. LEAVES are alternate, narrowly lanceolate, 1 to 2½ inches (2.5-7 cm) long, tapering to the stem and slightly hairy. The yellow meadow violet has elliptic basal leaves and ovate to broadly lanceolate stem leaves. Differences in leaf hairs make the yellow meadow violet appear a brighter green. GROWTH HABIT is low, 2½ inches (7 cm) and stems are short, with a clump of narrow dark green leaves topped with a bunch of yellow flowers. Plants of the yellow meadow violet are much less extensive and slightly shorter. HABITAT includes reasonably moist areas of the prairie in the south central and southwest. Two other yellow violets are occasionally observed in eastern parts of the area.

CROWFOOT VIOLET
Viola pedatifida G. Don

flower detail

Crowfoot violet

Crowfoot violet

FLOWERS are violet blue, large, ¾ inch (2 cm) across, on relatively short stems. The three lower petals are whitest at the base inside and heavily bearded in the cup of the flower. Approximate flowering date is June. FRUIT is a yellowish gray, ¼ inch (6 mm) capsule, which contains several light brown seeds. LEAVES are all basal, stemless, cleft almost to their bases into three lobes which are again divided into three or four lobes; hence, "crowfoot." They may be up to 4 inches (10 cm) wide and are slightly hairy at the margins. GROWTH HABIT is perennial, lacking a stem, with flowers and leaves arising from a short, vertical rootstock to 5 to 7 inches (13-18 cm) height. HABITAT includes grass-covered soil of the open prairie and hillsides where moisture conditions are relatively good. Because of their leaf shape they are rarely noticed in the grass until the flowers come into bloom.

WESTERN CANADA VIOLET
Viola rugulosa Greene

VIOLET FAMILY

F. R. VANCE

Western Canada violet

seed capsule

FLOWERS are white with pink to purplish veins on petals. Unopened buds are lavender pink with the white inside edges of petals showing. Flowers have five sepals and five petals, one of which has a prominent spur. They may be ½ to 1 inch (12-25 mm) diameter, and appear June-August. FRUIT is a dry, three-valved, many-seeded capsule which is studded with short spines to give it the appearance of a mace. LEAVES are alternate on long stalks, kidney-shaped or heart-shaped, smooth margined and pointed at the apex. They may be over 3 inches (7.5 cm) wide. GROWTH HABIT is erect, 8 to 24 inches (20-60 cm) tall, somewhat decumbent if moisture and light cause the plant to be very tall. This species is probably the longest flowering and most commonly observed violet. It is often called the wood violet. HABITAT includes shady places in aspen poplar groves and scrubby patches, and coulees throughout the entire region where moisture conditions are relatively good.

Western Canada violet

EVENINGSTAR

LOASA FAMILY

Mentzelia decapetala (Pursh) Urban and Gilg.

Eveningstar

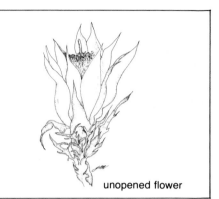

unopened flower

FLOWERS are creamy white with five sepals and ten petals, five of which are modified sterile stamens. There are numerous fertile stamens and a long thin pistil which persists after the other flower parts have fallen. Flowering occurs July-August. FRUIT is an oblong capsule 1½ inches (4 cm) long, up to ½ inch (12 mm) thick, occasionally covered by leafy bracts as well as sepals. LEAVES are alternate, gray green, oblong-lanceolate, sharply toothed, 2 to 6 inches (5-15 cm) long, covered with soft spine-like white hairs. Lower leaves have short stalks and the upper ones are stalkless. GROWTH HABIT is biennial, a rough branching plant with stout gray green, sticky stems and branches. Height is variable but may commonly range from 6 to 36 inches (15-90 cm). HABITAT includes rough hillsides, clay exposures and badlands in the south and southeast of the area.

Eveningstar

PINCUSHION CACTUS
Mamillaria vivipara (Nutt.) Haw.

Pincushion cactus

FLOWERS are violet purple due to sepals and petals, 1½ to 2 inches (4-5 cm) across, with a yellow center due to many stamens. Flowers arise at the convergence of the tubercles of the stem, and appear in July. FRUIT is a pale green fleshy berry which turns brown on ripening. It is edible and sweet but has a very bland flavor. LEAVES are absent; i.e., they are modified into three to eight short (⅛ inch or 3 mm) brownish green spines which cover each of the cone-shaped tubercles of the stem. GROWTH HABIT is perennial, cushion-like or tufted, in a group of branched balls, 1½ to 2 inches (4-5 cm) tall, each composed of several spine-tipped tubercles. HABITAT includes the open prairie, particularly south-facing slopes, of the south and southwest up to and along the Qu'Appelle Valley to the Fishing Lakes.

F. R. VANCE

Pincushion cactus   opened berry

PLAINS PRICKLY-PEAR CACTUS
Opuntia polyacantha Haw.

CACTUS FAMILY

Plains prickly-pear cactus

opened berry

Plains prickly-pear cactus

F. R. VANCE

FLOWERS are light lemon yellow to pink-sh orange, distinctly waxy, 2 to 3 inches (5-7.5 cm) across, with many sepals, petals and stamens. Flowers are numerous and bloom over an extended period, from mid-June to July. FRUIT is a soft, spicy-sweet, edible berry, round to ovate and about 1 inch (2.5 cm) long, filled with large bony discoid seeds (3/16 inch or 5 mm diameter). LEAVES are lacking, having evolved into clusters of five to nine straight spines, ½ to 2 inches (1-5 cm) long, on the surface of the pale green stem. GROWTH HABIT is perennial and prostrate, characterized by large clumps of jointed prickly stems. The brittle prickly-pear, (*O. fragilis* [Nutt.] Haw.), has rounder, more fleshy internodes in its stems. HABITAT includes dry hillsides, on even drier south slopes than those frequented by the pincushion cactus, all over the south, central and southwest of the area.

SILVERBERRY
Elaeagnus commutata Bernh.

Silverberry   fruit detail

FLOWERS are silvery yellow, ⅛ inch (3 mm) diameter and very fragrant. They are arranged in clusters of three or four, lack petals and have four sepals and four to eight stamens. Flowers bloom in June. FRUIT is a silvery-colored, tough skinned, dry, mealy berry, about ¼ inch (6 mm) in diameter, containing a large stony seed. LEAVES are alternate, silvery gray, scurfy on both sides, oblong to ovate, numerous, 1 to 3 inches (2.5-8 cm) long. GROWTH HABIT is perennial, a low shrub with purplish brown stems, moderately branched, 2 to 12 feet (60 cm - 4 m) high but rarely more than 7 feet (2 m). It is also called wolf-willow. HABITAT includes the moister areas of the plains and the parkland, edges of coulees, etc., in the southern half of the area, particularly where land is overgrazed.

Silverberry

SILVER BUFFALOBERRY
Shepherdia argentea Nutt.

Silver buffaloberry

FLOWERS are brownish yellow, about 1/16 inch (2 mm) diameter, with no petals and four sepals. They are in small clusters at the leaf axils. All flowers on any particular bush will be either male or female, not both. Flowers appear May-June. FRUIT is a round, bright red berry with an insipid taste and is reputed to be useful for jelly after a hard frost. The berry of Canada or russet buffaloberry, (*S. canadensis* [L.] Nutt.), has even less taste. It ripens earlier (July), is less plentiful and is not considered edible. LEAVES are oblong to ovate, 1 to 2 inches (2.5-5 cm) long, densely silvery-scurfy on both sides. They are smooth on the upper surface in russet buffaloberry, sometimes referred to as smooth buffaloberry. GROWTH HABIT: A tall thickly branched perennial shrub with rough spines well distributed along the silvery branches. The total height may be 7 to 15 feet (2-4 m). The russet species is more bushy and stems are not thorny. HABITAT includes wooded coulees and river terraces in the central portion of the area. Both species are often observed in parkland-prairie transition zones, but the russet buffaloberry is more common in the north and east.

G. W. SEIB

Canada buffaloberry

F. R. VANCE

Canada buffaloberry

PURPLE LOOSESTRIFE
Lythrum salicaria L.

LOOSESTRIFE FAMILY

Purple loosestrife

Purple loosestrife

FLOWERS are purple, numerous, tubular, up to ¾ inch (2 cm) across, arising in clusters in the axils of upper leaves, thus forming an interrupted leafy spike 8 to 16 inches (20-40 cm) long. Sepals and petals vary from four to eight and there may be up to sixteen stamens. Flowering usually occurs in August. FRUIT is a capsule about ¼ inch (6 mm) long with two cells (locules) containing many minute seeds which are responsible for the risk of this plant becoming a serious weed. LEAVES are dark green, stalkless, numerous, usually opposite but may be in whorls. They are 1¼ to 4 inches (3-10 cm) long, lanceolate, smooth, often cordate based, and rather thick with entire margins. GROWTH HABIT is perennial and erect on smooth, four-angled stems 12 to 60 inches (30-150 cm) long. Stems are not often branched and the long flowering spike is the most obvious part of the plant. HABITAT: This is an introduced plant. It favors wet ground and usually appears along lakes and streams. It is already common adjacent to cities in Saskatchewan and should be exterminated by cutting and burning.

F. A. SWITZER

FIREWEED
Epilobium angustifolium L.

Fireweed

F. R. VANCE

Fireweed

magnified flower

This is the floral emblem of the Yukon. FLOWERS are pink to light purple, rarely white, ½ to 1¼ inches (12-30 mm) diameter, in a long terminal raceme, with a small bract below each flower stalk, appearing July-August. FRUIT is a long narrow capsule, ¾ to 1¼ inches (2-3 cm). Each seed has a tuft of hairs. LEAVES are alternate, lance-shaped, gray green, slightly paler green on the lower side. They are short stalked, have smooth margins and may vary from 2 to 6 inches (5-15 cm) in length. GROWTH HABIT is erect, generally with a single stem dominated by the long terminal raceme. Height is highly variable but usually over 3 feet (90 cm) and under 6 feet (180 cm). HABITAT includes almost any disturbed area, particularly if it has been burned over, from scrubby patches on the prairie to the open parkland and forest.

YELLOW EVENING-PRIMROSE
Oenothera biennis L.

Yellow evening-primrose

FLOWERS are bright lemon yellow, 1 to 2 inches (2.5-5 cm) in diameter, with four reflexed sepals and four petals, erect in a long, dense, leafy terminal cluster. All flowers do not bloom at once and they usually open in the evening. Flowers appear July-August. FRUIT is a dry, coarse, slightly hairy, stalkless capsule about 2 inches (5 cm) long, with many small seeds. LEAVES are alternate, lance-shaped to oval, deep green, 1 to 5 inches (2.5-12 cm) long. Those on the lower stem have short stalks but they are stalkless on the upper stem. GROWTH HABIT is bushy and branched from a deep taproot. There are several varieties of this species. Shrubby evening-primrose, (*O. serrulata* Nutt.), is erect or decumbent in growth habit and has yellow flowers, but they resemble the white flowers of the gumbo evening-primrose, (*O. caespitosa* Nutt.), and white evening-primrose, (*O. nuttallii* Sweet), in the fact that they are less tubular and more radiate in shape, and open in the morning. Shrubby evening-primrose tends to occupy the same niches as this species and the white evening-primrose. HABITAT: Both species of yellow evening-primrose appear in field edges and in waste places, particularly in the south central parts of the area.

Yellow evening-primrose

seed capsule

GUMBO EVENING-PRIMROSE
Oenothera caespitosa Nutt.

EVENING-PRIMROSE FAMILY

Gumbo evening-primrose

seed capsule

Gumbo evening-primrose

FLOWERS are white when they open but fade to a delicate pink by the end of the same day. They have four petals, four sepals and eight stamens. Several flowers grow from the root crown, and appear June-August. FRUIT is a stalkless woody capsule arising from the root crown. LEAVES are clustered in a rough rosette on short petioles. They are dark, bright blue green, oblong to lance-shaped, slightly toothed or wavy-margined, 3 to 8 inches (7-20 cm) long. GROWTH HABIT is basal, little more than an inch (2.5 cm) above ground, from a thick woody root. HABITAT includes dry clay slopes and roadcuts throughout the south and central portion of the area, particularly where Cretaceous shales are near the surface.

WHITE EVENING-PRIMROSE
Oenothera nuttallii Sweet

EVENING-PRIMROSE FAMILY

White evening-primrose

White evening-primrose

FLOWERS are white, about 1½ inches (4 cm) across. They usually open in the morning and fade into a light pink by evening. They have a strong, rather unpleasant, heavy scent. The flowers develop in the axils of the upper leaves, and appear in July. FRUIT is a slender, somewhat curved capsule, ¾ to 1¼ inches (2-3 cm) long. LEAVES are alternate, pale green, linear, 1 to 4 inches (3-10 cm) long, with wavy margins and without teeth. GROWTH HABIT is perennial and much branched, 15 to 40 inches (35-100 cm) tall. Stems are white and shiny and have bark that shreds easily. Plants grow from a white, fleshy rootstock. The yellow species shown here is shrubby evening-primrose, (*O. serrulata* Nutt.). Its growth habit is very similar to the white species described. HABITAT includes road edges and margins of fields, particularly in sandy soils in the southern third of the area. It is named for Thomas Nuttall, a naturalist who collected plants in a journey up the Mississippi River in 1811.

Shrubby evening-primrose

WILD SARSAPARILLA
Aralia nudicaulis L.

GINSENG FAMILY

Wild sarsaparilla

W. C. BLIGHT

Wild sarsaparilla

J. W. SEIB

Wild sarsaparilla

FLOWERS are greenish white, under ⅛ inch (3 mm) diameter, borne on a flowering stalk 6 to 12 inches (15-30 cm) long, which is usually below the level of the leaves. Early June is the approximate flowering date. FRUIT is a round, purplish black, fleshy berry-like drupe, about ¼ inch (4-6 mm) in diameter, with three distinct compartments. LEAVES are light green on the upper surface and paler below. They are smooth-surfaced with finely-toothed margins. The single leaf stalk grows up for 6 to 12 inches (15-30 cm) and then divides into three parts which divide again into three to five leaflets. They are oval, sharply pointed at the apex, 3 to 5 inches (7-13 cm) long and turn a bronze color in autumn. GROWTH HABIT is perennial from a creeping rootstock. Leaf stem and shorter flower stem extend from a thick root base to 12 to 15 inches (30-40 cm). HABITAT: This plant is a characteristic feature of the understory of parkland groves and wooded ravines of the area in all parts except the extreme south and southwest.

SPOTTED WATER-HEMLOCK
Cicuta maculata L.

Spotted water-hemlock

FLOWERS are white, 1/16 inch (2 mm) diameter, numerous, in a rounded compound umbel which has narrow bractlets at the base of each umbellet, but no bracts at the base of the compound umbel. Flowers appear July-September. FRUIT is oval, about ⅛ inch (4 mm) long, nut-like with five thick ribs on the surface. LEAVES are alternate, compound pinnate, with narrowly lanceolate leaflets which are sharply toothed and 2 to 8 inches (5-20 cm) long. They are conspicuously wider than those of the water-parsnip, (*Sium sauve* Walt.), which are only singly pinnate (see sketch). GROWTH HABIT: A tall branching perennial, usually 1 to 3 feet (30-90 cm) but occasionally to 6 feet (180 cm), which grows from stout, tuberous, bulb-like rootstocks. Stems are smooth. HABITAT includes slough margins, ditches, lake shores, etc., often in association with water-parsnip. Two other species of water-hemlock grow in Saskatchewan, and all parts of the plants of all *Cicuta* species are very poisonous to human beings and livestock. Western water-hemlock, (*C. douglasii* [DC.] Coult. and Rose), replaces spotted water-hemlock in the west.

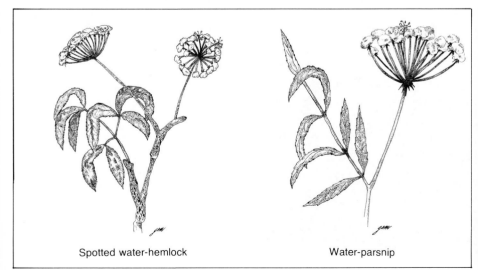

Spotted water-hemlock   Water-parsnip

POISON HEMLOCK
Conium maculatum L.

FLOWERS are white, numerous, and minute, arranged in a broad compound umbel about 2 inches (5 cm) across. The bracts at the base of the umbel are ¼ inch (6 mm) long with a green center and whitish edges. Bractlets may also be present at the bases of the umbellets. Flowering occurs in July and August.

seed stage

J. R. JOWSEY

Poison hemlock

J. R. JOWSEY

Poison hemlock

FRUIT is a small, barrel-shaped capsule with prominent thick ribs. LEAVES are dark green, alternate, and pinnately deeply cleft into many segments which are round at the apex. Leaves are large, up to 10 to 12 inches (25-30 cm) long and 4 inches (10 cm) across. GROWTH HABIT is biennial, a coarse, erect herb, up to 10 feet (3 m) tall but more often 3 to 6 feet (1-2 m) with a much branched, purple spotted, hollow stem arising from a woody taproot, which may be up to ¾ inch (2 cm) diameter. All parts of this plant are extremely poisonous, with the lower portions of the stem and taproot particularly deadly. Poisoning cases ending in death have resulted from children sucking on stems, leaves, or roots. HABITAT is low, moist, somewhat saline areas in edges of sloughs and in shallow watercourses. This is an introduced plant, and seeds may readily spread in spring flushes or grow in refuse piles. It has been observed in Saskatchewan at only a few locations.

PLAINS CYMOPTERUS
Cymopterus acaulis (Pursh) Raf.

Plains cymopterus

Plains cymopterus

R. CHARTERS

FLOWERS are white, small, and numerous on slender stalks, in compound umbels 1 ¼ to 1 ½ inches (3-4 cm) across. Each umbel, borne on a long stalk, 1 to 4 inches (2.5-10 cm), is divided into secondary groups (umbellets) which are subtended by one or more linear bractlets. Flowering occurs early in May; plants are inconspicuous by the end of June. FRUIT is a broadly oval, flattened, pod-like structure (schizocarp) about ¼ inch (6 mm) in diameter, encircled with winged ribs. LEAVES are bright green on long slender petioles, large, 3 to 8 inches (7.5-20 cm) long, and once or twice pinnately divided into linear, narrow segments. GROWTH HABIT is perennial, with leaf petioles and flower stalk arising from the top of a short stem which is rarely over 1 inch (2.5 cm) long. The plants, which are somewhat decumbent, may rise to a height of 3-10 inches (7.5-25 cm) and are sustained by a long, thick taproot. HABITAT is gravelly hillsides and dry prairie in the south and southwest where it is common.

COW-PARSNIP
Heracleum lanatum Michx.

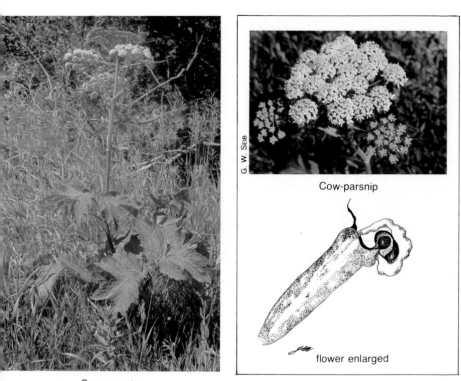

G. W. SEIB

Cow-parsnip

flower enlarged

Cow-parsnip

FLOWERS are white, slightly over 1/16 inch (2 mm) in diameter, with petals of varying length. There are hundreds of flowers in the slightly rounded, compound umbel which may be 12 inches (30 cm) across. Flowers bloom June-August. FRUIT is a flattened, oblong-ovate carpel up to ⅜ inch (1 cm) long. The dry umbels and stems are a conspicuous feature of the late fall and winter in the parkland. LEAVES are alternate, hairy, dark green on the upper surface and lighter underneath. They are 4 to 12 inches (10-30 cm) wide, palmately compounded into three toothed and divided leaflets. GROWTH HABIT is perennial, slightly branched, usually over 3 feet (1 m) tall and often up to 8 feet (2.5 m). Stems are hairy, ridged and hollow and may be up to ¾ inch (2 cm) in diameter. HABITAT includes moist open areas in aspen groves and moist meadows and ditches. It is commonest in the aspen parkland and very scarce in the southwest.

LEAFY MUSINEON
Musineon divaricatum (Pursh) Nutt.

Leafy musineon

Hairy-fruited parsley

F. R. VANCE

Musineon flowers and leaf

FLOWERS are powdery yellow with five petals and five sepals, and are supported by linear bractlets. The flowers are borne in a compound umbel, 2 to 2½ inches (5-7 cm) across, and appear in May. FRUIT is ovoid to oblong, 3/16 inch (4 mm) in length, laterally flattened. LEAVES are basal, doubly pinnate, with the main axis more or less winged. Leaflets are oblong, bright green and smooth, in contrast to prairie parsley, (*Lomatium* spp.), which has hairs on stems and leaves. GROWTH HABIT is erect, but low-growing and spreading. Flower heads are not usually more than 4 inches (10 cm) tall and the leaflets are beneath them. Common HABITAT includes the drier areas of the prairies of the south and southwest, usually among grass in well established swards.

SMOOTH SWEET CICELY
Osmorhiza aristata (Thunb.) Mak. & Yabe

PARSLEY FAMILY

F. A. SWITZER

Smooth sweet cicely

Smooth sweet cicely

FLOWERS are white and small with five petals and five sepals in a compound umbel, with a few loosely ordered linear bracts at the base of each umbellet of three to six members. The stalks of the rays of the umbel are rather long, ⅝ to 1 inch (1.5-2.5 cm), and very slender to give the whole umbel a loose appearance. Flowers appear in June. FRUIT is a long, angled capsule formed from two carpels and is roughly hairy, linear and pointed at the apex, borne on the long stalks of the rays of the umbel. Another species, *O. obtusa* (Coult. & Rose) Fern., is referred to as blunt-fruited sweet cicely because the fruits are shorter and lack the pointed tip. LEAVES are light green, thin, two or three times divided into three lanceolate or ovate leaflets, 1 to 2¾ inches (2.5-7 cm) long, pointed at the apex and coarsely toothed. GROWTH HABIT is perennial, erect on smooth, thin, branched stems 1 to 3 feet (30-90 cm) long. Roots are thick and fleshy and have a peculiar, sweet scent, hence the name of this species. HABITAT is shady moist areas of damp woods and deep coulees in the southern part of the area.

SNAKEROOT
Sanicula marilandica L.

Snakeroot

Snakeroot

FLOWERS are greenish white, arranged in a rounded, compound umbel of small umbellets, each about ¼ inch (6 mm) across. In each of these umbellets the pedicels (stalks) of the perfect flowers are short, but much longer on the few staminate flowers. Flowering occurs in late June. FRUIT is a dry, dense, green head about ¼ inch (6 mm) diameter, with hooked bristles on the two fused carpels. The slender, recurved style persists on the fruit with the appearance of two large hooks at the top of a prickly globe. LEAVES are dark green and smooth with sharply toothed edges. They are palmately compound with five to seven leaflets each up to 4 inches (10 cm) long and ⅜ to ¾ inch (1-2 cm) across. There is usually one very large basal leaf and several smaller, stalkless stem leaves. GROWTH HABIT is erect and perennial from a thick rootstock and fibrous roots. Plants are commonly 16 to 24 inches (40-60 cm) but may reach 40 inches (1 m). Stems are smooth, ridged, rather slender, and weak. HABITAT is most often the deep shade of aspen woods or scrubby thickets and banks of water courses throughout the area, where moisture conditions are good.

HEART-LEAVED ALEXANDERS
Zizia aptera (Gray) Fern.

flowers and leaves

Heart-leaved alexanders

FLOWERS are bright deep yellow, extremely small, under 1 mm in diameter, borne in a very flat, rather open umbel, appearing June-July. FRUIT is a flattened, nut-like, two-seeded capsule and has no ribbing as have fruits of many of the parsley family. LEAVES are bright green, smooth and finely toothed. The upper leaves clasp the stem and are three-lobed and smaller, ¾ to 1¼ inches (2-3 cm) wide. Basal leaves are borne on petioles and are heart-shaped, hence the common name. Another species, golden alexanders, (Z. *aurea* [L.] Koch), is very similar but all leaves are divided like the upper ones of the heart-leaved species. GROWTH HABIT is perennial and erect. Plants are slightly branched and usually 10 to 24 inches (25-60 cm) high. HABITAT includes moist meadows and scrubby margins of aspen poplar groves in the parkland and moister areas of the prairie. Golden alexanders or meadow-parsnip is more eastern in range and its presence in Saskatchewan has not been established with certainty.

Heart-leaved alexanders

BUNCHBERRY
Cornus canadensis L.

DOGWOOD FAMILY

flower detail

Bunchberry

FLOWERS appear white due to four large involucral bracts, ½ to ¾ inches (15-20 mm) long, which surround a cluster of minute green flowers. Flowers appear June-July. FRUIT is a small red orange drupe with a two-seeded stone. (The plant is also known as the pigeon berry.) LEAVES are oval, smooth, entire margined, dark green, 1 to 3 inches (2.5-7.5 cm) long and prominently veined. There are four to six leaves in a whorled arrangement at the head of the stem and a pair of smaller leaves halfway down. GROWTH HABIT is perennial, 3 to 6 inches (7.5-15 cm) high usually forming a dense mat once established in an area by spreading on a slender horizontal rootstock. Common HABITAT includes shady open areas in mixed or coniferous woods or occasionally in moist aspen poplar woods in the central, north and east and in the Cypress Hills.

Bunchberry

RED-OSIER DOGWOOD
Cornus stolonifera Michx.

DOGWOOD FAMILY

Red-osier dogwood

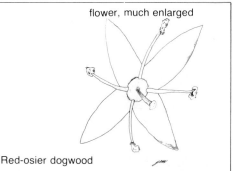

flower, much enlarged

Red-osier dogwood

FLOWERS are greenish white, 3/32 inch (1 mm) in diameter, borne in flat-topped cymose clusters of 1 to 2 inches (2.5-5 cm) diameter, with eight to twelve flowers in each. Flowering occurs in June. The FRUIT is a round, whitish, waxy berry, sometimes tinged with blue, about 3/16 inch (4 mm) diameter. It is not edible. LEAVES are opposite, ovate, with a rounded base and pointed apex. They are 1 to 3 inches (2.5-7.5 cm) long, not toothed, deep medium green above and slightly paler beneath due to short hairs on the under-side. GROWTH HABIT: A much branched shrub, 3 to 6 feet (90-180 cm) tall with distinctly reddish bark. Stems are not strong and some bushes appear semi-prostrate. HABITAT includes margins of woodlands and roadsides in the parkland and the coulees of the south and southwest. This is "kinnikinik" to the Crees and the pioneers who settled the parkland, and to those who learned first about plants from either.

PRINCE'S-PINE
Chimaphila umbellata (L.) Bart.

Prince's-pine

Prince's-pine

C. LETKEMAN

FLOWERS are lavender-pink to pinkish white in a cymose cluster of three to seven blooms. The five waxy petals are each about ⅛ to ¼ inch (3-6 mm) across, and the flower is shaped like a deep saucer about ⅜ inch (1 cm) across. The most prominent feature of the flower is the large, green, ribbed ovary. Flowers appear by the end of July. FRUIT is a small, ¼ inch (6 mm), globular, brown capsule which contains many seeds. LEAVES are dark green, leathery, bright and shiny, 1 to 1½ inches (2.5-4 cm) long, broadly ovate, serrated but not tipped at the apex. They are arranged in rough whorls of three to eight leaves around the base of the plant and along the lower part of the stem. GROWTH HABIT is evergreen and perennial, with a short weak stem. Plants are semi-decumbent, but total stem length, including flower stalks, may be 4 to 8 inches (10-20 cm). HABITAT is dry, sandy areas in coniferous woods. It is locally common in some areas of boreal forest and its edges and in the Cypress Hills.

ONE-FLOWERED WINTERGREEN
Moneses uniflora (L.) A. Gray

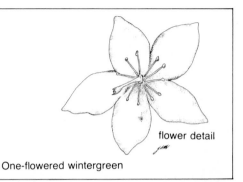

flower detail

One-flowered wintergreen

One-flowered wintergreen

FLOWERS are waxy white, fragrant, nodding and solitary. The five petals are widely spreading so the flower may be ¾ inch (2 cm) across. The pistil is elongated and conspicuous and the ovary is bright green. Flowers appear in July. FRUIT is a dry, brown, erect, many-seeded capsule. LEAVES are dark green, smooth, rounded and finely toothed. They are ½ to 1 inch (12-25 mm) long, borne in pairs or whorls near the base of the stem and remain more or less green in winter. GROWTH HABIT is perennial from a slender rootstock, low but erect, 2 to 6 inches (5-15 cm) tall. HABITAT is the forest floor, usually where conifers predominate, in areas of deep shade and high water table. It is found particularly in the north and east and in the Cypress Hills.

PINK WINTERGREEN
Pyrola asarifolia Michx.

Pink wintergreen

Pink wintergreen

seed capsules

FLOWERS are brownish red, pink when fully opened, about ⅜ inch (1 cm) diameter. They are borne in an open raceme of ten to fifteen flowers which are nodding and characterized by a long protruding style. Flowers appear June-July. FRUIT is a round, dry, many-seeded capsule. LEAVES are basal on short petioles, 1 to 1½ inches (2.5-4 cm) wide, dark green and shiny. They are rounded and stay green into severe autumn frosts. GROWTH HABIT is erect but only the flower-bearing stem rises appreciably above the forest floor. Stalks of the flowers may reach 15 inches (40 cm) but 6 to 8 inches (15-20 cm) is more common. HABITAT includes the forest floor of aspen poplar and mixed woods, where good moisture conditions prevail. It is widely distributed throughout the parklands.

GREENISH-FLOWERED WINTERGREEN
Pyrola chlorantha Sw.

Greenish-flowered wintergreen

F. A. SWITZER

White wintergreen (shinleaf)

One-sided wintergreen

FLOWERS are greenish white, (white in shinleaf wintergreen, *P. elliptica* Nutt.). There are ten to fifteen on short stems in a rather loose spike-like raceme. Each flower is about ½ inch (12 mm) across when fully open and appears in July. FRUITS of the greenish-flowered, shinleaf wintergreen and the one-sided, (*P. secunda L.),* species are the round, brown, many-seeded capsules typical of wintergreens. LEAVES are dark green, basal and elliptical, thick, and from 1 to 3 inches (2.5-8 cm) long. Stalks are longer than the leaf blades (in contrast to shinleaf wintergreen in which leaves are borne on shorter stalks). Leaves of the greenish-flowered species are rounded at the ends and are slightly toothed. GROWTH HABIT is perennial, low, 4 to 10 inches (10-25 cm), in which all the height is due to the flower stalks. The illustration of one-sided wintergreen shows the greenish white flowers which all grow to one side of the stem. Common HABITAT of the three species illustrated includes moist areas of deep coniferous woods, particularly pine stands and spruce bogs in the northern and eastern part of the area, but they appear in mixed woods occasionally.

PINESAP
Monotropa hypopithys L.

INDIAN-PIPE FAMIL

Pinesap

Pinesap

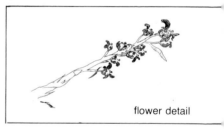

flower detail

FLOWERS are light brown to cream numerous, urn-shaped, in a rather short dense raceme. They are hairy, nodding, but erect when mature. There are four or five sepals, which are lance-shaped. Four or five petals closely surround the inner flower parts. Flowers bloom in July. The FRUIT is a many-seeded capsule. LEAVES are scale-like and brown, even more abbreviated than those of Indian-pipe, (*M. uniflora* L.). GROWTH HABIT is saprophytic; stems are light brown and clammy or fleshy. They may rise to 6 to 12 inches (15-30 cm). Common HABITAT is the richer forest soils. It is quite rare but may be found in the Cypress Hills.

INDIAN-PIPE
Monotropa uniflora L.

Indian-pipe

Indian-pipe   flower detail

FLOWERS are waxy white, occasionally with a pinkish tinge, with ten to twelve brownish yellow stamens. They are usually about ¾ inch (2 cm) long with two to four sepals and five petals. They are borne singly and droop until maturity when they move to an upright position. Approximate flowering date is July-August. The FRUIT is an erect many-seeded capsule held in the dried petals and sepals. LEAVES are short, ⅛ inch (3 mm) and appear as white or colorless scales, tipped with black as they mature. GROWTH

HABIT is saprophytic and plants may grow to a height of 12 inches (30 cm) but they are usually nearer 4 inches (10 cm). Stems are nearly translucent and the whole plant has the appearance of a thin rough candle. HABITAT includes deep shade of moist woods, particularly in mature stands of aspen poplar in east and central portions of the area.

PINEDROPS
Pterospora andromedea Nutt.

Pinedrops

Pinedrops

F. R. VANCE

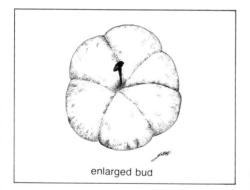

enlarged bud

FLOWERS are brownish cream in color, ¼ to ⅜ inch (6-10 mm) across. They are urn-shaped but much more rounded than those of pinesap, (*Monotropa hypopithys* L.). Flowers are nodding and grow on a long hairy spike, appearing in July. The FRUIT is a yellowish pink many-seeded capsule. LEAVES, more or less basal, are thick, brownish and scale-like. GROWTH HABIT is saprophytic; the stem is thick, coarse, somewhat ribbed, glandular and hairy. The plant grows from a rounded mass of roots and may reach a height of 40 inches, (1 m) of which 25 inches (60 cm) may be the flower spike. HABITAT includes coniferous forest, particularly pine stands. It is found in Saskatchewan in the Cypress Hills and in the foothills region of Alberta.

BOG ROSEMARY
Andromeda polifolia L.

HEATH FAMILY

Bog rosemary

FLOWERS are pinkish white, urn-shaped, ¼ inch (6 mm) long, with five small sepals and a round bell of five petals. Four or five flowers are borne on long stems in drooping umbels at the ends of stems and appear in June. FRUIT is a round, dry capsule with the style persisting at maturity. Each capsule contains numerous seeds. LEAVES are alternate, linear-oblong, smooth, dark green and evergreen above, white glaucous beneath. They are ⅜ to 1¼ inches (1-3 cm) long, sessile, with entire rolled margins. GROWTH HABIT is erect, a shrub with several weak stems which give the plant the appearance of a clump of vegetation 4 to 12 inches (10-30 cm) tall. HABITAT is swamps and bogs in clearings and road edges in the boreal forest. It is not common and should be preserved where it grows.

BEARBERRY
Arctostaphylos uva-ursi (L.) Spreng.

HEATH FAMILY

Bearberry

FLOWERS are pinkish white, urn-shaped and drooping, in dense terminal racemes. The corolla is four or five-lobed and about 3/16 inches (4 mm) long. Flowering occurs from May-July. FRUIT is a red drupe, ¼ to ⅜ inches (6-10 mm) diameter, which often persists into the next season. It is edible but dry, tasteless and contains five small nutlets. LEAVES are alternate, dark green and more or less evergreen, thick and oblong ovate. The older leaves are orange to reddish brown. The Indians of the plains called it "kinnikinik" and are reputed to have smoked the leaves in their pipes. GROWTH HABIT is prostrate. Trailing stems of this shrub may be 24 inches (60 cm) long and often form a mat on several square yards (meters) of ground. HABITAT includes dry sandy slopes of coulees or the edges of coniferous or mixed woods. It is general throughout the area from the Cypress Hills to the Qu'Appelle Valley and into the boreal forest.

Bearberry

fruit and seeds

BOG LAUREL
Kalmia polifolia Wang.

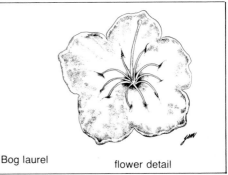

Bog laurel   flower detail

FLOWERS are pink to reddish purple, with five-lobed sepals and five petals in a wheel-shaped corolla. The ten stamens are held in creased pouches in the corolla. Flowers are ⅜ to ¾ inches (1-2 cm) across, borne in clusters in the upper leaf axils. Approximate date of flowering is June. FRUIT is an ovoid capsule about ¼ inch (6 mm) long. LEAVES are opposite, ½ to 1¼ inches (12-30 mm) long on short petioles. They are linear-lanceolate, dark green above and lighter beneath due to fine hairs on the underside. Their edges are usually somewhat rolled. GROWTH HABIT is more or less erect but the stems are weak. These shrubs may attain a height of 3 feet (90 cm) but are more commonly 10 to 12 inches (25-30 cm) tall. Each stem is sharply two-edged and arises from the rootstock. HABITAT includes sphagnum bogs in areas where spruce is dominant. This laurel favors rather sunny open areas, roadsides, etc., more than deep woods. It is known in most of the north and east but is not common. Its leaves are poisonous, particularly to sheep.

Bog laurel

LABRADOR TEA
Ledum groenlandicum Oeder

HEATH FAMIL

Labrador tea

FLOWERS are white, ¼ inch (6 mm) diameter when open. The five sepals are tooth-like and small and clasp the five spreading petals. The inflorescence is a dense, round-topped umbel at the end of each stem. Flowers appear June-July. FRUIT is an oblong, many-seeded capsule, about ¼ inch (6 mm) long with the style persisting at its apex. LEAVES are linear-oblong, dark gray green above and rusty-woolly below, ½ to 2 inches (1-5 cm) long, with strongly rolled margins. They were used as a substitute for tea by early trave lers in the Canadian north. GROWTH HABIT is perennial, a branched semi decumbent shrub from 1 to 4 feet (30-12 cm) tall, with brown bark on rather wea stems. HABITAT includes the boreal fores and its margins across the whole area, ex tending into the parkland in the valleys c some rivers.

C. W. CUTHBERT

Labrador tea

flowers and leaves

CANADA BLUEBERRY
Vaccinium myrtilloides Michx.

HUCKLEBERRY FAMILY

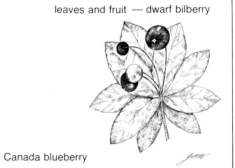

leaves and fruit — dwarf bilberry

Canada blueberry

FLOWERS are bell-shaped, greenish white in dense clusters or short racemes. The pinkish white flowers of the dwarf bilberry, (*V. caespitosum* Michx.) are single or fewer than in Canada blueberry. Flowers appear June-July. FRUIT is a sweet tasting blue berry about ¼ inch (6 mm) diameter, with a whitish bloom. LEAVES are alternate, dark green with very short petioles. They are elliptical, ¾ to 1½ inches (2-4 cm) long, (shorter and narrower in dwarf bilberry), and are lighter and slightly hairy on the underside. GROWTH HABIT: A low shrub 12 to 24 inches (30-60 cm) high, usually nearer the former height, with many branches. Dwarf bilberry is shorter, below 12 inches (30 cm) and is inclined to be semi-decumbent. Common HABITAT includes the floor of coniferous forests, particularly under jack pine or in open spaces among them. There are several species which are called blueberries, the commonest being the two described here. In combination they are widely distributed in the boreal forests of the area.

Canada blueberry

DRY-GROUND CRANBERRY

Vaccinium vitus-idaea L. var. *minus* Lodd.

Dry-ground cranberry

Dry-ground cranberry

Swamp cranberry

FLOWERS are rosy pink to nearly white, with a cup-shaped, four-cleft corolla ¼ inch (6 mm) long, and four short sepals and eight stamens, borne on short stalks ¼ to ⅜ inch (6-10 mm) in length in small terminal clusters. They appear in late June. FRUIT is a rosy red to dark scarlet edible acid berry, ¼ to ⅜ inch (6-10 mm) in diameter. The swamp cranberry, *Oxycoccus palustris* Pers., has similar fruit on stalks 1 inch (2.5 cm) long, larger pink flowers with reflexed petals, and small, linear-oblong, pointed leaves on a delicate trailing stem. LEAVES are alternate, numerous, ¼ to ¾ inch (6-20 mm) long, dark green and shiny above, paler with black dots on the underside. They are evergreen, thick, with rounded shape and rolled edges. GROWTH HABIT is perennial, a semi-erect, low herb with creeping branches which may be 6 to 12 inches (15-30 cm) in length but not rising more than 4 inches (10 cm) above the forest floor. HABITAT is dry open coniferous woods or dry bogs in the boreal forest.

PYGMYFLOWER
Androsace septentrionalis L.

PRIMROSE FAMILY

Pygmyflower

FLOWERS are minute, white with a pinkish tinge, three to forty borne in terminal umbels each on a flowering scape ⅜ to 4 inches (1-10 cm) long. The corolla has a short tube, but the five lobes spread out in a rather flattened saucer shape. The cup-shaped calyx is almost as long as the corolla. Flowers appear in early spring (May) but some plants may flower into August. FRUIT is a small, many-seeded, round capsule divided into five valves, held between the pointed sepals, the tips of which rise above the capsule. LEAVES are light green, numerous, linear to lanceolate, ¼ to 1 inch (6-25 mm) long, ⅛ inch (3 mm) wide, and may be entire or toothed, smooth or hairy. GROWTH HABIT: This is an annual or winter annual with a basal rosette of leaves and a random pattern of yellowish or reddish branched scapes which bear the flowers. Plants may be up to 4 to 6 inches (10-15 cm) tall. The flower stems and leaf rosettes are so small the plant is often not noticed. HABITAT includes edges of fields and gardens, often in disturbed soil, throughout the plains area, nearly to the edge of the boreal forest. It is sometimes called "fairy candelabra."

SALINE SHOOTINGSTAR
Dodecatheon pauciflorum (Durand) Greene

PRIMROSE FAMILY

Saline shootingstar

Mountain shootingstar

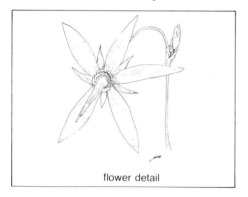

flower detail

Flowers are a striking color combination, produced by the reddish violet reflexed petals and their bright yellow throat or stamen tube. They are borne on a long stem in a terminal cluster which may have as many

as twelve flowers. Flowers bloom in June. A mountain species, *D. cylindrocarpum* Rydb., flowers in May, and has fewer blooms. The FRUIT is a five-valved, many-seeded capsule. LEAVES are basal, lance-shaped to spatulate, 1½ to 7 inches (4-17 cm) long, tapering into the petioles. GROWTH HABIT is perennial, from fibrous fleshy roots. The long flower stalks, 4 to 12 inches (10-30 cm), are usually smooth, but are glandular-hairy in some species. HABITAT is moist saline grasslands. It is often found in badly drained meadows near streams. Saline shootingstar is commonest in the south and central part of the area with mountain shootingstar and Cusick's shootingstar, (*D. cusickii* Greene), more common in the southwest.

SEA-MILKWORT
Glaux maritima L.

Sea-milkwort

flowers and leaves

FLOWERS are pinkish cream, but this color is due to the sepals. Petals are lacking and the cup-shaped calyx of five sepals encloses five stamens. Flowers appear in July. The FRUIT is an ovoid capsule 1/16 inch (2 mm) across which contains two to five seeds. It is enclosed by the calyx. LEAVES are opposite, linear to oblong, deep gray green and rather thick. They are stalkless. GROWTH HABIT is low and branching; stems of about 6 inches (15 cm) arise from a creeping rootstock. Numerous leaves per stem give the plant a bushy appearance. HABITAT includes saline meadows and slough margins throughout the area but the plant is not common. Some sites where it grows should be protected.

FRINGED LOOSESTRIFE
Lysimachia ciliata L.

PRIMROSE FAMILY

Fringed loosestrife

Fringed loosestrife

Tufted loosestrife

FLOWERS are bright yellow, ¾ to 1 inch (2-2.5 cm) in diameter. Petals are irregularly fringed at their tops. They are borne in groups of two or three in the upper leaf axils. Flowers appear in July. FRUIT is an ovoid capsule with five valves. LEAVES are opposite, light green, smooth, 2 to 6 inches (5-15 cm) long, oval to lance-shaped, pointed at the base and rounded at the apex. Petioles are ½ to ¾ inch (12-20 mm) long and have a hairy fringe on one side. GROWTH HABIT is erect, but the stem is weak and plants tend to fall over if not supported by other vegetation. Plant height is usually about 12 inches (30 cm) but some are about 3 feet (1 m). HABITAT includes wooded places, scrubby areas and roadside ditches in any part of the area where moisture is fairly plentiful. Tufted loosestrife, (*L. thrysiflora* L.), may be found in similar or more swampy habitat in the north and east.

MEALY PRIMROSE
Primula incana M. E. Jones

Mealy primrose

Mealy primrose

FLOWERS are pale lilac with a conspicuous yellow center. The whole flower is small, ¼ inch (6 mm) diameter. There are five petals, each with a deep notch at its apex. They are borne in an umbel-like cluster on a leafless flower stalk, 4 to 12 inches (10-30 cm) long. Approximate flowering date is June. The FRUIT is a short capsule, often covered by the dried sepals. LEAVES are pale green above and sulphur yellow below. They are arranged in a basal rosette, and are elliptic to ovate, 1 to 2¼ inches (2.5-6 cm) long. GROWTH HABIT is perennial and basal, except for the long flower stalk, which may be up to a foot (30 cm) high. HABITAT includes saline meadows, open moist slopes and slough margins throughout the area. The plant is not plentiful and should therefore not be picked, nor should its habitat be destroyed.

STARFLOWER
Trientalis borealis Raf.

PRIMROSE FAMILY

Starflower

Starflower

F. R. VANCE

FLOWERS are snowy white, slightly tinged with green near the base of the six to eight pointed petals which spread out in a star-like flower ¼ to ½ inch (6-12 mm) across. There are seven stamens and five to seven linear sepals, slightly shorter than the petals. One to three flowers are borne on slender stalks arising from a whorl of leaves and appear in June and July. FRUIT is a rounded capsule ¼ inch (6 mm) diameter, with five sections (valves), enclosed by the larger sepals. Two or three seeds mature in each valve. LEAVES are bright, medium green, oblong-lanceolate with a sharp tip, and tapering to the petiole. The five to nine main leaves are 1½ to 4 inches (4-10 cm) long and about ⅜ inch (1 cm) across, borne in a tight whorl at the tip of the stem, below which a few alternate, scale-like leaves ¼ inch (6 mm) long may be evident. GROWTH HABIT is perennial and erect, with a short stem 3 to 6 inches (7.5-15 cm) and a total height to the top of the inflorescence rarely more than 6 inches (15 cm). HABITAT is usually open, semi-shaded areas or in low shrubbery in the boreal forest or mixed forest.

OBLONG-LEAVED GENTIAN
Gentiana affinis Griseb.

Oblong-leaved gentian

Northern gentian

Oblong-leaved gentian

FLOWERS are dark blue to purple, usually just over 1 inch (2.5 cm) in length. They are tubular with fringed petals and are borne in a raceme-like cluster of a few flowers at the end of each major stem. Flowers may appear singly. The northern gentian,

(*G. amarella* L.), is somewhat smaller and variable in flower color from purplish blue to greenish yellow and white. Flowers appear August-September. FRUIT is a dry, oblong capsule, composed of two or more valves. LEAVES are opposite, stalkless, light green, oblong to lanceolate, and ½ to 1¼ inches (12-30 mm) long. GROWTH HABIT is erect, perennial, leafy, weak-stemmed and often prostrate, with several stems arising from a deep taproot. Height is usually 4 inches (10 cm) or less but may be nearly 12 inches (30 cm). HABITAT includes moist slough margins, particularly where the soil is sandy, and the moist edges of trees and scrub throughout most of the area, but the plant is most common in the east central portion.

CLOSED GENTIAN
Gentiana andrewsii Griseb.

GENTIAN FAMILY

Closed gentian

FLOWERS are blue with white streaks, 1 to 1½ inches (2.5-4 cm) long, and ⅜ inch (1 cm) in diameter. They always remain closed giving the impression of mature buds surrounded by the calyx tube of five pointed sepals, which are much shorter than the petals. The flowers are sessile, in terminal groups of three to five in a whorl of leaves, or in groups of two to three in the upper leaf axils. They mature in August and may bloom well into September. FRUIT is a linear capsule, 1 inch (2.5 cm) long, of several valves which each contain several oblong to linear, winged seeds. LEAVES are medium green, smooth and entire margined, 1½ to 5 inches (4-12 cm) long, pointed at the apex, and usually rounded at the base. They are oblong to lanceolate, stalkless, with three to seven prominent parallel veins. GROWTH HABIT is perennial and erect with abundant leaves on coarse, ridged stems, to a height of 1 to 2 feet (30-60 cm). HABITAT is wet meadows, roadside ditches, etc., usually among scrub or grassy vegetation of the parklands. This species is not often found west of Manitoba.

SMALL FRINGED GENTIAN
Gentiana procera Holm

A. H. SHORTT

Small fringed gentian

Small fringed gentian

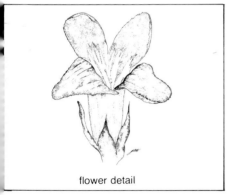

flower detail

FLOWERS are deep sky blue, ¾ to 1¾ inches (2-4.5 cm) long, ½ inch (12 mm) across. Both calyx and corolla are four-lobed and tubular, but the sepals are much shorter than the petals. Lobes of the corolla are fringed. They are borne singly at the ends of stems but the stems occasionally branch near the top. Flowers appear August-September. The FRUIT is an urn-shaped capsule, composed of two or more valves. LEAVES are rather light green, opposite, lanceolate to linear, simple, edges almost rolled, more or less clasping the stem, stalkless and ¾ to 1½ inches (2-4 cm) long. GROWTH HABIT is erect, annual, somewhat leafy, low growing, 4 to 10 inches (10-25 cm) tall. They are usually single stemmed but occasionally branch from the root crown. Some taxonomists separate the fringed gentians into another genus, *Gentianella*. HABITAT is moist ground, particularly near scrub or in open deciduous woods. The small fringed gentian and another species, *G. crinata* Froel., known simply as the fringed gentian, are common in the northern and eastern parts of the area.

SPURRED-GENTIAN
Halenia deflexa (Smith) Griseb.

GENTIAN FAMILY

Spurred-gentian

Spurred-gentian

FLOWERS are purplish green to brownish yellow due to the tubular bronze corolla enclosed in the four greenish brown sepals. The four or five stamens are inserted at the base of the corolla, which is about ¼ inch (6 mm) across. The corolla has four spurs which are downward projections of each lobe. Flowers appear in clusters at the top of each plant and in the axils of upper leaves in July. FRUIT is a stubby, bottle-shaped capsule ¼ to ⅜ inch (6-10 mm) long, projecting above the calyx. LEAVES are smooth and entire mar-gined, medium green, occasionally with a purplish tinge. Basal leaves are spatulate to oblong with petioles, and the stem leaves, 1 to 2 inches (2.5-5 cm) long, are half the size of the basal ones. GROWTH HABIT is usually annual. The stems are slender, ridged, and commonly reach a height of 6 to 18 inches (15-45 cm). HABITAT is the boggy edges of forest and wet road ditches of the parkland. The genus is named for Jonas Halen, a pupil of Linnaeus.

MARSH-FELWORT
Lomatogonium rotatum (L.) Fries.

GENTIAN FAMILY

Marsh-felwort

Marsh-felwort

FLOWERS are bluish white, ⅜ to ¾ inch (1-2 cm) across the star-like spreading petal lobes of the deeply cleft corolla, each lobe having a pair of hairy appendages at its base. The calyx is also cut into five . linear lobes of about equal length to the petals. Flowers, borne terminally and singly on long slender pedicels from the upper leaf axils, appear in August. FRUIT is an ovoid capsule ¼ to ⅜ inch (6-10 mm) long, in two parts (valves) which hold a few small, smooth seeds. LEAVES are opposite, sessile, medium green, ⅜ to 2 inches (1-5 cm) long, spatulate in the basal group and smaller and linear to lanceolate on the upper stem. GROWTH HABIT is annual, an erect herb with branches sharply erect and close to the stem. Height ranges from 4 to 16 inches (10-40 cm). HABITAT is the marshy, grassy edges of saline flats or the lower levels of drainage channels. It is locally common in Saskatchewan and Manitoba but not plentiful. The plant is considered rare in Alberta, where it is found in western and northern areas.

BUCK-BEAN
Menyanthes trifoliata L.

GENTIAN FAMILY

Buck-bean

Buck-bean

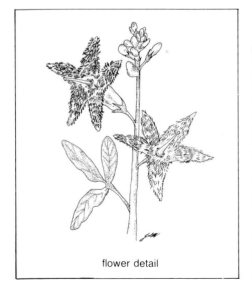

flower detail

FLOWERS are whitish inside, pinkish purple outside, about ½ inch (12 mm) long, with a tube-shaped, five-part corolla, bearded on the inside. They are arranged in a compact raceme at the end of a leafless stalk. Flowers bloom in June. FRUIT is an oval capsule ⅝ inch (15 mm) long, with several long, ⅜ inch (10 mm) seeds in each valve. LEAVES are bright green, elliptical, basal and trifoliate. Each leaflet is 3 to 4 inches (7.5-10 cm) long and the leaves are on long petioles which grow up from the rootstock. GROWTH HABIT is erect, basal in pattern with most stems 4 to 12 inches (10-30 cm) high. HABITAT includes moist and boggy places in marshes, forest bogs and shallow water of ditches. It is common in wooded sections, particularly on the east side of the area.

SPREADING DOGBANE
Apocynum androsaemifolium L.

DOGBANE FAMILY

F. R. VANCE

Spreading dogbane

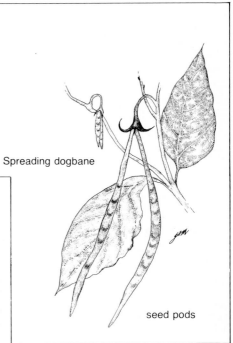

Spreading dogbane

seed pods

FLOWERS are pinkish white, ⅛ inch (3 mm) across, ¼ inch (6 mm) long, bell-shaped with five petals and five sepals. Petals are often streaked with a darker pink and may be reflexed downward. Flowering occurs June-July. FRUITS are pairs of many-seeded pods, 1 to 4 inches (2.5-10 cm) long. LEAVES are opposite, bright green, lighter and somewhat hairy on the underside, ovate to oblong, tipped at the apex, from 1 to 3 inches (2.5-7.5 cm) long. Leaves turn bright yellow or red in the autumn. GROWTH HABIT is perennial, a bushy shrub which grows from a horizontal rootstock. Some bushes may grow to a height of 3 to 4 feet (90-120 cm), but they are usually about 15 inches (40 cm) tall. Its branching and method of spreading makes it a major component of many patches of scrub. HABITAT includes wooded areas of parkland and moister coulees on the prairies, road allowances, etc.

INDIAN HEMP
Apocynum cannabinum L.

Indian hemp

FLOWERS have a greenish white tubular corolla up to ¼ inch (6 mm) long, including the five erect petal lobes. The five pointed calyx lobes are almost equal in length to the corolla tube. Numerous flowers are borne in cymose clusters both terminally and in upper leaf axils.

Indian hemp

This species blooms in July. FRUIT is a pair of long, slender, sickle-shaped pods 3 to 5 inches (7.5-12 cm) long, containing numerous seeds, each tipped with a long tuft of hairs, ¾ to 1¼ inches (2-3 cm) long. The pods are very similar to those of spreading dogbane, *A. androsaemifolium* L. LEAVES are pale green above, usually whitish on the underside, lanceolate to ovate-oblong, sharply pointed at the tip, 1¼ to 4 inches (3-10 cm) long. They are opposite and ascending on short, reddish petioles. GROWTH HABIT is perennial, from deep-branching roots. Plants are usually about 12 inches (30 cm) tall, but may grow much taller. Although branches may be fairly numerous on the upper stem, plants have a rather bare, erect appearance. The stem, which is filled with a milky sap, turns red at maturity. HABITAT is margins of thickets or aspen groves and roadside ditches on the prairies and southern parklands.

SHOWY MILKWEED
Asclepias speciosa Torr.

Showy milkweed

Showy milkweed

Dwarf milkweed

FLOWERS are pink to pinkish purple, /3 to ½ inch (8-12 mm) long, tubular, with the five petals and five sepals both reflexed downwards. Blooms are numerous and arranged in a dense globular umbel which may be 2 to 3 inches (5-7 cm) across. Their strong, sweet smell is said to have a stupefying effect on insects. Flowers bloom in July. FRUIT is a soft many-seeded pod which may be up to 3 inches (8 cm) long and nearly ½ inch (1 cm) thick at the base. The seeds are white-woolly and covered with soft projecting tubercles. LEAVES are dark green, opposite, thick and fleshy. They are oval, 3 to 6 inches (8-15 cm) long, smooth-margined and somewhat heart-shaped at the base. GROWTH HABIT is perennial, up to 6 feet (2 m) tall, often in large clumps. Their size and numerous

thick leaves cause some alarm, and while this species is more widely distributed than other species of milkweed, it is no real problem as a weed. When stems and leaves are broken a milky juice oozes out, and it is from this property that the whole genus gets its common name, "milkweed". HABITAT includes scrubby areas at the edges of fields or in pastures, particularly in moist areas in the grasslands and southern aspen parkland. Another species, dwarf milkweed, (*A. ovalifolia* Dcne.), is more common in the upper slopes of the Qu'Appelle Valley and the creeks which drain into it.

HEDGE BINDWEED
Convolvulus sepium L.

CONVOLVULUS FAMIL`

Hedge bindweed

Hedge bindweed

F. R. VANCE

Wild morning-glory

FLOWERS are white, faintly streaked with pink, 1½ to 2½ inches (4-7 cm) across, funnel-shaped with the five petals flaring widely at the top. Two large leaf-like bracts enclose the calyx. Field bindweed, (*C. arvensis* L.), is similar but has smaller, distinctly pink flowers. In this species the bracts subtending flowers are smaller and borne well below the calyx. Flowers appear June-August. FRUIT is a capsule which encloses four brownish black angular seeds. LEAVES are light green, alternate, smooth, broadly spear-shaped, 2 to 5 inches (5-13 cm) long and borne on long petioles. GROWTH HABIT is perennial and twining or creeping and stems are weak and slender. It may have stems several feet long which climb over snowberry, chokecherry and other shrubs. HABITAT includes the edges of roads and patches of scrub where moisture conditions are relatively good. It is widely distributed but most common in the Qu'Appelle Valley and its tributaries.

NARROW-LEAVED COLLOMIA
Collomia linearis Nutt.

Collomia

Collomia

FLOWERS are pink or pale purple, small, in a dense, head-like cluster at the top of the single stem. They have a calyx of five triangular sepals and five petals in a trumpet-shaped corolla about ⅜ inch (10 mm) long. There are five stamens placed irregularly in the corolla tube and the pistil has a three-lobed ovary. Flowers appear in late June and may be present until the end of the growing season. FRUIT is an extremely small round capsule about 2 mm diameter, partially enclosed by the calyx. In each locule there are one to three seeds, which are mucilaginous when moistened. LEAVES are alternate, gray-green, narrow linear and sharply pointed, ¾ to 1 ½ inches (2-4 cm) long. They are entire margined, narrow to the base and are sessile with small stipules. GROWTH HABIT: An erect annual, 3 to 18 inches (7.5-45 cm) tall, with numerous leaves, rarely branched. HABITAT: Common to the point of appearing to be a weed on dry, light, or heavy soils in field margins, road edges, and gardens on the brown and dark brown soils of the plains.

MOSS PHLOX
Phlox hoodii Richards.

Moss phlox

Moss phlox

flowers and leaves

FLOWERS are white to pale violet, ⅜ inch (1 cm) diameter; corolla is a short tube but is distinctly five-lobed. Flowers grow directly attached to the short main stems of the plant and form whitish patches on the ground, appearing in early MAY. FRUIT is a dry capsule enclosed by the five hairy sepals. LEAVES are gray green, ⅛ to ⅜ inch (6-10 mm) long, finely hairy, awl-shaped, closely clasping to the stems. GROWTH HABIT is short and tufted, not much more than an inch (2.5 cm) above the ground.

After the flowers fade the leaves and stem form an inconspicuous part of the ground cover. HABITAT includes the open prairie and dry eroded hillsides of the south and central part of the area. The plant is named for Robert Hood, midshipman on Sir John Franklin's expedition of 1819-22.

FRANKLIN'S SCORPIONWEED
Phacelia franklinii (R.Br.) Gray

WATERLEAF FAMILY

Scorpionweed

Scorpionweed

FLOWERS are blue to bluish white, ⅜ inch (10 mm) long, with a somewhat tubular corolla of five petals which open to about half their length. The five sepals are linear and hairy and the inflorescence is a dense coiled (scorpoid) cyme. Flowers appear from late June to the end of August. FRUIT is a round to ovoid capsule with numerous small, rough, brownish seeds in irregular rows. LEAVES are alternate, medium green, hairy, 1½ to 3 inches (4-7.5 cm) long, pinnately divided into irregular segments. They are numerous enough to shield the stem from sight. GROWTH HABIT is annual or winter annual. Plants have a coarse, hairy stem of 6-18 inches (15-45 cm) height with some branching near the top. HABITAT is roadsides, campgrounds, and otherwise disturbed areas in the north and east at the edge of the boreal zone. It is named for Sir John Franklin, of great fame as an Arctic explorer.

BLUEBUR
Lappula echinata Gilib.

BORAGE FAMILY

Bluebur

Bluebur

Stickseed

F. A. SWITZER

FLOWERS are pale blue, under ¼ inch (6 mm) across, on erect, leafy, branched racemes at the ends of stems. FRUIT is a nutlet about ⅛ inch (2-4 mm) across, with two marginal rows of sharp barbed prickles. Four nutlets are produced in each flower. LEAVES are alternate, gray-green, stiff and hairy, narrowly lanceolate and sessile. They are numerous and borne sharply erect and are ¾ to 2¾ inches (2-7 cm) long with rounded tips. GROWTH HABIT is annual or winter annual, low and much branched, usually 6 to 20 inches (15-50 cm) tall, and occasionally semi-prostrate. A similar but taller plant is nodding stickseed, *L. deflexa* (Wahl.) Garcke var. *americana* (Gray) Greene, which is erect on leafy hairy, thick stems. The nutlets of stickseed have marginal prickles in a single ring. HABITAT: An introduced weed of road edges, railway grades, and edges of fields and gardens, noticeable because of the persistent burs.

NARROW-LEAVED PUCCOON
Lithospermum angustifolium Michx.

Narrow-leaved puccoon

flowers and leaves

FLOWERS are bright lemon yellow with a tube nearly an inch (2.5 cm) long; the face of the flower is ¼ inch (6 mm) in diameter. Petals are distinctly fringed. Flowers are in a terminal cluster of three to four blooms, and appear May-June. FRUIT is four small, white nutlets enclosed in the hairy sepals. LEAVES are gray green, alternate, hairy and ½ to 2 inches (1.5-5 cm) long. GROWTH HABIT is semi-erect or decumbent, with slight branching. Plants grow from a woody taproot to a maximum height of about 8 inches (20 cm). HABITAT is the open prairie where moisture conditions are reasonably good, through the south and southwest of the area, replaced by the hoary puccoon, (*L. canescens* [Michx.] Lehm.), in the east and central portions.

Narrow-leaved puccoon

HOARY PUCCOON

BORAGE FAMIL*

Lithospermum canescens (Michx.) Lehm.

F. R. VANCE

Hoary puccoon

unopened flower

FLOWERS are deep orange to orange yellow, corolla tube ½ inch (1.5 cm) long, and the diameter of the flower is about ¼ inch (6 mm). They are borne in a rather compact leafy cluster at the top of the plant. In moist springs this flower sets pasture fields ablaze. Flowers appear in June. FRUIT is made up of four hard shiny white nutlets. LEAVES are gray green, alternate, stalkless, linear-oblong, ¼ to ½ inch (6-12 mm) long, covered with soft hairs.

GROWTH HABIT is erect; plants may be 6 to 18 inches (15-45 cm) tall, rarely branched. HABITAT includes moist meadows, edges of patches of scrub and aspen poplar, road ditches and railway grades throughout the central, east and northern parts of the area.

Hoary puccoon

ALL LUNGWORT
Mertensia paniculata (Ait.) G. Don

BORAGE FAMILY

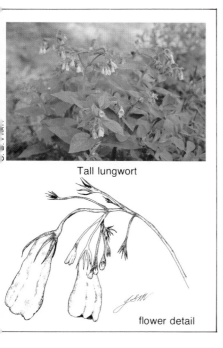

Tall lungwort

flower detail

FLOWERS are bright blue, often with a purplish tinge. The corolla tube is about ½ inch (1-2 cm) long. Drooping clusters of a few flowers are found at the ends of stems. Flowers appear June-July. FRUIT is four small nutlets encased in the five sepals. LEAVES are dark green, alternate, lanceolate, from 2 to 5 inches (5-12 cm) long, slightly hairy on both sides. GROWTH HABIT is tall, 1 to 3 feet (30-90 cm) and much branched. Stems are rather weak and 15 inches (40 cm) is a common height. HABITAT includes moist, shaded areas of aspen poplar groves and mixed forest of the northern parklands. The plant is plentiful and a pleasant sight in shady areas and on stream banks. Other species are also known in the area.

Tall lungwort

CLUSTERED OREOCARYA

BORAGE FAMIL

Oreocarya glomerata (Pursh) Greene

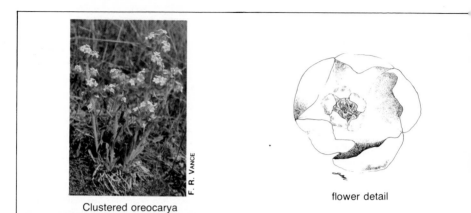

Clustered oreocarya

flower detail

Clustered oreocarya

FLOWERS are white with yellow cer
ters, ⅜ inch (1 cm) across, each with
short, tubular corolla. They are arranged i
compact clusters at the ends of stems an
appear in June. FRUIT is composed of fou
triangular nutlets which are encased in th
enlarged sepals. LEAVES are grayis
green due to short bristly hairs on their su
face. Lower leaves are spatulate, 1 to
inches (2.5-5 cm) long and upper leave
are shorter and linear. GROWTH HABIT i
erect, 2 to 12 inches (5-30 cm) high with
group of several hairy, branching stem
growing from a wóody root. HABITAT in
cludes dry open areas on the souther
grasslands, but the plant is often found i
crevices in rocks or on roadsides. It is occa
sionally referred to as "miner's candle".

GIANT-HYSSOP
Agastache foeniculum (Pursh) Ktze.

MINT FAMILY

F. R. VANCE

Giant-hyssop

Giant-hyssop

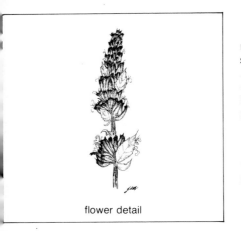

flower detail

FLOWERS are blue, ¼ to ⅜ inches (6-10 mm) across, borne in a dense spike. The spike may lack flowers for a short space and its total length may be 3 to 4 inches (7.5-10 cm). The corolla is tubular and two-lipped and the four stamens protrude. Approximate flowering date is July-August. FRUIT is made up of four small nutlets held in the cup-shaped calyx. LEAVES are opposite, dark green above and paler on the lower surface, 1 to 3 inches (2.5-7.5 cm) long. They have short petioles, are coarsely-toothed and pointed at the apex. GROWTH HABIT is tall, erect and branching on rather weak square stems, 1 to 3 feet (30-90 cm) in height. Plants have a pleasant anise-like odor. HABITAT includes the edges of aspen poplar groves and thickets in the parkland and prairie.

HEMP-NETTLE
Galeopsis tetrahit L.

MINT FAMILY

Hemp nettle

Hemp nettle

FLOWERS are deep pink to light lavender with yellow and purple spots, ⅝ to 1 inch (1.5-2.5 cm) long in dense terminal whorls, and clustered in the upper leaf axils. They have the two-lipped corolla with the upper lip arched over the three-lobed lower lip, characteristic of the mints. Flowers which have five needle-pointed calyx teeth appear in July to August. FRUIT is composed of four ovoid grayish brown nutlets enclosed in the enlarged calyx. LEAVES are opposite, light yellowish green with short petioles. They are ovate to lanceolate, coarsely toothed, hairy, and may be 4 inches (10 cm) long. GROWTH HABIT is annual; the square stems are coarse and hairy, swollen below nodes where leaves and axillary flower clusters join. Plants are commonly 2 feet (60 cm) high but may grow to 3 feet (90 cm). HABITAT is the moister areas of roadside ditches, edges of scrub piles, and rough wasteland, particularly in the central and eastern parklands where it is usually classed as a weed.

J. R. JOWSEY

WILD MINT
Mentha arvensis L.

Wild mint

Wild mint

flower detail

FLOWERS are bluish, occasionally with a purple tinge, about ⅛ inch (3 mm) long with a tubular calyx and four or five-lobed tubular corolla. As with many mints there are only four stamens. The flowers appear in crowded whorls at several of the upper leaf axils, July-August. FRUIT is four small oval nutlets, held in the tube formed by the sepals. LEAVES are opposite, bright green and rough. They are oval to lanceolate, pointed at the apex, ½ to 1½ inches (1-4 cm) long, almost hairless, with minute glandular dots on both surfaces. GROWTH HABIT is erect, perennial, on light green square stems, 4 to 18 inches (10-45 cm) tall. The stem and leaves have a pleasant mint smell when crushed and are occasionally used as flavoring. HABITAT includes grassy sloughs and moist places, particularly in the central, north and east of the area. The plant may grow in water but usually does not.

WESTERN WILD BERGAMOT
Monarda fistulosa L.

MINT FAMILY

V. ANDREWS

Western wild bergamot

seed head

FLOWERS are pink or lilac and occasionally white with a typical two-lipped corolla. They are fuzzy, ¾ to 1½ inches (2-4 cm) long, numerous in a globose head-like cluster, 1 to 1½ inches (2.5-4 cm) across when in full bloom. The calyx of each flower forms a narrow green tube, ½ inch (12 mm) long with purplish teeth, and the combination of these tubes forms the head. Flowers bloom July-August. FRUIT is composed of four small nutlets. LEAVES are opposite, gray green due to fine hairs, triangular-ovate on short petioles and pointed at the apex, 1 to 3 inches (2.5-7.5 cm) long. GROWTH HABIT is perennial and erect on stiff square stems which do not often branch. Leaves, stems and flower heads have a strong pleasant odor. HABITAT includes the edges of scrubby patches and aspen poplar groves and various moist waste places throughout the area. A variety, (*menthaefolia* [Graham] Fern.), with shorter leaf stalks and hairy leaves is more common, particularly in the west.

Western wild bergamot

ALSE DRAGONHEAD

hysostegia parviflora Nutt. var. *ledinghamii* Boiv.

False dragonhead

False dragonhead

FLOWERS are rose-pink to purple, ⅜ o ⅝ inch (1-1.5 cm) long, with a two-ipped corolla. The upper lip is erect with the lower one spreading out into three obes. The five-part, unevenly toothed, somewhat inflated calyx, less than half the length of the corolla, is covered with fine hairs and shows ten obscure veins or nerves. Flowers are borne in a dense, bracted, terminal spike 1 to 3 inches (2.5-7.5 cm) long, in which the lower flowers mature first, in July. FRUITS are four smooth, ovoid nutlets held loosely in the dried calyx of each flower. LEAVES are opposite, sessile, dark green, narrowly oblong to lanceolate, 3 to 7 inches (7.5-18 cm) long, sharply pointed, with coarse, rough teeth. They are larger midway along the stem, and the lower leaves may have short petioles. GROWTH HABIT is perennial and erect on thick, smooth, four-angled stems which rarely branch, although some branching may occur in the flowering spike. Plants are rough and leafy and height ranges from 12 to 36 inches (30-90 cm). HABITAT is moist places in ditches and stream banks, often near the water line and usually in some shade, particularly in the parklands.

238

SELFHEAL
Prunella vulgaris L.

MINT FAMIL

Selfheal

A. HANNERS

FLOWERS are violet-purple to blu
occasionally with streaks of white, ⅜
⅝ inch (10-15 mm) long, with a rounde
upper lip and a three-lobed lower lip i
which the middle lobe is the larges
There are four stamens which have fila
ments split near the tip. The calyx
about half the length of the corolla ar
two lipped, the upper square, the lowe
with two awn-like tips. Flowers are born
in short, dense, terminal spikes ¾ to
inches (2-5 cm) long, usually shielded b
the upper leaves, and appear in July an
August. FRUIT is composed of fou
smooth, ovoid nutlets which are about
inch (6 mm) long and project well abov
the somewhat shrunken calyx. LEAVE
are opposite, medium green, 1 to
inches (2.5-10 cm) long, sparingly hair
slightly toothed, pointed, and tapering 1
short petioles. GROWTH HABIT is perer
nial and erect on weak, ridged, usual
simple but occasionally branched stem
which may be smooth or hairy. Height
variable but ranges from 4 to 12 inche
(10-30 cm). HABITAT: Usually in moi
soils, at the edges of woodland (
scrubby patches, and in watercourse
This mint is not common but foun
occasionally in the southern parts of th
area.

MARSH SKULLCAP
Scutellaria epilobiifolia Hamilton

Marsh skullcap

F. A. SWITZER

Marsh skullcap

flower detail

FLOWERS are deep blue, ⅜ to ¾ inch (1-2 cm) long with a tubular calyx and a two-lipped corolla typical of the mints. A single flower or a pair develops in upper leaf axils and there are usually not more than two flowering groups per plant. Appearance of flowers is June-August. FRUIT is four small, tough nutlets held tightly in the calyx. LEAVES are opposite, bright green, oblong to lanceolate, wavy-margined, 1 to 2½ inches (2.5-7 cm) long. The lower ones are short stalked and the upper ones stalkless. GROWTH HABIT is perennial, erect but short, usually under 10 inches (25 cm), on slender square stems. HABITAT includes wet saline meadows and other wet places around sloughs and ditches, particularly in the parkland and the parkland-prairie transition area. These flowers are a pleasant find in long grass in upper levels of marshes.

MARSH HEDGE-NETTLE
Stachys palustris L.

MINT FAMILY

Marsh hedge-nettle

Marsh hedge-nettle

bud stage

FLOWERS are pale purple to white with dark purple spots, ⅜ to 1 inch (1-2.5 cm) long. The calyx is funnel-shaped. The corolla is two-lipped but the upper lip is more erect than in other mints and the lower more distinctly three-lobed. The flowers are found in spike-like axillary clusters near the top of the plant, July-August. FRUIT is four small nutlets held in the tube of the dried calyx. LEAVES are opposite, light green, coarsely toothed and hairy, lance-shaped to oblong, stalkless or on short petioles. They are generally rounded at the base. GROWTH HABIT is perennial, erect, occasionally branching, arising from creeping rhizomes. The stem is coarse, hairy and square and the height is usually about 12 inches (30 cm) but may reach up to 4 feet (120 cm). HABITAT includes marsh edges and roadside ditches throughout the area, particularly in the east and central section.

LARGE WHITE GROUND-CHERRY
Physalis grandiflora Hook.

POTATO FAMILY

Large white ground-cherry

Black henbane

Wild tomato

F. W. LAHRMAN

FLOWERS are white with a pale yellow center, wheel-shaped and somewhat bell-shaped too, 1¼ to 1½ inches (3-4 cm) in diameter, borne in the upper leaf axils. Flowers appear in July. FRUIT is a green berry partly enclosed in a persistent calyx, 1 inch (2.5 cm) long, and about ⅜ inch (1 cm) in diameter. LEAVES are dark green, prominently veined, ovate to lanceolate, 1½ inches (4 cm) long, smooth margined, somewhat sticky, borne on petioles 1 to 2 inches (2.5-5 cm) long. GROWTH HABIT is annual, erect from creeping rootstocks, but stems tend to flop over due to the weight of leaf growth. Stems are somewhat hairy and sticky. HABITAT is the floor of heavy woods in the north and east. The prairie ground-cherry, (*P. virginiana* Mill.), is more common on sandy prairies to the south. Fruits and flower parts of all three plants illustrated on this page warrant care and caution. They are dangerous poisons. The other members of the same plant family illustrated are the wild tomato, (*Solanum triflorum* Nutt.), and the black henbane, (*Hyoscyamus niger* L.).

BITTERSWEET
Solanum dulcamara L.

Bittersweet

Bittersweet

FLOWERS are deep purplish blue to violet, about ⅝ inch (1.5 cm) diameter, with five pointed petal lobes and five shorter, oblong, blunt sepals. The petals soon reflex, making the large yellow anthers very conspicuous. Flowers droop from long stalks and are borne in an irregular cyme. They usually appear in July and August. FRUIT is an ovoid to round red-orange berry about ⅜ inch (1 cm) diameter clasped by the sepals. The fruit is very shiny both in the green stage and after ripening. It is very poisonous. LEAVES are medium green, alternate, ovate, pointed, and entire margined. They are 2 to 4 inches (5-10 cm) long, 1 to 1½ inches (2.5-4 cm) broad, often with two small lobes at the base of the blade. Petioles are about ¾ to 1 inch (2-2.5 cm) in length. GROWTH HABIT is perennial, an introduced slender vine with a brown stem that is often woody at the base. Vines may be up to 40 to 90 inches (1-2.5 m) long. HABITAT is moist woods and stream banks; the plant is widely distributed but not common and most plants observed have escaped from adjacent gardens.

W. C. BLIGHT

WILD TOMATO
Solanum triflorum Nutt.

POTATO FAMILY

Wild tomato

Wild tomato

FLOWERS are white with a yellow center, wheel-shaped, ¾ inch (2 cm) across, with flower parts in fives. The petals are usually somewhat reflexed when flowers mature. Flowers are generally in threes and appear from late June to August. FRUIT is a smooth green berry, ¼ to ½ inch (6-12 mm) in diameter. It retains the sepals at the point of attachment as is the case with the horticultural tomato, *Lycopersicon esculentum* Mill. Fruit is poisonous but not as deadly as that of some other species of *Solanum*. LEAVES are alternate, dark green, oblong to ovate, 2 to 4 inches (5-10 cm) long, pinnately lobed in deep random divisions. They are entire margined and smooth except for a few coarse hairs scattered on their surfaces. GROWTH HABIT: A decumbent annual, with many leafy branches and thick stems which may form mats up to 2 feet (60 cm) across. HABITAT is garden edges, mounds raised by burrowing animals, and various other disturbed places. It is common throughout the area but particularly so in the south and southwest.

SCARLET PAINTBRUSH
Castilleja coccinea (L.) Spreng.

FIGWORT FAMILY

Scarlet paintbrush

Red Indian paintbrush

Lance-leaved paintbrush

FLOWERS are noticeable due to the colored bracts which surround them. The bracts are red in this species and yellow, cream or deep red in others. Actual flowers are within the bracts in a dense terminal spike. Flowers are yellow green and tubular. The corolla is two-lipped with a large upper lip (galea) and a three-lobed lower lip, about ¾ to 1 inch (2-2.5 cm) long, barely visible among the bracts. Note the differences in color in the two other species illustrated; red Indian paintbrush, (*C. mineata* Dougl.), and lance-leaved paintbrush, (*C. acuminata* [Pursh] Spreng.). Approximate flowering date is July. FRUIT is a dry, many-seeded capsule about ¾ inch (2 cm) long. LEAVES are alternate, simple, occasionally lobed and stalkless. They are 1 to 2 inches (2.5-5 cm) long, linear and pointed. GROWTH HABIT is usually perennial, leafy, 12 to 24 inches (30-60 cm) high. The plant is sometimes parasitic upon plant roots. HABITAT includes the margins of aspen groves, roadsides and patches of larger shrubs over most of the parkland. Scarlet paintbrush is the commonest of the species shown. The lance-leaved species is more common on open hillsides and edges of patches of scrub in the southeast and red Indian paintbrush is found in the Cypress Hills.

F. R. VANCE

TOAD-FLAX
Linaria vulgaris Mill.

Toad-flax

F. A. SWITZER

Toad-flax

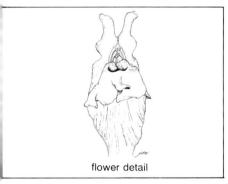

flower detail

FLOWERS are bright yellow with orange throats and have long spurs at the base. There are five sepals and five petals, and the corolla is distinctly two-lipped. Flowers are 1 to 1¼ inches (2.5-3 cm) long, arranged in a dense terminal raceme and appear June-July. FRUIT is an oval capsule, ⅜ to ⅝ inches (1-1.5 cm) long which contains several flattened seeds, each of which has a circular wing. LEAVES are alternate, gray green, linear and stalkless, ¾ to 3 inches (2-7.5 cm) long. Another species, (*L. dalmatica* [L.] Mill.), has an ovate to lanceolate leaf which clasps the stem. GROWTH HABIT is perennial, arising from creeping rootstocks. The stems, 8 to 24 inches (20-60 cm) tall, are somewhat branched and rather slender. HABITAT is variable but the plant is common in abandoned gardens, railway yards, roadside ditches, etc. Both species were introduced as garden plants.

COW-WHEAT
Melampyrum lineare Descr.

Cow-wheat

Cow-wheat

FLOWERS are dominantly white with a creamy yellow lower lip, up to ½ inch (12 mm) long. The upper and lower lips almost enclose the four stamens and the pistil. The shorter calyx has four pointed sepals covered with fine hairs. Flowers are borne singly in the upper leaf axils or in a terminal leafy spike during July and early August. FRUIT is a flat, oblong, beaked capsule which contains one to four minute blackish seeds. The capsule is ¼ to ⅜ inch (6-10 mm) long and partially enclosed by the calyx. LEAVES are opposite, yellowish green, linear lanceolate on short petioles. They are numerous and variable in size but commonly 1 to 2 inches (2.5-5 cm) long and ⅛ to ⅜ inch (3-10 mm) across. GROWTH HABIT is annual with slender, branching stems, usually to a height of 6 to 12 inches (15-30 cm). The stem is not strong and the plants are semi-decumbent if not supported. HABITAT is sandy, well-drained soil under pine stands either at the edge of or in open meadows within the boreal forest.

YELLOW MONKEYFLOWER
Mimulus guttatus DC.

FIGWORT FAMILY

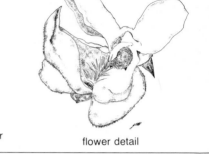

Yellow monkeyflower

flower detail

FLOWERS are deep yellow, usually spotted with red, and hairy in the ridges of petals. They are ¾ to 1¼ inches (2-3 cm) long, with four stamens in pairs. The corolla is two-lipped. Flowers are borne singly or in a short raceme on rather slender stalks. Two other species are known in the prairie provinces, one with blue flowers and one with red flowers. Flowers bloom in July. The FRUIT is a two-valved, many-seeded capsule. LEAVES are opposite, medium green, ovate or rounded, ½ to 2 inches (1-5 cm) long, lower leaves stalked and upper leaves usually clasping the stem. GROWTH HABIT is perennial, plants arising in branches from a common base 8 to 24 inches (20-60 cm) in height. Stems are erect but slender and often trail on other plants. HABITAT includes shady areas along the banks of running streams in the west of the area, and particularly in the Cypress Hills.

Yellow monkeyflower

OWL'S-CLOVER
Orthocarpus luteus Nutt.

Owl's-clover

FLOWERS are a dusty mustard yellow due to the two-lipped corolla which is ⅜ to ⅝ inch (10-15 mm) long. The upper lip is beak-like, enclosing the anthers; the lower lip is slightly shorter, helmet-shaped with three small teeth. The short, four-lobed calyx is glandular-hairy as are the three pointed bracts at the base of each flower. Flowers are in dense terminal leafy spikes and usually appear in August and September in Saskatchewan. FRUIT is a small, flattened capsule, ¼ inch (6 mm) long, containing several ridged seeds. LEAVES are dark green, alternate, ⅜ to 1¼ inches (1-3 cm) long. They are linear to lanceolate, stalkless, crowded and sharply erect on the stem. GROWTH HABIT is annual, erect and sessile, 6 to 18 inches (15-45 cm) high, and rarely branched. HABITAT: Open grassy plains, roadside ditches, and sunny dry margins of aspen groves in heavier soils. It is common across the plains and parklands.

Owl's-clover

LILAC-FLOWERED BEARDTONGUE

Pentstemon gracilis Nutt.

FIGWORT FAMILY

White beardtongue

flower detail—
Lilac-flowered beardtongue

FLOWERS are pale lilac, with a tubular corolla of five petals about ¾ inch (2 cm) long. The five sepals are deeply separated but the calyx is distinctly tubular. A white species, (*P. albidus* Nutt.), is also shown. Flowers appear June-July. FRUIT is the dry many-seeded capsule typical of the beard-tongues. LEAVES are opposite, gray green, more or less smooth, linear-oblong to lanceolate and slightly toothed, 1 to 3 inches (2.5-7.5 cm) long. GROWTH HABIT is erect and perennial on smooth slender stems usually 6 to 18 inches (15-45 cm) high. The white species and slender beard-tongue are both somewhat shorter. HABITAT includes moist grasslands and slough margins, particularly in the south and central part of the area.

Lilac-flowered beardtongue

250

SMOOTH BLUE BEARDTONGUE
Pentstemon nitidus Dougl.

FIGWORT FAMILY

Slender beardtongue

flower detail —
Smooth blue beardtongue

Smooth blue beardtongue

FLOWERS are bright blue with a slight lavender tinge, arranged in a spike-like raceme. The tubular corolla is about ¾ inch (2 cm) long, distinctly two-lipped and open. The lower lip is bearded with fine smooth hairs. Stamens are separated and one of the five stamens is bearded and sterile. Flowering occurs May-June. FRUIT is a dry, many-seeded capsule. LEAVES are opposite, gray green due to a velvety bloom on their surface, oval to lance-shaped, smooth-margined, 1 to 2 inches (2.5-5 cm) long. GROWTH HABIT is erect, usually branched, 4 to 12 inches (10-30 cm) high. Stems are hairless. HABITAT includes the dry eroded hillsides and river brakes of the grasslands and the plant is often found in sandy soils and under rather poor moisture conditions. Another distinctly blue species is slender beardtongue, (*P. procerus* Dougl.).

COMMON MULLEIN
Verbascum thapsus L.

FIGWORT FAMILY

Common mullein

Common mullein

FLOWERS are bright lemon yellow, ¾ to 1 inch (2-2.5 cm) long, ⅜ inch (1 cm) wide, with five petals in a soft, slightly irregular, tubular corolla enclosing five long stamens, three of which are densely hairy. The five sepals are woolly and much shorter than the petals. Inflorescence is a dense, spike-like raceme which may be 16 to 24 inches (40-60 cm) in length. Flowering occurs from June to September. FRUIT is an ovoid capsule about ¼ inch (6 mm) long, mostly enclosed by the woolly sepals. Seeds are longitudinally ridged. LEAVES are alternate, medium to dark green, and velvety due to many branched hairs. They are spatulate to elliptic, 8 to 16 inches (20-40 cm) long. The basal and lower leaves have short petioles but the upper ones are sessile, clasping the stem in a winged presentation. GROWTH HABIT is biennial, a coarse, rough herb 2 to 6 feet (60-180 cm) tall. Stems in the second year are very thick, up to ¾ inch (2 cm) at the base, giving the impression of a pyramidal shrub with few branches. Plants appear as a basal rosette the first year. A second species, black torch, *V. nigrum* L., is occasionally found where it has escaped from gardens. It is smaller, less coarse, and the flowers are a brighter yellow. HABITAT is roadsides, garden edges, field margins, or otherwise disturbed land. It is a horticultural introduction which is well distributed over North America but rare in the prairies. Its name arises from its reputed origin, the island of Thasos in Greece.

AMERICAN SPEEDWELL
Veronica americana (Raf.) Schwein

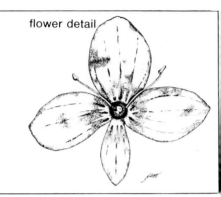

flower detail

American speedwell

FLOWERS are light blue, occasionally nearly white, and striped with purple, ¼ inch (4-6 mm) in diameter. They have a peculiar shape as they are slightly tubular, have one large petal at the "top" of the flower, two smaller side petals that stick out like wings, and a much smaller, more pointed petal at the bottom. Flowers are numerous on each plant, borne in a roughly racemose arrangement in upper leaf axils, and appear from late June to August. FRUIT is a minute, round, slightly flattened capsule with a small notch at the apex and is divided into locules that contain several flattened seeds. LEAVES are light green, oblong to ovate-lanceolate, 1 to 3 inches (2.5-7.5 cm) long, finely toothed, opposite, on short petioles. GROWTH HABIT: A smooth-stemmed perennial with weak stems 6 to 36 inches (15-90 cm) long which may root at each joint. Plants appear as a mat with blue flowers. HABITAT is moist stream banks, sandy slough edges, occasionally growing in shallow water. Not common but widely distributed in the boreal forest edges, the Cypress Hills, and in creek valleys on the plains.

American speedwell

WESTERN BUTTERWORT
Pinguicula macroceras Willd.

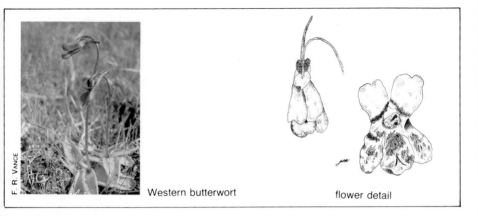

Western butterwort

flower detail

FLOWERS are deep purple, up to ¼ inch (6 mm) across, with a straight spur about ¼ inch (6 mm) long. The spur is curved in the other native species, (*P. vulgaris* L.). Petals are somewhat hairy, particularly near the mouth of the tube. Flowers appear in June. FRUIT is a two-valved capsule. LEAVES are basal, pale yellowish green, ¾ to 1½ inches (2-4 cm) long, ¾ inch (2 cm) wide, sticky. The edges are somewhat rolled and have shallow teeth. GROWTH HABIT is characterized by basal leaves and an erect flower stem 2 to 5 inches (5-13 cm) in length. Common HABITAT includes the edges of water runs and saline meadows of the Cypress Hills and a few other places in the southern portion of the area. It is replaced by *P. vulgaris* to the north and east. This plant is rare; do not pick it or dig it up.

Western butterwort

COMMON BLADDERWORT
Utricularia vulgaris L.

BLADDERWORT FAMILY

Common bladderwort

J. L. PARKER

Common bladderwort

flower detail

FLOWERS are deep yellow, ½ to ¾ inch (1-2 cm) long, stalked and widely spaced on a leafless spike. The corolla is two-lipped and has a short spur. Flowers appear in June. The FRUIT is a many-seeded capsule divided into two valves. LEAVES are brownish green, finely-divided and numerous, ¾ to 2 inches (2-5 cm) long. They bear numerous bladders which float the plant near the surface of the water. GROWTH HABIT is aquatic and stems and leaves combine to make a mat of plants near the surface so that flowers may be raised above the water. HABITAT includes most of the prairie sloughs of the whole area, where the striking yellow of bladderwort is a pleasant sight to the road-weary traveller.

CLUSTERED BROOM-RAPE
Orobanche fasciculata Nutt.

BROOM-RAPE FAMILY

Clustered broom-rape

FLOWERS are creamy yellow with a purplish tinge, ¾ to 1¼ inches (2-3 cm) long, about ¼ inch (6 mm) in diameter, tubular, somewhat two lipped, and nodding. There are five petal lobes, four stamens, and a short five-lobed calyx. Flowers are on long stalks, usually four to ten in a group, and appear from early July to mid-August. FRUIT is a one-celled, ovoid capsule with two valves containing many minute, dust-like, flattened seeds. LEAVES are yellowish to brown, lacking chlorophyll, scale-like, up to ¼ inch (6 mm) long, pressed close to the stem. GROWTH HABIT is parasitic, usually on wild sages (*Artemisia* spp.) and other composites. The pinkish brown naked stems raise the flowers 2 to 4 inches (5-10 cm) above the basal attachment to the host plant. HABITAT is open prairie areas of the southern plains. This species is common wherever there are sages. Another species, small broom-rape, *O.*

uniflora L., with one to three tall pedicels (stalks) bearing creamy white flowers, is occasionally reported growing in open woods but is very rare. The host plant for the clustered broom-rape in the illustration is pasture sage, *Artemisia frigida* Willd.

COMMON PLANTAIN
Plantago major L.

Common plantain

Common plantain   Saline plantain

FLOWERS are greenish white, minute, with four short sepals, and a corolla with four reflexed petals and four exerted stamens. The flowers are borne in a dense spike 3 to 10 inches (7.5-25 cm) long, shaped like a "rat tail," appearing in July. They flower and mature for some time and are still evident in late August. FRUIT is a special type of membranous capsule called a *pyxis,* which has a cap which breaks off at the middle to release five to fifteen minute brownish seeds which turn sticky when wet. LEAVES are basal, very dark green, ovoid, entire margined and numerous, with distinct longitudinal veins narrowing to the long fibrous petiole. Leaves are 3 to 8 inches (7.5-20 cm) long and stringy due to the strong venation when pulled or torn. GROWTH HABIT is perennial, from a short, thick rootstock. A second species, saline plantain, *P. eriopoda* Torr., is less fleshy, has a very woolly base, leaves are oblong to lanceolate and smaller, with a shorter, narrower flowering spike. HABITAT: Widely distributed in the complex of waste places, door yards, roadside ditches, and disturbed places, often where grasses have been crowded out with *P. eriopoda* more common under saline conditions.

NORTHERN BEDSTRAW
Galium boreale L.

Northern bedstraw

Northern bedstraw

Sweet-scented bedstraw

FLOWERS are white, ⅛ inch (3 mm) diameter with no sepals and a distinctly four-lobed wheel-shaped corolla. The pistil has two styles. Approximate flowering date is July-August. FRUIT is a pair of rounded nutlets, 1/16 inch (1 mm) long and densely covered with whitish hairs. LEAVES are bright green, arranged in whorls of four. They are linear, three-ribbed and pointed, 1 to 2 inches (2.5-5 cm) long. GROWTH HABIT is perennial and erect on slender square stems from thin brown rootstocks, 8 to 24 inches (20-60 cm) tall. The sweet-scented species, (*G. triflorum* Michx.), is a finer-stemmed plant, much more trailing in habit. HABITAT includes the aspen poplar groves and associated scrub of the parkland region to where parkland and forest meet. Sweet-scented bedstraw is more common in the boreal forest.

LONG-LEAVED BLUETS
Houstonia longifolia Gaertn.

Long-leaved bluets

Long-leaved bluets

FLOWERS are purplish blue to pale blue or nearly white, ¼ to ⅜ inch (6-10 mm) long, numerous in a loose terminal cyme on upper branches. They have a four-lobed tubular corolla which is enclosed by four linear-lanceolate sepals ⅛ inch (3 mm) long. There are four stamens inserted in the upper edge of the tubular section of the corolla. Flowering is common through late June and July. FRUIT is a very small round to ovoid capsule with its upper portion free of the enclosing sepals but clasped by the extended tips of each sepal. LEAVES are pale green, opposite, sessile, and narrowly linear oblong. They are ⅜ to 1 inch (1-2.5 cm) long but the basal group may be larger. Stem leaves have small white or purplish stipules. GROWTH HABIT is perennial rather tufted and much branched, varying in height from 3 to 10 inches (7.5-25 cm). Stems are somewhat square and often purplish in color. HABITAT: Parkland areas, usually on sandy soil or gravelly soils in open upland areas. The species is not common but is widely distributed in parkland and boreal areas.

TWINFLOWER
Linnaea borealis L.

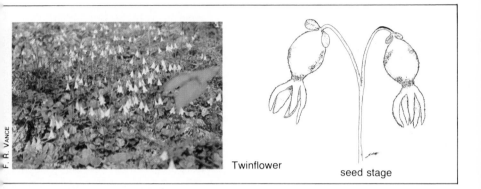

Twinflower

seed stage

FLOWERS are pinkish white, ⅛ inch (3 mm) across, bell-shaped, paired and nodding from a stem about 4 inches (10 cm) long. These flower stalks are numerous along the creeping stem. Approximate flowering date is June-July. FRUIT is an oval, hairy, one-seeded capsule. LEAVES are opposite, oval, short-stalked, somewhat wavy-margined, ⅜ to ⅝ inch (1-1.5 cm) wide. GROWTH HABIT is creeping and evergreen. Stems may be up to 30 inches (75 cm) long. HABITAT includes open and semi-shaded areas of mixed woods and coniferous woods, particularly in the north and east. It is named for Linnaeus, founder of our system of taxonomic botany.

Twinflower

TWINING HONEYSUCKLE
Lonicera glaucescens Rydb.

Twining honeysuckle

Twining honeysuckle

Twining honeysuckle

FLOWERS are yellow, turning red as they age, tubular, ¾ to 1 inch (2-2.5 cm) long, held at the stem tip in a whorled leaf. Flowers appear July-August. The FRUIT is a round berry, bright red when ripe. LEAVES are light green, opposite, often joined at the bases, and joined to form the whorled leaf at the base of the flower cluster. The margins are smooth. GROWTH HABIT: A woody shrub, more or less twining, often attaining a height of 6 feet (180 cm) or more, but usually under 3 feet (90 cm). Common HABITAT includes edges of aspen poplar groves or shady roadsides where it twines on other shrubs. It is found throughout the parkland area and in occasional coulees in the prairie area.

INVOLUCRATE HONEYSUCKLE

Lonicera involucrata (Richards.) Banks

HONEYSUCKLE FAMILY

Involucrate honeysuckle

Blue fly honeysuckle

F. A. SWITZER

Involucrate honeysuckle

FLOWERS are a soft bright yellow, tubular with five petal lobes, five small sepal lobes, and five stamens. Flowers are ⅜ to ⅝ inch (10-15 mm) long, borne on stalks (peduncles) about ¾ inch (2 cm) length, which arise from the leaf axils. Flowers, in twos, supported by two pairs of bracts ⅜ to ⅝ inch (10-15 mm) long, appear in July. FRUITS are deep purplish black and shiny, ¼ inch (6 mm) diameter, in pairs, and partly surrounded by the bracts which turn deep red as the fruits ripen. LEAVES are opposite, medium green, smooth margined, 2 to 4 inches (5-10 cm) long, oblong to oval,

and pointed at the apex. They are slightly hairy on the underside and have a prominent midrib. GROWTH HABIT is perennial, a rather slender leafy shrub 24 to 36 inches (60-90 cm) tall. Stems are brownish green, sometimes downy, and rarely over ¾ inch (2 cm) diameter at the base. The blue fly honeysuckle (*Lonicera caerulea* L. var. *villosa* [Michx.] T. and G.) is a shorter shrub with smaller, less pointed leaves, yellowish white flowers in pairs, and ovoid blue-black berries. HABITAT: Moist low places in woodlands and along stream banks and open meadows in the boreal forest.

RED ELDER
Sambucus racemosa L.

HONEYSUCKLE FAMILY

Red elder

FLOWERS are creamy white, very small (2 mm), somewhat wheel-shaped, with a three- to five-part tubular corolla, and five stamens and an inconspicuous calyx. They are borne in a large, rather ovoid cymose cluster 2 to 3 inches (5-7.5 cm) long and about 2 inches (5 cm) diameter. Flowers appear by late May. FRUIT is a bright red, berry-like drupe with three to five seed-like nutlets. The fruit ripens early, by the end of July. LEAVES are medium green, odd pinnate with five to seven toothed, pointed leaflets. The leaflets have short stalks and are each about 2 to 5 inches (5-12 cm) long and ¾ to 2 inches (2-5 cm) across, smooth above and slightly hairy on the underside. GROWTH HABIT: A low shrub which is usually 3 to 9 feet (1-3 m) tall. Stems are weak with a wide brown pithy center. HABITAT is the margins of boreal forest growth in eastern Saskatchewan and Manitoba or on road edges that have been cleared. This plant requires good moisture conditions.

J. L. PARKER

Red elder

WESTERN SNOWBERRY
Symphoricarpos occidentalis Hook.

HONEYSUCKLE FAMILY

Western snowberry

G. W. SEIB

Thin-leaved snowberry

Western snowberry

FLOWERS are pink and white, about ¼ inch (6 mm) long, with several tubular five-lobed flowers in a dense terminal or axillary cluster. Stamens and pistil project above the corolla in western snowberry but not in thin-leaved snowberry, (*S. albus* [L.] Blake). Flowers appear in July. FRUIT is a waxy white berry which later dries to a light brown. LEAVES are opposite, gray green, ovate to oval, somewhat hairy on the underside, 1 to 3 inches (2.5-7.5 cm) long. In the thin-leaved snowberry the leaves are usually slightly toothed. GROWTH HABIT is perennial, a low bushy shrub, 1 to 4 feet (30-120 cm) high with hollow stems. They grow in dense clumps from creeping rootstocks. Common HABITAT includes the ravines and low spots of the open prairie and the margins of patches of chokecherries and other shrubs throughout the area. It is commonly known as "buckbrush."

HIGH BUSH-CRANBERRY
Viburnum trilobum Marsh

High bush-cranberry

High bush-cranberry

Low bush-cranberry

FLOWERS are white in the sterile florets to creamy white in the fertile florets, with five petals, five sepals and five stamens. The outer sterile flowers are ½ to ¾ inch (12-20 mm) across and have five large petals. The whole flower cluster may be 2 to 6 inches (5-15 cm) across. Both sterile and fertile florets are present in each cluster. Flowers appear in June. FRUIT is a red berry, tart and edible, nearly a ¼ inch (6 mm) in diameter with a large flat seed. LEAVES are opposite, deeply three-lobed, 2 to 4 inches (5-10 cm) wide, coarsely and irregularly toothed. They are palmately-veined, deep green above and lighter beneath. GROWTH HABIT: A tall shrub with a few smooth, reddish gray branches, 3 to 12 feet (1-4 m) in height. In another species, the low bush-cranberry, (*V. edule* [Michx.] Raf.), the plant reaches about 4 feet (120 cm) and has many slender branches. HABITAT includes open areas in aspen poplar groves or scrubby areas of the parkland, river valleys and low places. The low bush-cranberry is more frequent in moister, heavily-wooded areas. Neither of these species should be confused with *Vaccinium oxycoccus* L. and *Vaccinium vitis-idaea* L. which are known as cranberry, but are of the same genus as the blueberries.

HAREBELL
Campanula rotundifolia L.

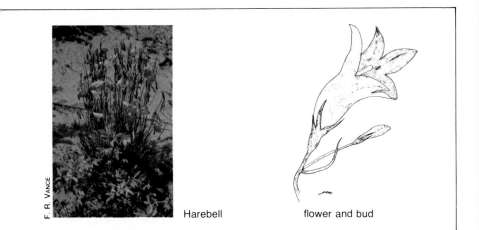

F. R. VANCE

Harebell
flower and bud

FLOWERS are bell-shaped, blue of varying depth, this color increasing with the intensity of the shade in their location. They are ⅝ to ¾ inch (1.5-2 cm) long and about ⅜ inch (1 cm) diameter, often borne singly but sometimes in a loose raceme. Flowers bloom June-September. FRUIT is a papery, many-seeded capsule. LEAVES are linear to linear-oblong, ½ to 3 inches (1-7.5 cm) long. Basal leaves appear at an early stage of growth, are about 1 inch (2.5 cm) long, ovate and heart-shaped at the base. GROWTH HABIT is perennial and erect. Height may vary from 4 to 18 inches (10-45 cm). HABITAT includes the meadows, cultivated hayfields and roadsides throughout the area, even to the edge of the boreal forest.

Harebell

WILD CUCUMBER
Echinocystis lobata (Michx.) T. and G.

Wild cucumber   dry fruit

FLOWERS are greenish white and unisexual. Male flowers are in panicles or racemes and the female flowers, on the same plant, are less plentiful and located in the axils of leaves. Flowers appear in June. FRUIT is a large, ovoid, fleshy berry, 1 to 1½ inches (2.5-4 cm) long, known as a pepo, with a thick, pale green skin. It is covered with long weak spines. Each fruit contains several large flat, roughened dark brown to black seeds. LEAVES are alternate, thin, pale green, palmately veined, rough on both sides, 2 to 5 inches (5-12.5 cm) across, deeply divided into five to seven large lobes. GROWTH HABIT is annual. The stem is twining, 10 to 20 feet (3-6 m) long and somewhat angled. Twining is aided by frequent long, spirally-twisted tendrils. Vines twine through bushes 3 to 5 feet (90-150 cm) above the ground. HABITAT includes moist places along creeks and rivers in the southeast and south central parts of the area.

Wild cucumber

KALM'S LOBELIA
Lobelia kalmii L.

Kalm's lobelia

Spiked lobelia

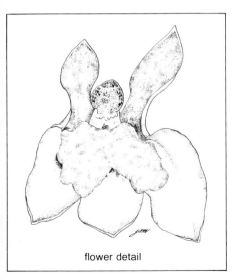

flower detail

FLOWERS are light blue, fading to white on the inside near the base, ⅜ inch (1 cm) long. Each flower has two wing petals above and three below and they are borne in a loose raceme of a few flowers. The corolla is split to separate the lower lip from the upper three petals. The spiked lobelia, (*L. spicata* Lam. var. *hirtella* A. Gray), is also shown. Flowers appear in July. FRUIT is a short pod-like capsule. LEAVES are alternate, spatulate on the lower stem and linear above, ½ to 1 inch (12-24 mm) long, bluish green and numerous. They are borne on short petioles. GROWTH HABIT is biennial or perennial, 4 to 12 inches (10-30 cm) high on a slender branching stem. Common HABITAT includes bogs, wet meadows and road ditches through the central parklands; the plant is frequently found in calcareous soils.

LARGE-FLOWERED FALSE DANDELION
Agoseris glauca (Pursh) Raf.

COMPOSITE FAMILY

Large-flowered false dandelion

Large-flowered false dandelion

Common dandelion

FLOWERS are deep orange yellow, made up of ray florets only. Flowers are usually about 1 inch (2.5 cm) in diameter but may be nearly 2 inches (5 cm). The flower stem is 8 to 15 inches (20-40 cm) high and there is usually one flower per plant. The common dandelion, (*Taraxacum officinale* Weber), is shown for contrast. Flowers bloom July-August. FRUIT is a dry, beaked achene with a white pappus. LEAVES are bluish green, usually basal, narrowly lanceolate, sometimes with a few teeth, usually about 3 to 5 inches (7-12 cm) long but may be up to 10 inches (25 cm). GROWTH HABIT is perennial, with basal leaves in a dense rosette and a long flower stalk of up to 15 inches (40 cm). HABITAT: Widely distributed over the prairie and to the edges of the parkland in moister grassy areas, roadside ditches, etc.

NARROW-LEAVED HAWK'S-BEARD
Crepis tectorum L.

COMPOSITE FAMILY

Narrow-leaved hawk's-beard

flowers and seed heads

FLOWERS are deep yellow, in heads up to ½ inch (12 mm) in diameter, composed of ray florets only. They are ringed with short bracts and grow on branched stalks, July-September. FRUIT is an achene, 3/16 inch (4 mm), with a reddish brown seed, slight beak and white pappus. LEAVES are dark green, oblanceolate to spatulate and often slightly toothed with backward-pointing teeth. Basal leaves may be up to 6 inches (15 cm) long but stem leaves are shorter and distinctly linear, 1½ to 3 inches (4-8 cm) long. GROWTH HABIT is annual or occasionally perennial, from a thick, branched root supporting a dense mat of leaves and the tall flower stalks. Stems exude a milky juice when broken. They may be hairy or smooth and vary in height from 8 to 36 inches (20-90 cm). Hawk's beard species are easily confused with the hawkweeds, (*Hieracium* spp. [Tourn.] L.). Hawkweeds have a distinctly brown pappus on their seeds and are fibrous rooted. HABITAT includes edges of moist meadows, field edges and margins of aspen poplar groves or patches of scrub.

Narrow-leaved hawk's-beard

270

BLUE LETTUCE
Lactuca pulchella (Pursh) DC.

COMPOSITE FAMILY

Blue lettuce

Blue lettuce   flower detail

FLOWERS are bright powdery blue, up to an inch (2.5 cm) across, with ray florets only, borne in a loose panicle of three to five blooms, August-September. FRUIT is a dry achene with a small white pappus. LEAVES are alternate, pale bluish green, with a distinct bloom, linear-lanceolate, often with lobes that point backward toward the stem. They may be up to 7 inches (18 cm) long. GROWTH HABIT is perennial with tall slightly-branched stems growing from running rootstocks. Stems and roots exude a milky sap when broken. Plant height varies from 15 to 36 inches (40-90 cm). HABITAT includes the margins of roads, gravel pits and fields where the soil is fairly heavy and moist, although the ground where this plant grows usually appears rather inhospitable. It is common throughout Saskatchewan but more common in the southern third.

LOBED PRICKLY LETTUCE
Lactuca scariola L.

COMPOSITE FAMILY

Lobed prickly lettuce

Lobed prickly lettuce

FLOWERS are deep yellow in ligulate heads of six to twelve ray florets each. The conical heads, ¼ to ⅜ inch (6-10 mm) across, are arranged in panicles on the terminal and upper branches. There are several series of bracts with the shortest ones nearest the base. Flowering commonly occurs in August. FRUIT is a ridged achene about ⅛ inch (3 mm) long with a white pappus at the end of the long beak. LEAVES are dark bluish green, oblong to lanceolate, sometimes pinnately lobed bearing a row of stiff prickles along the midrib. They vary in size from 2 to 8 inches (5-20 cm) long and clasp the stem with ear-like modifications at the base of the leaf. GROWTH HABIT is either winter annual or biennial, erect and much branched. Stems are rather weak and average 12 to 30 inches (30-75 cm) but may grow taller under ideal conditions. HABITAT is the margins of cultivated fields and gardens, fence rows, etc.

272

SKELETONWEED
Lygodesmia juncea (Pursh) D. Don

Skeletonweed

Skeletonweed

FLOWERS are pale lavender, in a head of three to seven flowers, about ½ inch (12 mm) diameter, with ray florets only. The solitary heads at the ends of branches are enclosed by five linear bracts. Flowers appear in August. FRUIT is an achene up to ¼ inch (6 mm) long with a soft pale brownish pappus. LEAVES are alternate, linear lanceolate, up to 2 inches (5 cm) long and ⅛ inch (3 mm) wide, but only the lower leaves are broad enough to be noticed as leaves, with upper ones reduced to scales. GROWTH HABIT is perennial from deep tough rootstocks. The plant, 4 to 16 inches (10-40 cm) high, appears as a "jungle" of bare, rigid, tough stems topped by a few flower heads. The stems release a milky juice when broken. HABITAT is the light sandy soils and dry uplands in the south and central plains.

GLAUCOUS WHITE-LETTUCE
Prenanthes racemosa Michx.

C. B. PRATT

Glaucous white-lettuce

Glaucous white-lettuce

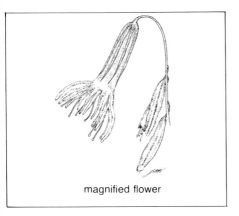

magnified flower

FLOWERS are greenish or yellowish white, ½ to ¾ inch (12-20 mm) diameter, disc-shaped, composed of ray florets only. They are slightly scented and borne in drooping heads in a long terminal panicle. Heads are enclosed in a group of linear purplish bracts. Flowers appear in August. FRUIT is an elongated ribbed achene with a pale cinnamon brown pappus. LEAVES are alternate and mainly stalkless, 1 to 2 inches (2.5-5 cm) long, up to an inch (2.5 cm) wide. The lower leaves may be stalked and are triangular or heart-shaped. The upper leaves are lance-shaped. GROWTH HABIT is perennial; the smooth erect stem may be 2 to 5 feet (60-150 cm) tall, but it is usually nearer 2 feet (60 cm). Stems exude a milky sap when broken. HABITAT includes the open areas in aspen poplar groves in the northeast and central portions of the area.

PERENNIAL SOW-THISTLE
Sonchus arvensis L.

O. STILL

Perennial sow-thistle

Annual sow-thistle

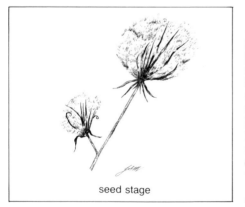

seed stage

FLOWERS are deep yellow, ½ to 1¼ inches (1-3 cm) in diameter. Only ray florets are present. Several flower heads are ar-

ranged in a rounded panicle, and appear June-September. FRUIT is a dry, flattened achene with a white pappus. The seeds produced per plant are a major factor in the problem of this plant as a weed. LEAVES are bluish green with backward pointing lobes and prickly margins, 4 to 10 inches (10-25 cm) long. The upper leaves are stalkless, less lobed and shorter; the lower leaves have short petioles. GROWTH HABIT is perennial in this species and annual in the other species shown, (*S. oleraceus* L.). Stems exude a milky sap when broken. They have few branches and leaves are mostly basal. Height of plants varies from 1 to 5 feet (30-150 cm). HABITAT includes gardens, roadsides and weedy fields throughout the area. It is sometimes a significant source of pollen and nectar for honeybees.

GOAT'S-BEARD
Tragopogon dubius Scop.

Goat's-beard

Goat's-beard

FLOWERS are yellow with only ray florets and the outer ones are wider. Blooms may be 1½ to 2 inches (3.5-5 cm) across. All flowers are complete as far as sex structures are concerned. Beneath the ray florets are ten to fourteen green, pointed involucral bracts which are longer than the outer ray florets. Approximate flowering date is July-August. The FRUIT is a narrow, beaked achene, 1 to 1¼ inches (2.5-3.5 cm) long, with a plume-like pappus. The whole fruiting head is a striking sight. LEAVES are erect and grass-like, 4 to 12 inches (10-30 cm) long and under ½ inch (1 cm) wide. They are stalkless and clasp the stem. GROWTH HABIT is biennial, stems are coarse, up to ⅝ inch (1.5 cm) diameter, 6 to 24 inches (15-60 cm) high, from a fleshy taproot. They contain a milky sap. Flowers appear at ends of stems and stems are thickened below the flower head. HABITAT includes yards, roadsides, railway grades and waste land; the plant is more common on prairies than parkland. This species was probably introduced from western United States. Another species, meadow goat's-beard, (*T. pratensis* L.), is similar but smaller and flowers are chrome yellow with shorter bracts.

Goat's-beard

YARROW
Achillea millefolium L.

COMPOSITE FAMILY

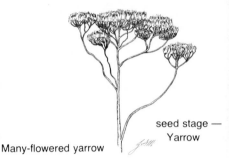

seed stage —
Yarrow

Many-flowered yarrow

Yarrow

FLOWERS are usually white, but occasionally light pink. Color is mainly due to the sterile ray florets. The ten to thirty disc florets are yellow to light cream. Involucral bracts overlap in three or four rows. The flower heads are 1½ inches (4 cm) across and are densely packed in a round topped terminal cluster. The many-flowered yarrow, (*A. sibirica* Ledeb.), has flowers in a flat topped cluster. Flowers appear June-August. FRUIT is a small flattened dry achene with no pappus. LEAVES are woolly, blue green, 1½ to 6 inches (4-15 cm) long, 1 inch (2.5 cm) wide, divided into many segments. Leaves average 3 inches (7.5 cm) long. The leaves of many-flowered yarrow are linear and deeply toothed but not in segments, and somewhat less hairy. GROWTH HABIT is perennial, with several stems arising from a branched rootstock. Stems are not much branched and are very woolly-hairy. HABITAT includes roadsides and open prairie throughout the area with the other species more common at the edges of aspen poplar groves in the north and east. Yarrow is one of the commonest white flowers of the summer scene in Saskatchewan.

LOW EVERLASTING
Antennaria aprica Greene

Low everlasting

Prairie everlasting

Rosy everlasting

FLOWERS are white to cream color, occasionally slightly pink, in heads ¼ to ½ inch (7-12 mm) tall. Ray florets are absent; disc florets are creamy white and have either stamens or pistil, (sometimes both sexes are on the same plant). Bracts are thin, white, or translucent and overlap the flower heads. Several flower heads are present in each compact cluster which is so shaped that the flower is often called "pussy toes." Flowering date ranges from June-July. The FRUIT is a dry achene with a white pappus. LEAVES are woolly white on both sides and form a close mat on the ground. Individual leaves are spatulate or wedge-shaped, ⅜ to ¾ inch (1-2 cm) long. Stem leaves, if present, are ⅜ inch (1 cm) long and linear. The prairie everlasting, (*A. campestris* Rydb.), has yellowish green leaves which are almost devoid of hairs on the upper surface. GROWTH HABIT is basal, and even with the flower stems, plants are rarely over 6 inches (15 cm) tall in low everlasting as well as in rosy everlasting, (*A. rosea* Greene). However one species, the showy everlasting (*A. pulcherrima* [Hook.] Greene), may grow to 20 inches (50 cm). HABITAT includes dry prairie or dry meadows of the parkland in the case of the low and prairie everlasting. About a dozen species are known for the area and one, (*A. dimorpha* Nutt.), is rare and worthy of serious protection.

COTTON BURDOCK
Arctium tomentosum Mill.

COMPOSITE FAMILY

Cotton burdock

Cotton burdock

FLOWERS are purple, in discoid heads ½ to 1 inch (12-25 mm) diameter, ⅜ inch (10 mm) high in a rough corymbose cluster on long, 2 inch (5 cm) stalks (peduncles). The heads are covered with hairy white-tipped bracts to give the appearance of a cottony globe with a pinkish purple top. The bracts are particularly noticeable as the heads mature due to coarse, hooked bristles. Another species, *A. minus* (Hill) Bernh., has shorter involucral bracts, and the heads are borne on shorter stalks, ¾ inch (2 cm). Flowering occurs from late June to August in Saskatchewan. FRUIT is a small, brownish, three- to five-angled, oblong achene with a pappus of short whitish bristles, enclosed in the spiny bur-like involucre. Another composite, cocklebur, *Xanthium strumarium* L., has inconspicuous flowers and forms a rough prickly bur in the fruiting stage and is occasionally confused with the burdocks. LEAVES are dark green, alternate, ovate to oblong, round tipped, and coarse. They are often slightly toothed, lighter in color underneath. Petioles are long and coarse and leaves vary from 4 to 12 inches (10-30 cm) in length. GROWTH HABIT is biennial, coarse and bushy in appearance, to a height of 2 to 6 feet (60-180 cm). HABITAT is usually road edges, railway grades, and locations where garden refuse may have been piled. This introduced plant is not common, but it is found occasionally in the parkland.

HEART-LEAVED ARNICA

Arnica cordifolia Hook.

Heart-leaved arnica

Shining arnica

Heart-leaved arnica

FLOWERS are deep orange yellow due to many wide ray florets and the closely-grouped disc florets. Each stem usually has a single flower head, 1 to 2 inches (2.5-5 cm) diameter, June-July. The FRUIT is a dry hairy achene with a barbed, white to creamy pappus. LEAVES on the stem are heart-shaped, opposite, usually stalkless and bright green and smooth, 1 to 3 inches (2.5-7 cm) long. They are distinctly smaller and less lobed than the basal leaves. Another species is referred to as shining arnica, (*A. fulgens* Pursh), and has smaller, linear-lanceolate leaves. GROWTH HABIT is perennial and erect, with leaves growing along the coarse stem which may be 8 to 24 inches (20-60 cm) tall. HABITAT includes the reasonably moist soils and slough edges in grassy areas where the plants may not be noticed until flowers open. Both species are common in the south and southwest. The heart-leaved arnica is more common in the west and in the Cypress Hills.

SAGEBRUSH
Artemisia cana Pursh

Sagebrush

Prairie sage

Prairie sage

FLOWERS are minute, dusty yellow florets in flower heads of five to twenty units, with several crowded into upper and terminal leaf axils. The leafy appearance of the upper stem tends to obscure the small flowers. The numerous involucral bracts which enclose each head are thin, spine-tipped, and very pubescent. Flowering occurs in August. FRUIT is a small achene, lacking a pappus. LEAVES are alternate, numerous, silvery-hairy on both sides. They are linear to linear-lanceolate, ⅜ to 1¼ inches (1-4 cm) long. They are usually entire margined, sessile, and pointed at both ends. GROWTH HABIT is perennial, a coarse, much-branched, leafy shrub from 15-50 inches (40-125 cm) tall. The larger stems or older plants have a white shreddy bark and a very twisted appearance. Another lower growing, wider leafed, and branching species is prairie sage, *A. ludoviciana* Nutt. This white woolly species dies back to the ground each season and is much less woody in appearance. HABITAT is the uplands and overgrazed areas of the southwest, a sign of the true prairies. Prairie sage is much more widely distributed and extends into the parklands and forest edges.

PASTURE SAGE
Artemisia frigida Willd.

COMPOSITE FAMILY

Pasture sage

Pasture sage

FLOWERS are light yellow disc florets clustered in small, dense heads clasped by many hairy involucral bracts ⅛ inch (3 mm) high. Numerous yellowish heads form narrow leafy clusters at the tops of the stems and are most often observed in August. FRUIT is a minute, smooth achene with no pappus. LEAVES are alternate, gray-green, finely dissected into numerous hair-like leaflets ¼ to ½ inch (6-12 mm) long, which are silvery-hairy on both sides. They are numerous, especially near the base of each plant.

GROWTH HABIT is perennial from a woody root crown, forming a mat of grayish leaves first, then giving rise to numerous spindly stems by flowering time. Plants may spread by roots and range in height from 6 to 18 inches (15-45 cm), and the whole plant has a distinct "sage" odor. HABITAT is overgrazed pastures and disturbed places in the drier south and west of the area. It is less common in the parkland but occasionally observed on sandy hillsides.

SMOOTH ASTER
Aster laevis L.

COMPOSITE FAMIL

Smooth aster

Lindley's aster

Showy aster

FLOWERS are bright violet blue due to their ray florets; disc florets are dark yellow. The heads, about ¾ inch (2 cm) across, are borne in a loose panicle and each head has a circle of green-tipped bracts loosely grouped beneath it. Also illustrated are two other asters of similar flower color, Lindley's aster, (*A. ciliolatus* Lindl.), and showy aster, (*A. conspicuus* Lindl.).

Lindley's aster is deeper blue than the othe two. Flowers appear August-Septembe The FRUIT is a ribbed, flattened acher with numerous pappus bristles. LEAVE are alternate, dark green, thick an smooth-surfaced, usually somewha toothed, ovate to lanceolate. Basal leave have wide-margined stalks and uppe leaves are stalkless and often clasping Lindley's aster has conspicuously-winge petioles. GROWTH HABIT is usually pei ennial and erect but "flopping." Height va ies from 1 to 4 feet (30-120 cm), usuall nearer the former. Stems are more or les smooth. HABITAT includes the woode areas of the parkland, scrubby roadsid ditches and some moist open places on th prairie. Lindley's aster is more common i open spaces among trees than the smootl aster.

MANY-FLOWERED ASTER
Aster pansus (Blake) Cronq.

COMPOSITE FAMILY

Many-flowered aster

Willow aster

seed stage — White prairie aster

FLOWERS have white ray florets and yellow disc florets. The flower heads are relatively small, ⅜ inch (1 cm) diameter but very numerous. They are mostly found on one side of the curved stems, where 4 to 7 inches (10-17 cm) of the end of each stem may bear flowers. Bracts are arranged in three series around the heads. Flowers appear August-September. FRUIT is an achene with distinct ridges and a pappus with hairs of variable length. LEAVES are alternate, gray green, narrow, linear, ½ to ¾ inch (12-20 mm) long with smooth margins. They are quite numerous. Leaves of the willow aster, (*A. hesperius* A. Gray), are much longer, up to 6 inches (15 cm) and occasionally slightly toothed. GROWTH HABIT: A cluster of several wiry hairy stems arising from a thick tufted rootstock to a height of 8 to 24 inches (20-60 cm). The willow aster is more branched and much taller, up to 40 inches (1 m). HABITAT includes grassy edges of fields, open meadows and edges of scrubby patches. The plant is common throughout the area, but more common on the open prairie than the willow aster. The white prairie aster, (*A. falcatus* Lindl.), is also illustrated (seed stage).

284

NODDING BEGGARTICKS
Bidens cernua L.

COMPOSITE FAMILY

Nodding beggarticks

flower detail

FLOWERS are usually nodding, ¾ to 1¼ inches (2-3 cm) in diameter, deep yellow in color, with the center darker or speckled yellow and black. The outer bracts are nearly 1 inch (2.5 cm) long and slightly reflexed, and are slightly longer than the ray florets. Approximate flowering date is August-September. FRUIT is a spear-shaped achene, about ¼ inch (6 mm) long with four barbed awns which are backward pointing. LEAVES are dark green, opposite, somewhat paler on the underside stalkless and clasping, 2 to 6 inches (5-15 cm) long, toothed and linear lanceolate GROWTH HABIT is annual, erect and leafy on coarse, angled stems, height 24 to 30 inches (60-75 cm). HABITAT includes wet slough edges and the margins of sloughs which have recently dried up, particularly in the eastern part of the area.

Nodding beggarticks

NODDING-THISTLE
Carduus nutans L.

COMPOSITE FAMILY

Nodding-thistle

Nodding-thistle

Russian-thistle

FLOWERS are deep purple, borne in single heads, 1 to 2 inches (2.5-5 cm) in diameter. The heads are on nodding, angled, spineless stems, 8 to 10 inches (20-25 cm) in length. Involucral bracts are in many series, purple at maturity and possessing a prominent mid-vein that develops into a spine. Flowers appear July-August. FRUIT is a smooth, spotted, brown achene, about ¼ inch (6 mm) long, with a white pappus that lacks a plume. LEAVES are alternate, deeply divided, gray green, well covered with spines and clasping the stem. GROWTH HABIT is biennial, branching and tall, 3 to 5 feet, (90-150 cm) with many flower heads per plant. The stem is angular and somewhat ridged. HABITAT includes roadside ditches, fence edges, field borders, etc., particularly in the central part of the area. Nodding-thistle was introduced and is not the same genus as the native thistles. The third illustration shows another introduction, Russian-thistle, (*Salsola pestifer* A. Nels.).

HAIRY GOLDEN-ASTER
Chrysopsis villosa (Pursh) Nutt.

Hairy golden-aster

Hairy golden-aster

seed stage

FLOWERS are bright yellow due to the ray florets while tubular florets range from orange to brown. There may be one or several flower heads, 1 to 1¼ inches (2.5-3 cm) across, present at the ends of each branch July-September. FRUIT is a flattened hairy achene. The pappus is double on each fruit. LEAVES are alternate, gray green due to their hairiness, oblong to lanceolate, 1 to 2 inches (2.5-5 cm) long and numerous. They are usually short-stalked or stalkless. GROWTH HABIT is bushy, with branches arising from a woody taproot. Branches are often nearly prostrate but some plants reach a height of 24 inches (60 cm). HABITAT includes dry sandy prairie and hillsides, particularly in the south and south-central part of the area.

RABBITBRUSH
Chrysothamnus nauseosus (Pall.) Britt.

COMPOSITE FAMILY

FLOWERS are bright yellow and lack ray florets. Heads are ½ inch (12 mm) diameter, enclosed in two or three series of hairy involucral bracts ⅜ to ⅝ inch (10-15 mm) tall in a head of ½ inch (12 mm) diameter. Heads are numerous and borne in terminal panicles and are common in August and early September. FRUIT is a slender, hairy achene with a bristly pappus of creamy white hairs. LEAVES are light gray-green, alternate, thin to the point of being thread-like, and covered with matted hairs. They are ⅜ to 2 inches (1-5 cm) long, and very nu-merous, making the plant appear as sagebrush, but the lack of an aromatic odor indicates that it must be something else. GROWTH HABIT: A coarse, semi-prostrate, branching shrub which ranges in height from 8 to 24 inches (20-60 cm). The root and lower stem are dispropor-tionately large for the size of the shrub. Branches are twisted and white woolly due to the felt-like, persistent hairs on stems. HABITAT is dry and poorly vege-tated prairie of the south and west, on eroded banks and occasionally on saline clay flats.

Rabbitbrush

CANADA THISTLE
Cirsium arvense (L.) Scop.

Canada thistle

Canada thistle

Wavy-leaved thistle

FLOWERS are lavender blue to purple and occasionally white. All florets are disc or tubular type and all florets on a plant are of the same sex. The florets are arranged in loose corymbose heads at the ends of stems. The male heads are up to 1 inch (2.5 cm) across and the female heads nearer ½ inch (12 mm). In the wavy-leaved thistle, (*C. undulatum* [Nutt.] Spreng.), flowers are purple to pink and are larger: 2 inches (5 cm) across and solitary at ends of branches. Flowers bloom July-September. FRUIT is a small, flat, smooth achene with a white pappus. LEAVES are alternate, dark green, stalkless, sometimes clasping. They are lanceolate, curled or wavy and deeply incised into spined segments. In the wavy-leaved thistle the lower leaves are stalked. GROWTH HABIT is perennial, growing to 1 to 3 feet (30-90 cm) from deep running rootstocks. It often appears in patches and is rather slender. HABITAT includes roadsides and cultivated fields where moisture conditions are fairly good. The wavy-leaved thistle is more common in the south and west.

SHORT-STEMMED THISTLE
Cirsium drummondii T. and G.

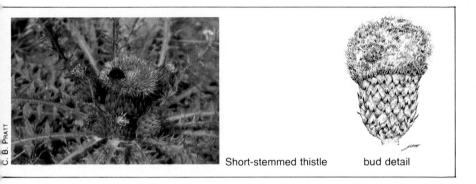

Short-stemmed thistle   bud detail

FLOWERS are unusual because of their large size, with heads up to 2 inches (5 cm) across and equally tall. They are deep rose purple and the center head usually matures first with up to five lesser heads blooming around it later. The other species illustrated is Flodman's thistle, (*C. flodmanii* [Rydb.] Arthur), which has flowers of similar color but somewhat smaller heads, 1 to 1½ inch (2.5-4 cm) across. Flowers appear in July. The FRUIT is a flat achene, 3 to 5 mm long with a creamy white bristly pappus. LEAVES appear basal due to the shortness of the stem; they are smooth and green on both sides when mature, stalkless, 3 to 6 inches (8-15 cm) long, triangular-lobed with weak spines. GROWTH HABIT is perennial, low and squatty, 4 to 12 inches (10-30 cm) tall, usually nearer the lower figure. Flodman's thistle is much taller, up to 36 inches (90 cm). HABITAT includes the eastern and north eastern portions of the area (Togo and Parr Hill Lake); the plant is usually found in grassy meadows in woods. Flodman's thistle is common across the prairies and parkland throughout the area.

Flodman's thistle

COMMON TICKSEED
Coreopsis tinctoria Nutt.

Common tickseed

F. R. Vance

Common tickseed   seeds

FLOWERS have deep orange yellow ray florets and reddish brown disc florets. They are usually about an inch (2.5 cm) across and borne on long, slender, smooth stems. The ray florets are broad, three-lobed at the apex, and may be tinged with purple at the base. Flowers bloom August-September. FRUIT is an achene that lacks a pappus and is curved so that it distinctly resembles a tick or small insect. LEAVES are mainly opposite, stalkless or nearly so, 2 to 4 inches (5-10 cm) long, once or twice divided into linear or lanceolate lobes. Upper leaves are less divided than the lower ones, and lower leaves are more often stalked. GROWTH HABIT is erect and annual; stems are slender, hairless and much branched, usually about 12 inches (30 cm) tall but may be as tall as 36 inches (90 cm). HABITAT includes moist places in road ditches and edges of grassy marshes in rather sandy soil. The wild species may be noticed particularly because of the flowers deep orange color and dark center. Other species are hardy garden annuals.

TUFTED FLEABANE
Erigeron caespitosus Nutt.

COMPOSITE FAMILY

Tufted fleabane

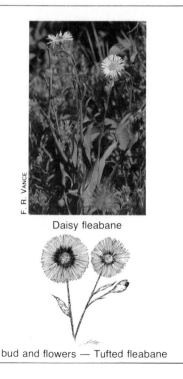

Daisy fleabane

F. R. VANCE

bud and flowers — Tufted fleabane

FLOWERS are white with a yellow center, 1 inch (2.5 cm) in diameter and often appear singly. Ray florets are numerous, (60-90), and about ⅜ inch (1 cm) long. Each head is surrounded by three or four series of bracts thickened at the back. Daisy fleabane, (*E. strigosus* Muhl.), is similar but bracts are not thickened and ray florets are more numerous. Flowers appear in July. FRUIT is a dry achene with a bristly pappus, typical of the fleabanes. LEAVES are gray green, smooth-margined and three-veined. Basal leaves are oblong-lanceolate, 1 to 3 inches (2.5-7 cm) long and have petioles, but upper leaves lack petioles, are reduced in size and linear oblong in shape. GROWTH HABIT is, as the name implies, tufted, with several curving stems, 6 to 12 inches (15-30 cm) tall from a thick root crown. HABITAT includes dry prairie and hillsides of the south and central part of the area.

SMOOTH FLEABANE
Erigeron glabellus Nutt.

Smooth fleabane

Smooth fleabane

Philadelphia fleabane

FLOWERS have purple (occasionally nearly white) ray florets which are ¼ to ⅝ inch (8-15 mm) long and numerous (125-175). Disc florets are yellow with stamens and pistil. Flower heads have linear bracts, ¼ inch (6 mm) long, with a conspicuous brown mid-vein. There may be one to five heads on each plant and each is about ½ inch (12 mm) diameter. Flowers appear June-August. FRUIT is a dry achene with a bristly double pappus. LEAVES are mostly basal, 2 to 4 inches (5-10 cm) long, oblong-lanceolate and hairless. Upper leaves are alternate, toothed, much smaller and linear-lanceolate, with a single prominent vein. The basal leaves of the smooth fleabane have petioles but all the leaves of the Philadelphia fleabane, (*E. philadelphicus* L.), are clasping at the base and spatulate in shape. GROWTH HABIT is perennial, occasionally biennial, with simple or slightly branched stems arising 6 to 18 inches (15-45 cm) from tufted fibrous roots. HABITAT includes the open prairie and edges of scrubby patches through the moister parts, particularly in the north, central and east. The Philadelphia fleabane occupies the same type of habitat, usually in areas that are even more moist than where smooth fleabane grows.

JOE-PYE WEED
Eupatorium maculatum L.

COMPOSITE FAMILY

Joe-pye weed

FLOWERS are composed of purplish pink tubular florets in heads ⅜ inch (1 cm) high and ¼ inch (6 mm) across. Each head is encased in several series of unequal, pinkish, linear involucral bracts ¼ to ⅜ inch (6-10 mm) high. Numerous heads are clustered in a rather flat-topped inflorescence 6 to 8 inches (15-20 cm) across, which appears in August. FRUIT is a small, five-angled achene with a white bristly pappus. LEAVES are dark green, short petioled, in whorls of three to six, ovate to lanceolate, 4 to 6 inches (10-15 cm) long, pointed at the apex, and sharply toothed. They are smooth on the upper surface and somewhat hairy beneath. GROWTH HABIT is perennial, erect, and branching on a coarse stem which is 2 to 6 feet (60-180 cm) tall. Stems are somewhat purplish spotted and slightly hairy near the top. HABITAT is low, moist woodland glades and stream banks in the eastern parklands. It is also known as purple boneset, in contrast to *E. perfoliatum* L., which is white boneset.

Joe-pye weed

GAILLARDIA
Gaillardia aristata Pursh

COMPOSITE FAMILY

Gaillardia

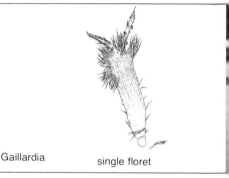

single floret

FLOWER heads are up to 4 inches (10 cm) across with yellow orange ray florets toothed at the apex and set in a rounded brownish purple disc. The ray florets are often purple at the base. Flowers appear July-August. FRUIT is a dry hairy achene with a scaly pappus. LEAVES are alternate, grayish green and hairy, with lower leaves stalked and spatulate; upper leaves are stalkless and smaller than the lower ones, which may be 2 to 5 inches (5-12 cm) long. Upper leaves may be slightly lobed. GROWTH HABIT is erect, a slightly branched, hairy stemmed perennial growing from a slender taproot, usually 8 to 24 inches (20-60 cm) tall. HABITAT includes roadsides, railway grades and drier uplands as far up as the forest edge.

Gaillardia

GUMWEED
Grindelia squarrosa (Pursh) Dunal

Gumweed

flower detail

F. R. VANCE

Gumweed

FLOWERS are bright yellow, due to both ray and disc florets and are somewhat wheel-like. The heads are ¾ to 1¼ inches (2-3 cm) across and develop on the ends of the plant's many branches. The plant gets its name from the rows of sticky bracts which cover the involucre. Flowers appear July-September. FRUIT is a four or five-ribbed achene with a pappus of two or more awns. LEAVES are alternate, dark green, smooth and glistening. They are oblong-lanceolate, stiff and dotted with glands. The lower leaves have petioles but the upper ones are clasping. The edges have teeth of varying size and are pointed at the apex. GROWTH HABIT is much branched and stems arise from a deep taproot. Plants grow 8 to 24 inches (20-60 cm) high, usually nearer the former. HABITAT includes roadsides, saline flats and slough margins, particularly where there has been overgrazing. The plant is very common in the prairie section and encroaches into the parkland in some places.

BROOMWEED
Gutierrezia diversifolia Greene

COMPOSITE FAMILY

Broomweed

Broomweed

magnified flowers

FLOWERS are deep yellow, about ⅛ inch (3 mm) high, 1/16 inch (1 mm) across, in close clusters at the ends of branches. The few ray florets have no stamens; the disc florets have both stamens and pistil. There are usually five or six ray florets and eight to ten disc florets, giving the cluster the appearance of a head of deep yellow, tubular flowers. Approximate flowering date is June-August. FRUIT is a dry, five-angled achene with a scaly pappus. LEAVES are gray green, narrow-linear, 1/16 inch (1 mm) wide, stalkless, and lack marginal indentations. GROWTH HABIT is biennial or perennial, more or less erect on many slender brittle stems which grow from a woody taproot. HABITAT is the dry prairies of the southern third of the area.

NARROW-LEAVED STENOTUS
Haplopappus armerioides (Nutt.) A. Gray

Narrow-leaved stenotus

Narrow-leaved stenotus

FLOWERS are bright yellow in heads of eight to ten ray florets, borne singly on 8 to 10 inch (20-25 cm) tall, nearly leafless stems. Each head, about ¾ to 1 inch (2-2.5 cm) across, is surrounded by ovate, ridged, overlapping, conspicuously green-tipped involucral bracts. Flowering begins by late June. FRUIT is a small, elongated, rather hairy achene with a pappus of soft white bristles. LEAVES are numerous, mostly basal, light green, rigid, linear or narrowly spatulate, 1 to 3 inches (2.5-7.5 cm) long. They are mostly crowded at the ends of numerous short, woody branches, forming a mat. A few smaller stem leaves appear on the flowering stalks. GROWTH HABIT is perennial and tufted, with flowering stems arising from a woody root crown. The height of the plant is 4 to 8 inches (10-20 cm) but appears greater due to the length of the flower stalks. HABITAT: This plant is not common but may be found on overgrazed pastures and dry eroded hillsides on the southern prairies in Saskatchewan.

SNEEZEWEED
Helenium montanum Nutt.

COMPOSITE FAMILY

Sneezeweed

FLOWERS are dark yellow, in several heads per plant, 1 to 1½ inches (2.5-4 cm) across, with ten to twenty toothed, fertile ray florets. These ray florets are deflexed around the numerous disc florets distributed on a convex receptacle up to ⅜ inch (1 cm) high and ¼ to ¾ inch (6-20 mm) wide. The involucral bracts are dark green and short, under ⅜ inch (1 cm), and usually reflexed. Flowering is most common in late July and August. FRUIT is a slightly hairy, small, four-angled achene with a brownish pappus of five to eight tooth-like scales. LEAVES are alternate, bright green, thick and numerous, oblong to lanceolate, pointed, finely toothed, stalkless with blade of leaf extending down the stem as narrow wings. They are large, 1½ to 4 inches (4-10 cm) long, ¾ to 1¼ inches (2-3 cm) across, covered with fine, soft hairs. Leaves are bitter to taste and somewhat poisonous to cattle and sheep, and reputed to impart a taint to milk. GROWTH HABIT is perennial, herbaceous, 8 to 24 inches (20-60 cm) tall, coarse and branching, with stout, erect stems covered with fine hairs. The roots are fibrous and the stem arises from the crown of these roots. HABITAT is low meadows or slough edges in the eastern prairies and throughout the parkland. It is not common but often spreads through introduction in poor quality hay. The genus was, according to Linnaeus, named by Helen of Troy, so perhaps it grew on the plains near that ancient city.

RHOMBIC-LEAVED SUNFLOWER

COMPOSITE FAMILY

Helianthus laetiflorus Pers. var. *subrhomboideus* (Rydb.) Fern.

Narrow-leaved sunflower

FLOWERS are yellow heads 1 to 3 inches (2.5-7 cm) across with reddish purple or brownish disc florets. Ray florets vary from ⅝ to 1½ inches (1.5-4 cm) in length. Flower heads are often solitary and appear August-September. FRUIT is a dry achene with the pappus reduced to two awn-like scales. LEAVES are dark green, usually opposite and with the rhombic shape for which it is named. They have three distinct veins and are 2 to 4 inches (5-10 cm) long. GROWTH HABIT is perennial from a thick branching rootstock. The long stem of the single flower is easily noticed and the stems appear bare of leaves and slightly hairy. The narrow-leaved sunflower, (*H. maximilianii* Schrad.), appears even less leafy and the leaves are much narrower and somewhat folded. HABITAT characteristically includes roadsides and field margins. The rhombic-leaved species is more common in dry areas on light soils than the other sunflowers.

Rhombic-leaved sunflower

Rhombic-leaved sunflower

PRAIRIE SUNFLOWER
Helianthus petiolaris Nutt.

Prairie sunflower

Prairie sunflower

seed head

FLOWERS have bright yellow ray florets and yellow brown disc florets, 1 to 3½ inches (2.5-9 cm) across. The scales between the disc florets each have a small tuft of hairs. Approximate date of flowering is July-August. FRUIT is a smooth, dry, slightly ribbed achene which contains a single seed. LEAVES are alternate, deep green and entire margined. They are rough on both surfaces, 1 to 3 inches (2.5-8 cm) long, ovate to lanceolate, with long stalks. GROWTH HABIT is annual, 1 to 3 feet (30-90 cm) tall with some branching of the stem. HABITAT includes roadsides and other disturbed places, particularly where the soil is sandy. The showy sunflower, (*H. lenticularis* Dougl.), will displace it on heavier soils.

COLORADO RUBBERWEED
Hymenoxys richardsonii (Hook.) Cockerell

COMPOSITE FAMILY

Colorado rubberweed

Colorado rubberweed

FLOWERS are bright yellow, due to both ray and disc florets. The few ray florets are about ½ inch (12 mm) long and lack stamens. The disc florets have both stamens and pistil. The flower heads are borne at the ends of branches in a flat-topped cluster about ¾ inch (2 cm) across. An illustration of spiny iron plant, (*Haplopappus spinulosus* [Pursh] DC.), is also shown. It flowers in August, about a month later than the Colorado rubberweed. Approximate date of flowering is June-July. FRUIT is an achene and the pappus is short-awned. LEAVES are alternate, dark green, mostly basal, divided into narrow linear lobes up to 1½ inches (4 cm) in length. GROWTH HABIT is perennial, stems rise to 12 inches (30 cm) from a coarse woody taproot which appears as a woolly crown full of dead leaves. The plant is more or less tufted and stems are slightly straggling and slightly hairy. HABITAT includes overgrazed pastures and roadside ditches under rather indifferent moisture conditions throughout the prairies of the area.

Spiny iron plant

DOTTED BLAZINGSTAR
Liatris punctata Hook.

COMPOSITE FAMILY

Dotted blazingstar

Dotted blazingstar

Meadow blazingstar

FLOWERS are deep rosy purple, up to ½ inch (12 mm) diameter, with the heads arranged in a dense crowded spike of disc florets. Each head contains four to six tubular florets with plumose pappus hairs among them. The meadow blazingstar, (*L. ligulistylis* [A. Nels.] K. Schum.), has a round head about 1 inch (2.5 cm) diameter and a "shingling" of purplish bracts around it. Flowers appear in August. FRUIT is a ribbed, hairy achene, ¼ inch (6 mm) long with a bristly pappus. LEAVES are bright green with a whitish midvein, stiff and linear, 2 to 6 inches (5-15 cm) long, usually nearer the former. Lower leaves are wider and almost lanceolate. GROWTH HABIT is perennial in a clump of stems which may be somewhat decumbent, but up to 18 inches (45 cm) tall. The stems arise from a thick corm-like rootstock. HABITAT includes open grassy meadows and hillsides in the prairie area, with meadow blazingstar much more common in moister areas, particularly through the parkland-prairie.

WILD CHAMOMILE
Matricaria chamomilla L.

Wild chamomile

Pineapple weed

Ox-eye daisy

FLOWERS have wide white ray florets with yellow disc florets in a center about ½ inch (12 mm) diameter. Ray florets may be up to 1 inch (2.5 cm) and are pistillate. Flower heads are numerous at the ends of branches, July-August. FRUIT is a small (under 1/16 inch or 1 mm) dry achene with three to five faint ribs and no pappus. LEAVES are alternate, light green, stalkless ¾ to 3 inches (2-7.5 cm) long, divided into many threadlike segments. Both leaves and flowers have a pineapple odor when crushed. In contrast, leaves of the ox-eye daisy, (*Chrysanthemum leucanthemum* L.), are broader and spatula-shaped, with toothed margins. They have no odor. GROWTH HABIT is annual, erect and much branched, 6 to 30 inches (15-75 cm) high. Some of the slender stems on taller plants droop somewhat. HABITAT includes roadsides, field margins and meadows, particularly where moisture conditions are good. Another member of the same genus, pineapple weed, (*M. matricarioides* [Less.] Porter), is shown also. It is more widely distributed and frequently appears in yards, gardens and at the edges of walks.

SCENTLESS CHAMOMILE
Matricaria maritima L.

COMPOSITE FAMILY

Scentless chamomile

Scentless chamomile

FLOWER heads have a "daisy-like" appearance due to twelve to twenty-five white ray florets ¼ to ¾ inch (6-20 mm) long around a dense, flat, yellow center of disc florets. The heads, varying from ¾ to 1½ inches (2-4 cm) diameter, are numerous in a corymbose cluster on the upper branches. Flowers may appear as early as June but flowering persists until September. FRUIT is a small, brownish achene with three ribs. The pappus is inconspicuous but shows under a microscope as a short four-pointed crown or merely a terminal ridge. LEAVES are alternate, light green, bipinnately compound, ¾ to 3 inches (2-7.5 cm) long, finely dissected into hair-like minor segments each ⅜ to 1 inch (1-2.5 cm) long, which give the plant a feathery appearance. GROWTH HABIT is annual, occasionally biennial, usually erect but continuing to bloom even when knocked over by field cultivation. Common height is 8 to 15 inches (20-38 cm) but may grow to 3 feet (1 m). HABITAT: An introduced weed which is becoming a persistent problem in some areas of the parkland and eastern prairie. It will readily invade stands of grasses and cereal crops if moisture conditions are good.

ARROW-LEAVED COLT'S-FOOT
Petasites sagittatus (Pursh) A. Gray

Arrow-leaved colt's-foot

Arrow-leaved colt's-foot

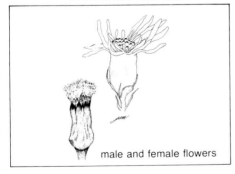

male and female flowers

FLOWERS are white, minute, in dense terminal clusters, either male or female, and sexes are usually on separate plants. The bracts which surround the cluster are in a single series and scaly in appearance. Flowers appear before leaves, May-June. The FRUIT is a dry achene, 3/16 inch (4 mm) long with a white pappus, an unusual sight in the lush green of mid-June. LEAVES are light grayish green above and dense white-woolly beneath, borne on long stems which arise from the root crown. They are triangular-ovate with short marginal teeth. The palmate-leaved colt's-foot, (*P. palmatus* [Ait.] A. Gray), is very similar except for the shape of the leaf, which the common name describes. GROWTH HABIT is perennial; the thick coarse flower stem rises from the root crown to 8 to 30 inches (20-75 cm). This soon dies back and the flannel-like leaves develop. HABITAT includes edges of water-filled ditches and sloughs as well as marshy areas, deep in aspen poplar groves throughout the forest and parkland areas.

PRAIRIE CONEFLOWER
Ratibida columnifera (Nutt.) Woot. and Standl.

COMPOSITE FAMILY

Prairie coneflower

Brown coneflower

Purple coneflower

FLOWERS have bright yellow ray florets which are usually reflexed. The receptacle (disc) is columnar, ½ to 1½ inches (1-4 cm) high. The disc florets are yellowish brown and bear both stamens and pistil. Another form, (forma *pulcherrima* [D.C.] Fern.), has purplish brown ray florets but it is quite rare. Ray florets in either are ½ to 1¼ inch (1-3 cm) long and up to ¼ inch (6 mm) wide. Flowers appear July-September. FRUIT is a grayish black, flattened achene, 1/16 inch (2 mm) long, with the pappus reduced to a few scales and one or two small teeth. Leaves are alternate, gray green, pinnately divided and somewhat hairy, 2 to 4 inches (5-10 cm) long. Basal leaves are often not divided. GROWTH HABIT is perennial, erect, stems are hairy and somewhat grooved longitudinally, 10 to 24 inches (25-60 cm) high, with the flower stems ac- counting for at least a third of this height. HABITAT is dry prairie, roadsides, railway grades, etc., of the south and west, being replaced by the black-eyed susan, (*Rudbeckia serotina* Nutt.), to the east and north. Another similar plant illustrated on this page is the purple coneflower, (*Echinacea angustifolia* DC.), which is very rare in Saskatchewan.

BLACK-EYED SUSAN
Rudbeckia serotina Nutt.

COMPOSITE FAMILY

Black-eyed susan

Black-eyed susan

flower profile

FLOWERS have ten to twenty striking orange yellow ray florets which are not reflexed. They enclose a dense, flattened, dark brown disc of complete florets. The disc is ½ to 1 inch (1.5-2.5 cm) across and the ray florets are often 1 to 1½ inches (2.5-4 cm) long. Flowers appear July-September. FRUIT is a smooth four-angled achene. LEAVES are medium green, hairy, lanceolate to oblanceolate in the western forms, more oval in the eastern one, (*R. hirta* L.). GROWTH HABIT is biennial, 12 to 18 inches (30-45 cm) tall and hairy, with stem occasionally purplish in color. Leaf stalks account for a third or half the total height. HABITAT includes the edges of aspen poplar groves and scrubby patches or open meadows in the parkland where moisture conditions are good.

ENTIRE-LEAVED GROUNDSEL
Senecio integerrimus Nutt.

Entire-leaved groundsel

Entire-leaved groundsel

Entire-leaved groundsel

FLOWERS are bright yellow, borne on slender stems in a terminal cluster of five to thirty-five heads, each ½ to 1 ¼ inches (12-30 mm) across, with eight to twelve ray florets. The numerous bracts are very obvious in the bud stage, light green and linear, ¼ to ⅜ inch (6-10 mm) long, with one variety (var. *exaltatus* [Nutt.] Cronq.) having sharp black tips. Flowers appear by late May and some plants may flower until August. FRUIT is a slender, ribbed, brownish achene ⅛ inch (3 mm) long with a white pappus. LEAVES are alternate, smooth, and thick, particularly in the basal rosette. They are entire margined, oval to spatulate, pointed, 2¼ to 10 inches (6-25 cm) in length, including the long petiole, and ⅜ to 2¼ inches (1-6 cm) wide. The upper leaves are much smaller, lanceolate to linear, irregularly toothed or notched and sessile GROWTH HABIT is perennial, with an erect, thick, smooth, solitary stem 12-20 inches (30-50 cm) tall arising from a stout stem base or caudex and coarse, fleshy fibrous roots. The plants are first obvious in May with their rough, dark green basal rosettes. HABITAT is moist soil or hillsides and disturbed road allowances through the south and central portion of the area, with the variety with black tipped bracts found only in the Cypress Hills.

MARSH RAGWORT
Senecio palustris (L.) Hook.

Marsh ragwort

FLOWERS are bright, rather pale yellow in ½ to ¾ inch (12-20 mm) heads crowded into a dense terminal cluster which may be somewhat nodding. Flowers appear June-July. FRUIT is a small, dry achene with a white pappus. The seed heads form a woolly cluster and may be present while some flower heads are still blooming. LEAVES are coarse, light gray, 2 to 6 inches (5-15 cm) long, the lower ones with winged stalks and wavy margins, lanceolate to spatulate in shape. The upper ones are somewhat smaller, lobed, stalkless, clasping and linear lanceolate. GROWTH HABIT is annual, with a coarse, hairy, angled, hollow stem, 6 to 24 inches (15-60 cm) high. Stems may be cobwebby when young but soon lose this cover. HABITAT: The immediate margins of prairie and parkland sloughs and lakes across the area; in some years it practically forms a yellow ring around them. The other member of the genus illustrated is silvery groundsel, (S. *canus* Hook.), which is from 12 to 36 inches (30-90 cm) tall with mainly basal leaves.

Marsh ragwort

F. R. VANCE

Silvery groundsel

COMMON GROUNDSEL
Senecio vulgaris L.

Common groundsel   Common groundsel

FLOWERS are bright yellow in discoid heads up to ¼ inch (6 mm) diameter and ⅜ inch (10 mm) tall with black tips on some of the linear involucral bracts. The heads are borne in groups of two to four in small corymbose clusters at the ends of branches and flower from June to September. FRUIT is a small, bottle-shaped, slightly hairy achene, gray, with a white pappus of about the same length. LEAVES are gray-green, numerous, deeply and irregularly lobed in a pinnate pattern, 2 to 6 inches (5-15 cm) long. Lower leaves taper to the petiole while upper leaves are sessile and somewhat clasping. GROWTH HABIT is annual, usually 6 to 18 inches (15-45 cm) tall, often nearer the former under poor conditions. Stems are deep green, hollow hairless, and somewhat ridged. HABITAT: An introduced weed, common in gardens and borders, persistent due to numerous seeds, with a range of maturity that allows the plant to be found at all stages throughout the summer and early fall.

.OW GOLDENROD
Solidago missouriensis Nutt.

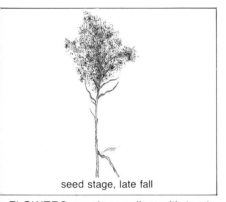
seed stage, late fall

FLOWERS are deep yellow with ten to wenty heads in a rather rounded compact erminal panicle 2 to 3 inches (5-7 cm) long. he individual heads are ⅛ to 3/16 inch 3-5 mm) high and are supported by blunt near bracts. In contrast, mountain golden-

rod, (*S. decumbens* Greene var. *oreophila* [Rydb.] Fern.), blooms later and has the flower heads separated on the upper stem in a longer, narrower panicle. Flowers appear July-August. FRUIT is a small hairy achene with a creamy white pappus. LEAVES are deep green, some basal, some alternate on the stem, and triple veined. Basal leaves are oblanceolate and stalked, 1 to 4 inches (2.5-10 cm) long, but the upper ones are smaller, mostly stalkless and lanceolate to linear. In mountain goldenrod leaves are wider, thicker and more rounded at the tip. GROWTH HABIT is erect and perennial, 4 to 15 inches (5-45 cm) tall. The stems are hairless and usually somewhat reddish. HABITAT includes the dry prairie and hillsides of the south and southwest where it is the first goldenrod to herald the autumn.

Low goldenrod

Mountain goldenrod

312

VELVETY GOLDENROD
Solidago mollis Bartl.

COMPOSITE FAMILY

Canada goldenrod

FLOWERS are bright deep yellow. The heads are dense in a pyramid-like panicle in both velvety goldenrod and Canada goldenrod, (*S. canadensis* L.). The bracts, in several series, are yellowish and somewhat thick and pointed. The whole inflorescence may be 4 inches (10 cm) high and 1½ inches (4 cm) across. The stiff or rigid goldenrod, (*S. rigida* L.), with which velvety goldenrod is often confused, has flower heads in a flat topped inflorescence. Flowers appear August-September. The FRUIT is a small dry achene with a rather bristly pappus. LEAVES are alternate, pale green oval and stalked. The upper leaves are elliptic and stalkless with three distinct veins. They are covered with short, fine, velvety hairs. Leaves are larger and smooth in Canada goldenrod. GROWTH HABIT is perennial, erect, on stems which tend to be solitary and arise from a horizontal root stock. Height varies from 8 to 18 inches (20-45 cm). The Canada goldenrod is taller up to 24 to 30 inches (60-75 cm). HABITAT principally includes the prairie and roadsides of the south and central part of the area. The three species illustrated are probably the commonest of the goldenrods and the most widely distributed. Canada goldenrod is more common in the eastern part.

Velvety goldenrod

Stiff goldenrod

ANSY
anacetum vulgare L.

COMPOSITE FAMILY

COMPOSITE FAMILY

Tansy

Tansy

FLOWERS are deep orange-yellow in discoid heads, each about ¼ inch (6 mm) diameter. In a few heads the stunted ray florets are rolled into the edges of the heads. Heads are numerous, twenty to one hundred in a rough corymb. Flowering occurs in August. FRUIT is a small, ribbed achene with the pappus reduced to a microscopic ridge or crown at one end. LEAVES are alternate, light green, and pinnate with deeply divided leaflets. Some of the basal leaves may be 12 inches (30 cm) long and even the smallest upper leaves can be 4 inches (10 cm) long. GROWTH HABIT: A coarse perennial herb with many stems which grow from a rhizome to a height of 16 to 36 inches (40-90 cm). Stems and leaves have a rank odor when bruised. HABITAT: Tansy is an introduced garden plant, still commonly cultivated in gardens, that has escaped to grow wild in road ditches, abandoned farm yards, and hedgerows throughout the prairies.

LOW TOWNSENDIA
Townsendia sericea Hook.

COMPOSITE FAMIL

Low townsendia

FLOWERS are white to cream, ⅜ inch (1 cm) long, occasionally tinged with pink or light blue due to the ray florets. The conspicuous yellow center is due to disc florets. The flower heads, ½ to 1¼ inches (12-30 mm) are borne on very short stalks and the involucral bracts are flattened to the head and partly overlapping. Approximate flowering date is May-June. The FRUIT is a dry achene with a pappus of forked or barbed hairs. LEAVES are alternate or basal, narrowly spatulate to linear, 1 to 2 inche (2.5-5 cm) long, pale gray due to fine hairs They have deeply cleft, divided margins GROWTH HABIT: A low perennial rarel over 1½ inches (4 cm) high, on a short sten which grows from a woody root. HABITA includes sunny slopes of dry hills of th south and southeast. It appears along wit moss phlox, leafy musineon, and othe flowers of early spring.

Low townsendia

Townsendia (pink form)

F. R. VANCE

GLOSSARY

ACHENE	A one-seeded, one-celled, dry, hard fruit that does not open when ripe
AWN	A bristle-like part of the inflorescence
AXIL	The upper angle formed where a leaf stalk or a branch joins a stem
AXILLARY	In an axil
BARB	A short, stiff point or short bristle
BERRY	A pulpy fruit with several seeds
BLOOM	The whitish, powdery covering of some fruits
BRACT	A small leaf or scale, often borne below a flower or flower cluster
CALCAREOUS	Pertaining to soil high in calcium salts
CALYX	The outer floral ring or sepals
CAPSULE	A dry fruit consisting of more than one chamber
CARPEL	A seed-bearing chamber at the base of the pistil of a flower
CATKIN	A tight, scaly cluster of flowers of one sex, in which the flowers usually lack petals
CLEFT	Refers to deeply lobed leaves (Fig. 8)
CORM	A thick enlarged base of a plant stem
COROLLA	The petals or inner floral ring
CORYMB	A flower cluster with a flat or rounded top in which flower stalks arise from different points on the stem. (Fig. 3)
CRETACEOUS	The last geological period of marine type rock deposition in Saskatchewan
CYME	A loose flower cluster in which the central flowers open first (Fig. 3)
DECIDUOUS	Trees with leaves that are dropped yearly, not evergreen
DECUMBENT	A stem with the base on or near the ground, with tip or main stem erect
DICOTYLEDON	A plant with two cotyledons or seed leaves
DIOECIOUS	Having the flowers with pistils or with stamens on separate plants
DISCOID	Having only disc flowers
DRUPE	A pulpy or fleshy fruit containing a single seed enclosed in a hard shell or stone
ENTIRE	Refers to a leaf, having a margin not toothed or cleft
FLORET	A single flower, usually of a composite head or cluster
FOLLICLE	A fruit with a single chamber that opens along one side
GLABROUS	Leaves or stems which lack hairs, i.e., smooth
GLANDULAR	Bearing secreting organs or glands
GLAUCOUS	Covered with a bloom
GLOBOSE	Spherical or nearly so

GLOBULAR	Globe-like
GRANULAR	Covered with very small grainy structures
HIP	The berry-like, enlarged calyx tube of roses, containing many achenes
INFLORESCENCE	The arrangement of groups of flowers on a plant (Fig. 3)
INTERNODE	The part of a stem between two nodes
INVOLUCRE	The whorl of bracts below a flower cluster
KEEL	The two lower united petals of flowers of legumes
LANCEOLATE	Narrow leaves, broadest at the base and tapering to the tip. (Fig. 7)
LIGULE	A strap-shaped organ, as in ray florets of Compositae
LINEAR	Leaves, long and narrow, with parallel margins (Fig. 7)
LIP	The main lobe of a two-lobed corolla or calyx, particularly in the orchid family
LOBE	A rounded projection of a leaf or a leaf-like part of a plant
LOCULE	One of the compartments of a pistil or anther
LOMENT	A pod in which there are constrictions between the seeds
MONOCOTYLEDON	A plant with only one cotyledon or seed leaf
MONOECIOUS	Having pistils and stamens in separate flowers on the same plant
NODE	The place on a stem where leaves grow or normally arise
OBLANCEOLATE	Leaves of a shape longer than broad and tapering to the tip (Fig. 7)
OBOVATE	Leaves of an egg shape with the broader end towards the tip (Fig. 7)
OVAL	Leaves of an egg shape with ends equally tapered (Fig. 7)
OVARY	The part of the pistil of a flower containing the cells that become seeds
OVATE	Leaves of an egg shape broader towards the petiole (Fig. 7)
OVOID	Egg-shaped with the wide part near the point of attachment
PALMATE	A simple or compound leaf divided into finger-like parts or leaflets (Fig. 8)
PANICLE	A flower cluster in which the lower branches are longer (Fig. 3)
PAPPUS	The bristly or scale-like appendage on fruits of Compositae
PETAL	A separate part of the corolla or inner floral ring, usually brightly colored (Fig. 4)
PETIOLE	The stalk of a leaf
PINNATE	Refers to compound leaves with leaflets on each side of the stalk (Fig. 8)
PISTIL	The central ovule-bearing organ of a flower, made up of stigma, style and ovary
PLUMOSE	Having fine hairs
POD	A dry fruit, opening when mature
POME	A fleshy fruit
PUBESCENT	Leaves or stems which are covered with fine hairs
RACEME	A flower cluster with each flower borne on a short stalk arising at different points on a common stem (Fig. 3)
RECEPTACLE	The end of the flower stem bearing flower parts
REFLEXED	Bent sharply backwards, as with sepals or petals
RHIZOME	An underground, root-like stem
SAPROPHYTIC	Living on dead organic matter
SCAPE	A flowering stem growing from the root crown and not bearing proper leaves

SCURFY	Refers to leaves and stems, covered with small scale-like particles
SEPAL	One of the separate parts of a calyx, usually green and leaf-like (Fig. 4)
SPADIX	A dense or fleshy spike of flowers
SPATHE	A large leaf-like bract enclosing a flower cluster
SPATULATE	Leaves which are spoon-shaped with a broad, rounded tip, tapering to the petiole (Fig. 7)
SPIKE	A flower cluster with stalkless individual flowers on a common stalk (Fig. 3)
SPUR	A hollow projection, usually at the base of a flower
STAMEN	The pollen-bearing part of a flower consisting of anther and filament
STIGMA	The upper part of the pistil where the pollen is received
STIPULE	An appendage at the base of a leaf
STYLE	The part of the pistil joining the stamen and ovary
TAXONOMY	The study and practice of classification of organisms
TRIFOLIATE	Three leaves attached to a common petiole (Fig. 8)
TUBERCLE	A rounded protruding body attached to some part of a plant
UMBEL	A flower cluster in which all flower stalks arise from one point (Fig. 3)
WHORL	A group of three or more leaves arising from the same node (Fig. 2)
WOOLLY	Covered with tangled soft hairs

BIBLIOGRAPHY

Bailey, L. H. *Manual of Cultivated Plants Most Commonly Grown in the United States and Canada.* Rev. ed. New York: Macmillan Co., 1949.

Boivin, Bernard. *Flora of the Prairie Provinces: A Handbook to the Flora of the Provinces of Manitoba, Saskatchewan and Alberta.* Reprinted from *Phytologia* 15-23 (1967-1972).

Breitung, August J. *Annotated Catalogue of the Vascular Flora of Saskatchewan.* Reprinted from *American Midland Naturalist* 58 (1957).

Britton, Nathaniel Lord, and Addison Brown. *An Illustrated Flora of the Northern United States and Canada* 1-3 (1913). 2nd ed. New York: Dover Publications, 1970.

Budd, A. C. and J. B. Campbell. "Flowering Sequence of a Local Flora," *Journal of Range Management* 12 (1959): 127-132.

Budd, Archibald C. and Keith F. Best. *Wild Plants of the Canadian Prairies.* Publication 983. Ottawa: Canada Department of Agriculture, 1964.

Canada Weed Committee. *Common and Botanical Names of Weeds in Canada.* Publication 1397. Ottawa: Canada Department of Agriculture, 1975.

Carmichael, Lloyd T. *Prairie Wildflowers.* Toronto: J. M. Dent and Sons (Canada) Limited, 1961.

Cormack, R. G. H. *Wild Flowers of Alberta.* Edmonton: Alberta Department of Industry and Development, 1967.

Looman, J. and K. F. Best. *Budd's Flora of the Canadian Prairie Provinces.* Publication 1662. Ottawa: Research Branch, Agriculture Canada, 1979.

Moss, E. H. *Flora of Alberta: A Manual of Flowering Plants, Ferns and Fern Allies Found Growing Without Cultivation in the Province of Alberta, Canada.* Toronto: University of Toronto Press, 1959.

Scoggan, H. J. *Flora of Canada Pts. 1-4.* Botany Publication No. 7. Ottawa: National Museums of Canada, 1979.

Scoggan, H. J. *Flora of Manitoba.* National Museum of Canada Bulletin No. 140. Biological Series No. 47. Ottawa: Canada Department of Northern Affairs and Natural Resources, 1957.

INDEX

Common and Scientific Names

INDEX

Plant Families

Aceraceae (maple family) 165
Alismaceae (water-plantain family) 20–21
Anacardiaceae (sumach family) 163–164
Apocynaceae (dogbane family) 221–222
Araceae (arum family) 22
Araliaceae (ginseng family) 185
Asclepiadaceae (milkweed family) 223
Balsaminaceae (touch-me-not family) 159
Betulaceae (birch family) 54
Boraginaceae (borage family) 228–232
Cactaceae (cactus family) 174–175
Campanulaceae (bluebell family) 265
Cannabinaceae (hemp family) 56
Capparidaceae (caper family) 90
Caprifoliaceae (honeysuckle family) 259–264
Caryophyllaceae (pink family) 69–73
Chenopodiaceae (goosefoot family) 63–65
Cistaceae (rock-rose family) 168
Compositae (composite family) 268–313
Convolvulaceae (convolvulus family) 224
Cornaceae (dogwood family) 194–195
Crassulaceae (orpine family) 98
Cruciferae (mustard family) 91–95
Cucurbitaceae (gourd family) 266
Droseraceae (sundew family) 96
Elaeagnaceae (oleaster family) 176–177
Ericaceae (heath family) 203–206
Euphorbiaceae (spurge family) 162
Fagaceae (beech family) 55
Fumariaceae (fumitory family) 89
Gentianaceae (gentian family) 215–220
Geraniaceae (geranium family) 153–155
Hydrophyllaceae (waterleaf family) 227
Iridaceae (iris family) 34–35
Juncaginaceae (arrow-grass family) 19
Labiatae (mint family) 233–240
Leguminosae (legume family) 126–152
Lentibulariaceae (bladderwort family) 253–254
Liliaceae (lily family) 23–33
Linaceae (flax family) 157–158
Loasaceae (loasa family) 173
Lobeliaceae (lobelia family) 267
Lythraceae (loosestrife family) 178

Malvaceae (mallow family) 166–167
Monotropaceae (indian-pipe family) 200–202
Nyctaginaceae (four-o'clock family) 66
Nymphaeaceae (water-lily family) 74
Onagraceae (evening-primrose family) 179–184
Orchidaceae (orchid family) 36–50
Orobanchaceae (broom-rape family) 255
Oxalidaceae (wood-sorrel family) 156
Plantaginaceae (plantain family) 256
Polemoniaceae (phlox family) 225–226
Polygalaceae (milkwort family) 160–161
Polygonaceae (buckwheat family) 59–62
Portulacaceae (purslane family) 67–68
Primulaceae (primrose family) 209–214
Pyrolaceae (wintergreen family) 196–199
Ranunculaceae (crowfoot family) 75–88
Rosaceae (rose family) 104–125
Rubiaceae (madder family) 257–258
Salicaceae (willow family) 51–53
Santalaceae (sandalwood family) 58
Sarraceniaceae (pitcherplant family) 97
Saxifragaceae (saxifrage family) 99–103
Scrophulariaceae (figwort family) 244–252
Solanaceae (potato family) 241–243
Sparganiaceae (bur-reed family) 18
Typhaceae (cattail family) 17
Umbelliferae (parsley family) 186–193
Urticaceae (nettle family) 57
Vacciniaceae (huckleberry family) 207–208
Violaceae (violet family) 169–173

COLOR INDEX TO PLANTS

Red - Pink

Purple - Blue

White

Greenish white - Cream

cattail   17
broad-fruited bur-reed   18
seaside arrow-grass   19
early coralroot   40
long-bracted bog orchid   46
twayblade   48
pussy willow   53
bur oak   55
common hop   56
stinging nettle   57
western dock   61
sand dock   62
greasewood   65
low whitlowwort   71
meadow rue   88
alumroot   99
bishop's cap   100
wild black currant   102
Canadian milk-vetch   127
American milk-vetch   127
narrow-leaved milk-vetch   131
cushion milk-vetch   133
wild licorice   134

cream-colored vetchling   137
late yellow locoweed   144
leafy spurge   162
poison ivy   163
skunkbush   164
silver buffaloberry   177
greenish-flowered wintergreen   199
pinesap   200
pinedrops   202
Canada blueberry   207
northern gentian   215
spurred-gentian   218
lance-leaved paintbrush   244
cow-wheat   246
clustered broom-rape   255
common plantain   256
wild cucumber   266
sagebrush   280
pasture sage   281
Russian-thistle   285
pineapple weed   303
arrow-leaved colt's-foot   305

Yellow

ABOUT THE AUTHORS

Fenton R. Vance, the main photographer for *Wildflowers Across the Prairies,* received a B.Sc. in Electrical Engineering from the University of Manitoba in 1941. He has been a serious photographer for some years and has developed a library of nearly 500 slides of Saskatchewan wildflowers.

James R. Jowsey is currently employed as a problem wildlife specialist with the Saskatchewan Department of Agriculture. He received a Ph.D. in Agricultural Chemistry from McGill University in 1953, as well as a B.Ed., B.Sc. in Agriculture, and M.Sc. from the University of Saskatchewan. He is a member of the Saskatchewan Natural History Society and maintains active interests in ornithology, education, the natural history of plants and animals, and the quality of the environment.

James S. McLean, employed by CP Rail in Moose Jaw, drew the line drawings for *Wildflowers Across the Prairies.* He paints in oils and watercolors and does ink drawings, and his illustrations have appeared in literary and scientific books and publications. He is also a writer of fiction, non-fiction, and drama, and his book of poetry, *The Secret Life of Railroaders,* was published in 1982.